Story of "J"

Story of "J"

The Author of *The Sensuous Woman* Tells the Bitter Price of Her Crazy Success

by *Terry Garrity*
with *John Garrity*

William Morrow and Company, Inc.
New York   1984

Library of Congress Catalog Card Number: 84-60479

ISBN: 0-688-00997-2

Printed in the United States of America

First Edition

1 2 3 4 5 6 7 8 9 10

BOOK DESIGN BY ABBY KAGAN

To Grace Stuart and Mary Casey, who were born too early for medicine to help them

And to Arthur Halper for his loyalty and compassion in difficult times

ACKNOWLEDGMENTS

We are very grateful to Donald Engel and Dr. Moke Williams, who opened up their files and memories to us and who were also extremely generous with their valuable time, patiently answering our many questions and reviewing sections of the manuscript.

Several other friends were also helpful to us in piecing together incidents from the early 1970's: Jacqueline Thompson, Evelyn and Arthur Halper, John McDonnell. Two other dear friends will be cherished forever for the support they extended during the dark times; they are Orrin Stine and Norman Monath. We would also like to thank Laurie Lister and Deborah Baker of William Morrow and Company for their hard work on what proved to be a recalcitrant manuscript.

PART
ONE

PALM BEACH, FLORIDA, 1978

The building staff must have gossiped for hours about the screwball in 2-A.

Her apartment bordered the courtyard garden, not twenty feet from the glassed-in security office, where polite and cheerful doormen in green blazers fed the fish in the office aquarium and helped people in and out of cars. But they never saw 2-A anymore. They heard her sometimes, at midnight or later, her sandals slapping the marble tiles as she scurried behind the iron gate to the freight elevator. Sometimes—again, late at night—they saw her blue Caprice swinging in or out of the basement garage, the garage door gliding shut behind her. But she shunned the passenger elevators, which opened opposite the office windows at the building entrance.

Every few days, a delivery truck arrived from Palm Beach's most expensive market with a box or two of "groceries" for 2-A: cans of diet soda; several pints of Howard Johnson's ice cream in assorted flavors; three or four Sara Lee cherry pies. On Miss Garrity's instructions (she always sounded so bright and cheerful on the phone), a doorman would leave the grocery boxes on her kitchen floor just inside a jalousie door which was right next to her apartment's front door. The kitchen and the apartment beyond always seemed dark and still, as if no one were home.

In the office, mail choked box number 2-A. The staff bundled it, made a pile of the dozens of magazines and catalogues that arrived every week, and, as with the groceries, left it on the kitchen floor.

Miss Garrity never appeared in her tennis outfit any more, carrying her racket in a Vuitton racket cover. She never walked along the ocean as she had before, almost nightly. The elegant white shutters in her guest bedroom window, which looked out on the swimming pool and the gardens remained shut, the louvres closed. She received no visitors.

This last fact was probably the most interesting to the gossips. Miss Garrity had made her money, they knew, under the pen name "J". She was The Sensuous Woman. When she had moved in, in the fall of 1970, her neighbor in apartment 2-C had jabbered that no one could sleep at night because of the sounds of orgiastic revelry emanating from Miss "J"'s bedroom.

The staff doubted these stories. Miss Garrity's visitors were few, even then, and never stayed the night. Everyone smiled when they learned that "J" had sound-proofed her bedroom by covering the walls and ceiling with luxurious white carpeting. The nosy and imaginative neighbor, unaware of this fact, kept telling her tales of debauchery, until she, too, learned about the soundproofing. She then fell silent.

Eight years later, the carpeted walls were seen as cruel irony. Miss Garrity saw no one.

In a small town, her house would have been avoided by children, proclaimed "haunted," made the stuff of local legends. In Palm Beach, where wealth softens madness into "eccentricity," her secrets were guarded, her whims indulged by that dedicated staff.

But they must have wondered: Just what was she doing in there?

1

"J" was born in New York City in the spring of 1969. Joan Theresa "Terry" Garrity came into the world some thirty years earlier in Minneapolis, Minnesota.

We are one and the same person, but for a time in the 1970's, we thought, we felt, and acted separately.

And that's one of several reasons why I term the fame and fortune that writing *The Sensuous Woman* brought me "my crazy success." But I'm getting ahead of myself. To understand the person(s) I became, you need to know the person I was.

I did not grow up in a den of sex fiends, as some later critics supposed. Just the opposite. Mine was a wholesome-as-apple-pie upbringing in Kansas City, Missouri, and then Lake Lotawana, Missouri: camp fire girl meetings, organizing lemonade stands on hot summer days, writing plays that neighborhood kids performed for families and friends in our garage, ice-skating parties in the winter, golf and swimming in the summer, Saturday-afternoon movies, camping out overnight in a tent in the backyard, Saturday-night song-fests with my brother Tommy (Johnny was still a baby) and my parents, who drank highballs or California wine while we kids swigged Coca-Cola and Dr. Pepper and we all har-monized on "Harbor Lights," "I'm Lookin' Over a Four-Leaf Clover," and "Smoke Gets in Your Eyes" or listened to my father's solo rendition of "Where the River Shannon Flows" and other Irish favorites.

Sex was not mentioned in my own or friends' households, so I remained completely unaware of its existence until I was twelve years old. I remember mentioning to my mother that a neighbor had lent me a copy of the novel *Forever Amber*, and I was finding it very interesting because of the descrip-tions of the reign of Charles II (one of Mother's Stuart ances-tors).

My mother almost dropped her teeth and the dish she was washing.

"I forbid you to read that book until you're older," she said agitatedly.

"*Forbid* me? Why? I've always been able to read any book I wanted."

"Because you're too young to understand the sexual situa-tions in that book."

"What's sex?" I asked in confusion.

"It's something that happens between men and women when they're married, but you're not old enough to be inter-ested in sex now, and besides, that book doesn't present it right. So you return that book to Dorothy *right now*."

What was in *Forever Amber* that I wasn't supposed to know about? I'd read practically the whole book (including the sex scenes that were so shocking at that time) and hadn't noticed anything special. I returned *Forever Amber* to Doro-thy but rushed off to the library, took the book off the shelves, and perused it carefully at a table (making sure to keep a copy of *The Saturday Evening Post* in front of the book so that no one could see what I was reading). I searched through *Forever Amber* until the library was ready to close, but I never did figure out what sex was. But the question stayed in my head, and at slumber parties the next winter girl friends and I spent hours discussing this mysterious thing called sex.

"It's what you've seen dogs and cats do to have puppies and kittens. Humping. People get on top of each other and do the same thing," said Sue knowledgeably.

"*My* parents would never do a disgusting thing like that," said Joyce.

"Well, they had to have or you wouldn't be here," Sue pointed out.

"Oh, you don't know that for sure, and besides, even if they did do it, it was only once, and I'm sure they never did it again," cried Joyce.

"Yeah, that's probably right," agreed Linda. "Parents only do 'it' to get children. Then there's no other reason to want to do such an *uhhhkky* thing again. *Uhhk. I'm* never going to do 'it,' that's for sure."

"My mother says that sex is beautiful if a man and woman really love each other and that when I'm grown up I'll feel the same way," reported Dionne.

"I don't know," I said thoughtfully. Pictures of neighborhood dogs copulating kept going through my mind, and it was hard to envision my ever feeling such an act was beautiful.

By the time I was eighteen, I began to suspect I was wrong—sex could be beautiful—but this was the fifties, the twilight years of the philosophy that men married only virgins, that becoming "used goods" would ruin your life. In Missouri, the specter of Hawthorne's Hester Prynne hung over the parked cars on lovers' lanes and kept me and many other girls from "going all the way."

Florida girls were just as worried about the repercussions

of losing their virginity as Missouri girls, I discovered when my family moved to Florida the following year. Today's teen-agers, whose only fears are getting caught or pregnant, would undoubtedly be at a loss to understand my genera-tion's obsession with "purity," but twenty-five years ago only spinsters and the gifted had careers. Most girls' life goal was to make a good marriage, and then stay home and raise babies. If you got labeled "fast," there was a very real chance that "nice" boys, the good-husband types, would reject you as wife material. The stakes were too high to give in to curi-osity or a momentary surge of hormones.

Nevertheless, I risked all on my twenty-first birthday. My rationale was that since I was going to be a professional actress, society and my future Mr. Right would excuse a sex-ual romance or two in my past. Artists, after all, aren't ex-pected to lead traditional lives.

I was mad about my seducer. He was tall, dark, charming, and at least ten years older than I. He was an actor, and I'd met him at the Palm Beach Playhouse where I was appear-ing in a minor role in *Sabrina*, starring Constance Bennett.

"Did you come?" asked my lover interestedly after a few moments of activity.

"I'm here, aren't I?" said I, puzzled.

He looked at me strangely. "Did you have an orgasm?"

"Was I supposed to?"

"*All* women have orgasms, if they're *normal*," said he. "Al-though maybe not the first time or two," he allowed gener-ously.

"Oh. What's an orgasm?"

"It's a climax, an explosion. Look, why don't we try again, and maybe it'll happen now that you know you're supposed to come."

We made love every night after the curtain came down on *Sabrina*, but the Palm Beach earth failed to move or even quiver.

I had never had sexual anxieties before because I didn't know enough to. So I didn't brood over this orgasm business. I was young. Apparently orgasms were just supposed to "happen" . . . sooner or later. In my case, it would apparently be later. I met other men in the next few years, and experience suggested that I was probably not *frigid* (a word you don't hear much anymore). I felt tenderness with them, affection, love, and pleasure, but I didn't attain those ecstasies and climaxes that I'd read about and seen hints of in movies. I waited . . . and waited. . . .

And when it didn't happen, I started doing what most women do when they don't have orgasms.

I faked.

It was fall, my first autumn in New York. I was a struggling actress, dreaming of Broadway, but instead I was juggling fedoras and overcoats in a cramped restaurant cloakroom. Lucky Pierre's was by no means a dive. It was a very elegant restaurant on the West Side, around Fifty-seventh Street, near the Manhattan auto showrooms. The specialty was food cooked at your table with a blowtorch.

Lucky Pierre was creative, but he was not a good businessman. He was always short of money and often didn't have everything on the menu. When an order would go in, the chef would sometimes have to run next door to another restaurant to fill it.

Lucky Pierre may have had a cash-flow problem, but I didn't. Tips were good, and my only aggravation was that the male clientele kept pinching my bottom whenever I bent over to retrieve their umbrellas. Luckily, it was a dry autumn.

This was my Greenwich Village period. I shared a small second-floor apartment with two other actresses in a Mafia neighborhood near Prince Street. It was bohemian, but not picturesque bohemian (when the building burned down a few years ago, *The New York Times* described it as a tenement). Claire Justice, who was working as a waitress between acting jobs, left to live at a hotel, so Elmarie Wendell and I moved upstairs to a sixth-floor walk-up which, when we fixed it up, was a pretty cute apartment.

Of course, I always puffed after climbing five flights of stairs, and there was no air conditioning. The refrigerator didn't work either, but we used it as a closet for clothes and shoes. In cold weather we left our perishables on the windowsill. When my father came to New York from Kansas City on a business trip with his second wife, Jack, I arranged to meet them on a midtown corner because I knew he would be very upset if he saw my building. My father is anything but stuffy—"The hell you say!" is his response to most surprises—but he would have been afraid for me. He and Jack took me to Gallagher's Steak House for dinner, and the steaks were wonderful, but I was more impressed afterward when we returned to their room in the Vanderbilt Hotel. It had one of those big old-fashioned bathtubs you could lie down in. I took a great bath.

Elmarie, my roommate, was a version of *My Sister Eileen*. She was a very colorful, very volatile girl from Eugene, Oregon. Her heritage was Slavic—gypsy, she implied, but she changed her story from time to time. She claimed she could read palms. (She really didn't know anything about it, but people liked what she did.) She was very earthy. She taught me the word *sakaraneski*, which I think is a dirty word in Slavic.

Elmarie was more adventurous than I. One Christmas she bought a Christmas tree from the Mafia, on credit, and then wouldn't pay for it. I nearly had a heart attack when I found out. "Elmarie," I pleaded, "you're not dealing with the Little Sisters of the Poor. You *gotta* pay the Mafia!" I worried about reprisals. The mother of the head of the New York Mafia

lived on our corner in a nice brownstone, and I expected her
son to come pounding on our door, shouting threats. But he
never did. He probably couldn't get up the stairs.

Elmarie was a wonderful singer, with considerable summer stock and repertory behind her. When we lived together,
Elmarie auditioned tirelessly and worked as a waitress to
make ends meet. Mostly she sang in dives in New Jersey—
she called them toilets—which was a waste of her talents.

But at least she was singing! After Lucky Pierre's folded I
tried my hand at free-lance envelope addressing. I rode the
subway downtown to an insurance company on Wall Street
where, for three dollars per thousand, I addressed envelopes.
I was so good at it that one day the insurance people invited
me back and offered me another three dollars to seal the envelopes and put stamps on them. So I briskly set about the
task, not taking into account the fact that it was a very hot
day. I had piled up thousands of envelopes before I realized
that they had all stuck together. All the rest of that week I
had to take the subway back down to Wall Street and la-
boriously unstick all those envelopes with a steamer. Of
course, I wasn't making any money—I was just salvaging
my original three dollars' worth of work. The insurance people felt sorry for me and took me out to lunch.

After that, I went back to just addressing.

I was making the rounds of the theatrical agents, of
course, and auditioning when I could muster the courage.
But since Elmarie and I were Village bohemians, we stayed
up all night, and it wasn't easy dragging myself out of bed in
the morning to look for work. One morning the phone rang
at the crack of dawn—seven-thirty or eight A.M.—and I answered it, very foggily. I was meticulous in those days about
writing down what people said on the phone, even in my
sleep, so when I woke up later, around five o'clock in the
afternoon, I looked at my note pad. I was astonished to discover that I had accepted a job with a puppet troupe. As a

puppeteer! They had accepted me sight unseen on the recommendation of a friend, and I was expected at the first rehearsal within an hour. I knew nothing about puppets, but it sounded better than addressing envelopes, so I threw on my clothes and raced off to rehearsal.

Two weeks later, I was on a Volkswagen tour of the Northeast as a member of the Susari Marionettes. We played summer theaters and summer camps in New England, New York State, and Pennsylvania for fifty dollars a week and all the terrible camp food we could eat, and I hated every minute of it. There were only three of us, so I had to do twelve characters. Voices were easy enough, but I had certain limitations as a puppeteer, the worst of which was a lack of coordination with all those strings. The Lilac Fairy, one of the characters in *Sleeping Beauty*, had fourteen strings and could do anything a great ballerina could do, if you knew how. But I didn't know how. I had strings curled around my fingers, my elbows, my arms, and my ears. It didn't help that I had to do all the female voices. Working the Lilac Fairy while talking for two other characters took enormous concentration, and I was strung out after every performance.

There was little opportunity for romance on a shoestring-budget puppet tour, but I did have a sleeping companion. I found Charlie Charles Charles in the northern woods that summer. He had been abandoned as a tiny little kitten, and I carried him with me on the tour. The company stayed in places where you weren't allowed to have pets, so I had to carry Charlie around in a metal lunch box with a breathing hole cut in it. That was fine when Charlie was truly tiny, but he kept getting bigger and bigger, and I'd think I was making it through a hotel lobby when this big orange paw would lunge out of the breathing hole, drawing questioning looks from everyone. I brought him back to Manhattan when the tour was over.

I was still waiting for an orgasm.

I began to suspect that something was wrong with me. Orgasm was like a train that never arrived. I went to my closest women friends and pleaded, "Can you give me any clues?"

They said, "It just happens!" I was getting nowhere.

One cold winter afternoon I went to a gynecologist on Park Avenue. He was a man in his late fifties, and he listened patiently as I chronicled my menstrual woes of recent years. But he began to squirm when I asked him a direct question about orgasm. "I don't understand why I can't have the orgasms that all women are supposed to have," I said, feeling embarrassed myself. "Do you see a medical reason?"

He looked very uncomfortable. (I learned, after a while, that doctors didn't like to talk about sex. They either turned suddenly pompous or stuffy, or they began to play with the papers on their desks, shifted their weight, and avoided eye contact.)

"I see nothing organically wrong," he said, stopping to clear his throat. "Nothing that should preclude your . . . functioning normally. If your menstrual discomfort persists, we might consider a D and C (dilation and curettage) down the road, but as far as your . . . other problem is concerned . . . I don't see that there's . . ."

He could have talked all afternoon and turned several more shades of crimson, but I gathered that his advice about my "sex problem" was simply to "live with it."

I decided not to "live with it." Not yet, anyway. I also decided that my gynecologist lacked warmth. "I feel no rapport with him," I told my friends. "I think I'll drop him."

My second gynecologist was a much younger doctor, a bright and capable practitioner whose office was in the Mount Sinai Medical Center. He agreed with the first doctor's assessment: that I displayed no abnormality that would prevent my having orgasms. "All you have to do is fall in love," he said.

My heart sank. "But I *am* in love," I said.

"Oh," he said. He looked sort of baffled. Crestfallen.

Still, that doctor taught me a lot. He sat me down and drew pictures of the ovaries and the uterus, really explained the female organs to me. I *needed* patient tutoring, because I was truly ignorant of the workings of my own body.

He was also the one who suggested that I see a psychologist.

She was a middle-aged Viennese psychiatrist with an office in a lovely brownstone in Greenwich Village, overlooking Washington Square. She was a very pleasant, motherly woman with gray hair and a strong accent. Her office was cozy and old-fashioned, full of overstuffed chairs and big windows.

I presented my problem to her with some shyness, but she simply nodded and began taking down my history in a folder. Then she said, "Come into the next room," and we got on with the tests. We did a word association test first, and I did fine. She said, "Salt," and I said, "Pepper." She said, "Black," I said, "White." She said, "Happy," I said, "Sad."

Then she began the inkblots, the Rorschach test. The inkblots were projected on a screen, and she asked me to relate to her whatever I saw in their random patterns. Everything went smoothly for a slide or two, and she wrote nothing down. But then we got to one that I stared at intently. She asked, "What do you see?"

"Oh!" I finally exclaimed. "I see one of the Seven Dwarfs!" I turned to her and saw that her pen was poised in midair. There was an alertness in her eyes that had been missing a moment earlier.

"Dwarf?" she said. "Where?" I pointed it out, and she said, "Can you tell me more about this dwarf?"

"Well, I'm not sure which one it is," I said. "It could be Doc, it could be Sleepy, it could be Grumpy. . . ."

"Do you *know* any midgets?" she asked.

"What?"

"Do you know any midgets or dwarfs?"

"No," I said. "Why?"

"Well, the reference . . ."

I suddenly realized that she had misunderstood my impression of the blot. "No." I smiled. "I just saw a rerelease of *Snow White and the Seven Dwarfs.*"

"Seven Dwarfs? Snow White?"

"You know . . . the Walt Disney film?"

She said, "Walt Disney?"

". . . from Kansas City? . . . The great cartoonist who makes all the movies?" I saw that she was writing down, "*Walt Dizny . . . Kansas City . . .*" She was writing down everything I said at this point. "It's a fairy tale," I started to explain, but she looked up sharply at the word *fairy*. Everything I said seemed to make things worse, so I finally just stopped talking. She scribbled away like mad for another minute or so, and finally changed to the next inkblot.

"Tell me what you see," she said.

It was a pretty busy inkblot, and I named a couple of things before I blurted, without thinking, "Oh, there's Thumper!" She looked baffled, and I thought, *Oh, God, no, another Disney character*! I said, "Bambi? The deer?" She stared at me. "There's this children's story, it's a movie, and there's this rabbit in it named Thumper. . . ." And she wrote all this down and began asking me questions about animals. They were strange questions that I didn't understand. Later, I figured out that they related to bestiality, but at the time I just figured that we had a complete language block.

I thought, *If I keep seeing these characters in every slide, we'll never get anywhere.* So from there on in, I just saw all the usual vaginas and penises in the inkblots. And she stopped writing so much.

I went back a week later, when she had had time to ponder

the results of her tests. "Many women are born with low sex drives," she said. "You are probably one of those. You would do well to forget about sexuality, as far as fulfillment goes, and find yourself a lifetime, intellectually stimulating pursuit."

Low sex drive? That sounds funny now, but it was not an uncommon diagnosis twenty years ago. She was telling me, in effect, to find myself a really exciting hobby for the rest of my life.

I listened politely, and probably nodded from time to time, but the Scottish side of me, inside, was protesting. "That's not so! I am *normal!*" I rejected the diagnosis.

So I went to another psychiatrist. This man was in his forties and practiced out of an office in the West Fifties, but he gave me essentially the same diagnosis: "You were just born that way." He added, "Most women are. . . . It should be enough for you to give your partner pleasure. Don't let orgasm become an obsession. This is going to be the pattern of your life, and, when you think about it, it's not the end of the world."

I said to him, "Doctor, how would you feel if *you* never had an orgasm?"

He bristled. "That's an entirely different matter. Men *do.*"

On that note, I left him. And never went back.

I was stubborn.

If medical doctors and psychologists were incapable of answering my questions, I decided I would find the answers on my own. I was convinced that there *was* an answer, a piece to the puzzle, that was out there somewhere.

But where? I remember standing in a vaulted room in the New York Public Library, surrounded by thousands upon thousands of drawers of catalog cards. I was completely intimidated. I didn't know how to look anything up; I didn't know who to ask for help, or even what I was looking for! I went, instead, to a neighborhood library on the East Side and checked out a couple of marriage manuals, which was all they had. I read them eagerly, but they disappointed me: not a word about how to achieve orgasm.

I went to other libraries. I studied home medical guides, more marriage manuals, psychology books. I told librarians I was looking for books about "gynecological problems," because you didn't say "sex." You didn't walk into a library and say, "I'd like a book on sexuality." The few medical books that contained sex material were locked in glass cases in the library, and only "professionals" had access to them. (It turned out, later, that those books didn't have much in them anyway.) From my standpoint, the female orgasm was a secret more closely guarded than that of the hydrogen bomb. William H. Masters and Virginia E. Johnson had not yet published *Human Sexual Response*. They had begun to publish articles in professional journals like the *New England Journal of Medicine*, but I didn't know that, and I wouldn't have understood the terminology if I had come upon them. There was no book, it seemed, that explained what really happened inside a woman's body during sex. Not one.

But I didn't know that yet. I was still looking.

I was down in Gimbels' basement one afternoon for a wonderful shoe sale. They had shoes from Saks Fifth Avenue that were very expensive if you bought them at Saks, but were very cheap at Gimbels—$6.95, maybe $7.95, for $50.00 and $60.00 shoes. I was a master at bargain shopping in those days, and I worked my way through the other women, turning up spectacular buys by burrowing under mountains of shoes. I sort of complimented myself, saying, "I've really learned how to do this. I not only have talent, I've learned the techniques."

And it suddenly hit me! Maybe I had to *learn* to have orgasms!

Simple? Sure it was. I thought, *I had to learn to walk, I had to learn to talk, I had to learn to do everything.* Instinct played a large role in mastering those skills, I knew, but maybe my natural instinct had failed me in sexual matters. I realized that I was dealing with sexual ignorance. Not only was I badly informed about the bodies of women in general, I knew practically nothing about how *my* body reacted and functioned.

I paid for my shoes and hustled out of Gimbels, truly excited. I was about to embark on my private voyage of discovery.

The missing piece of the puzzle was self-knowledge.

As I have learned since, the female's sexual mechanism is more complex than the male's, and very few women embark on their sex lives in their teens and find instant fulfillment. There's so much more for a woman to know than that the penis goes into the vagina. I used to say that a woman's body was to a man's as a Rolls-Royce was to a Model T, and I drew criticism for that statement. I simply meant that women seemed to require more "fine tuning" to function sexually as easily as men. Male orgasm was no mystery. As with the Model T, every man knew how to find the crank and how to turn it. We women were in the front seat of the Rolls, looking for the starter and baffled by all the knobs on the instrument panel.

When I got home from Gimbels, I was like the woman behind the wheel of the Rolls. If I were ever to start the damn thing, I was going to have to try all the knobs.

Masturbation.

It's an ugly-sounding word, isn't it? It's a frightening word to many women: Say it and they draw back. It's not a "pretty" word. It's not even lively or wicked, like a four-letter word. *Autoeroticism* is a lot better, although it sounds like a psychologist coined it. *Erotic* has all sorts of wonderful, mysterious connotations, whereas *masturbation* just sounds like something from a hygiene class.

But I was determined to learn about my own body, to discover what excited and pleased me.

So I masturbated.

I was a little self-conscious at first, but not for long. After all, I approached it like a research project. I was intellectually curious. I noted my response to every experiment in self-stimulation: Touching myself *here* gave me shivers and quickened my breath, while stroking *there* was as erotic as brushing my teeth. I was in no hurry, either. A few years later, Masters and Johnson would publish their "sensate focus exercises," which involved masturbation, "stop-start" touching and sensitivity drills, and similar means for tuning in to your own sensations for the first time. They would recommend the removal of all "performance" considerations. That's exactly what I was doing by masturbating: escaping all distractions (the greatest of which, with a man, was my earnest desire to give him sexual pleasure). Now I had an ultimate goal, but no immediate goal. I was truly "discovering" my body.

Then it came. It was a surprise. An utter surprise. One evening, perhaps two months after I had started "training," I was masturbating with a vibrator when suddenly the mildly pleasurable sensations I was used to escalated. I suddenly felt myself in the grip of dizzying, gasping, ecstatic, pulsating . . . *"Orgasm!"* I cried out. I was thrilled, and as the sensation leveled out into a relaxed, warm feeling of contentment, I savored it. I lay there in bed, my breathing and pulse returning to normal, and savored my first, my very first orgasm.

And then I got on the telephone!

"I did it!" I crowed to my three closest women friends. "I had an orgasm! I did it!"

"How did you do it?" each asked, her excitement unconcealed.

"Just the way you did," I said. Each time the sudden silence on the other end of the line betrayed the truth: *She didn't know how!* For years I had asked friends how they had achieved orgasm, and they had always put me off with, "It just happens." They had *lied.* They were too embarrassed to admit that their sex lives were as vacant as mine had been. I was on the phone with this blockbuster news—orgasm could be learned! My "orgasmic" friends were begging *me* to tell *them* how.

I was shocked. All along, I had assumed that other women were having orgasms the way I had breakfast—they *told* me they were—and now I discovered that they had been in the same fix I was in. They faked orgasm with their husbands and lovers. They lied to their women friends. And they suffered privately—awful pangs of sexual inadequacy that made them feel unwomanly. To them, it was worth the embarrassment of confession to learn my secret! "How did you do it?" they asked. "How did you do it?"

I told them.

It started that way, on the telephone, one to one. Then, three or four of us would get together where we could really share information. We began to talk about our sex lives candidly, which in itself helped dispel the crushing sense of inferiority some of us felt. We discovered that, although we had similar problems, we had different sexual patterns. Carol (to make up a name) was a one-orgasm woman; she could achieve one blockbuster orgasm, but then she was turned off to sex, much like a man. Virginia, once she got past the obstacle of that first orgasm, was capable of whole strings of orgasms. Louise had one mild orgasm, then a much stronger orgasm, after which she could relax, fulfilled.

These were not seminars. I had initiated the White Elephant Trades, where six young women, all wearing similar sizes, would get together and bring at least one dress we hated. We'd put the dresses in a pile and take turns picking out what we liked until we all had new things. These parties were ideal forums for talk about sex. (The White Elephants in our lives were sometimes men!) We also talked at lunch, at dinner parties, or when friends dropped by for drinks after work. We shared worries, swapped knowledge, unaware, of course, that we were precursors of the consciousness-raising groups that began to flourish in the 1970's. What was very rewarding to me at that time was the feeling that we women were no longer competing with each other. It was also satisfying that after hearing me promote my "formula," other women went home, masturbated, and within weeks came back to gloat, "I did it, too! And it was wonderful!"

That first orgasm, I must admit, did not make me predictably orgasmic from that day forward. I continued my "research," as I described masturbation. Now that I knew the puzzle could be fitted together, I found even more satisfaction in working it. Orgasms came more and more often. There were disappointments, too. Even after I found I could achieve orgasm with my hand or with a vibrator, I still had difficulty climaxing with a man. I overanticipated that final glory, and I had to study that problem separately. With a man it was more difficult to focus on my own sensations. I had to learn a higher degree of selfishness.

I succeeded, finally. And, as before, I was overwhelmed by my sense of accomplishment. It was as if a great inner resource had been unleashed. I felt erotic. Attractive. Lovable. *Sensuous.* Not only were the physical sensations of orgasm delightful, but they relieved me of the sexual role of the Good Hostess.

"What's the Good Hostess?" my friends asked.

"I have yet to meet a woman who talks candidly about sex who hasn't at one time or another faked orgasm," I said. "Even the women who are orgasmic. If we think we're lagging too far behind the man in our responses, with little hope of catching up, we fake an orgasm to make sex 'come out right.' It makes men happy when we 'end together.' We're like the good hostess at a dinner party, who serves dessert even if she's not hungry."

No more, I vowed. (Or not as often, anyway.)

I had given up acting by this time; I had "retired." One reason, as I explained in letters and expensive long-distance calls to Mother in Florida, was that I found most actors shallow and boring. "They're always talking shop," I complained, "and frankly, I need more variety in my life." Mother clung to this explanation and built on it, telling her friends and co-workers that my career was thwarted by virtue. "Terry isn't willing to compromise herself to get ahead as an actress," she said, meaning, without being explicit, "the casting couch." The casting couch was a subject of much excited speculation and gossip in Mother's conversational circles, so my alleged incorruptibility seemed like a valid excuse for my not being a star yet.

Actually, I had a much more compelling reason for quitting acting. No work! I was very shy for an actress, overly sensitive to the steady diet of rejection that is a performer's lot. It was agony for me, making the rounds. I would start off for an audition and instead walk past the stage door or around the block and not go in. Fortunately, the bohemian life-style did not require that you actually *be* what you professed to be. The actors were waiting on tables, the musicians were working in mail rooms, the writers stayed up all night drinking and talking. We were all doing creative things, and it was fun. We attended off-off-Broadway parties, drank cheap wine, and got free tickets to see all the shows. Some of us used to meet regularly at Tony's, a spaghetti place in the Village that had a basketball net in its courtyard. You could get a whole plate of spaghetti and a glass of red wine for a dollar. It was great fun, if you could keep the actors from talking about themselves.

I wasn't quite ready to give that up, so I determined to become a playwright, a master of light farce, someone in the Kaufman and Hart tradition.

Part of the appeal of writing, I confess, was the freedom. I could never stand regular work. I hated routine. For two summers I had worked in the box office and done publicity for the Canal Fulton Summer Theater in Ohio, and in 1959 I had done the same for the Pocono Playhouse in Pennsylvania. Working in a box office was a terrible job—fast, noisy, pressured, and poorly paid—which, I decided, is why most veteran ticket sellers looked and acted like Alastair Sim playing Ebenezer Scrooge. At the end of every season I collapsed into depression and lethargy. I would go to bed and sleep for days, hibernating like a bear.

One fall I went back to Kansas City to stay with my father who had remained in Missouri following my parents' divorce. Autumn was so beautiful there, and the sight of flaming elms and maples and the smell of burning leaves picked up my spirits. Other times I visited Mother in Palm Beach. She lived in a modest garden apartment in an old Addison Mizner building close to the beach and close to her job as receptionist and switchboard operator for the Boynton Landscape Company. Mother had very little money, and her hands were full raising my youngest brother, Johnny, but she was always glad to see me. She would nurse me back to health and high spirits with homemade custards, tapioca, fresh orange juice, and beef stew, and then stay up almost all night talking with me, her glass of sherry at her side, a cigarette in one hand. She never criticized me for my collapses, and never accused me of malingering. In a few weeks, my flesh tanned and my adrenaline restored, I would return to New York and get a new job.

For a time, I did secretarial work. At Clarendon Press I answered phones and did simple bookkeeping. (I was very neat, but none of the figures ever came out right.) Then I went to Thompson Newspapers, again as a secretary. (At my interview I didn't bother to mention that I couldn't type or take dictation. I just implied that my dictation was "rusty," and then rushed out and took a crash course in Speedwriting.) One winter, I did research for a writer who was compiling a book on "services for the rich"—the best tailors, pet doctors, etc. Another winter, I wrote travel brochures for a travel agency. It was excellent experience for a writer, since I had never been to any of the places I was writing about. A year later, I returned to Palm Beach and did publicity for the Biltmore Hotel. Then, back in New York, I worked three months in Best's Better Blouses. (The nice part about that job was that I got a terrific discount on sample monogram blouses, which I bought in quantity. The only catch was, the initials were SK. I told everyone my name was Sue Katz.)

All that time, I was writing stories and plays on weekends and late at night. I sent humor pieces to *The New Yorker,* which showed up in the return mail two days later. (I decided that *The New Yorker* editors had benches next to the post office conveyor belt and rejected manuscripts while they were still moving.) I never sold a story.

I was getting nowhere fast, but it was during this period of frantic and brief employments that I made one of the more significant friendships in my life. I was dating a young man named David Pelham, who was an assistant to David Merrick, the Broadway impresario. One night in 1959, David Pelham took me to a dinner party at the apartment of Jim Moran, the world-famous publicist and author. Jim's renown was built upon a series of zany publicity stunts he had perpetrated in Hollywood during the movies' heyday, when films needed wonderful, amusing exploitation. He had sold an icebox to an Eskimo. He had changed horses in midstream. He had sat on, and hatched, an ostrich egg (to publicize the book *The Egg and I*). He had searched for, and found, a needle in a haystack. Now he was living in New York in the East Sixties, across the street from a fire station, in a wonderful airy apartment with lots of plants and beautiful tile work. He did publicity for David Merrick and others.

Actually, Jim Moran was a bookish man, an expert on many esoteric subjects. He maintained a personal library of about ten thousand volumes and, if I had a question about crustaceans or Buddhism or Shakespeare's sonnets, I could call him and count on getting an answer. He was portly and fiercely bearded, and he had a wonderful sense of humor. He loved to explode the pompous, surrounding himself with eccentrics and beautiful young women—mostly the latter. He came as close as an American can come to maintaining a harem in his apartment.

My best friend, Jacque Thompson, remembers meeting me for the first time at Jim's apartment. "You were painting a room for Jim," she says, "and you were dressed in your pink-and-white-checked smock. You were doing it because it was therapeutic, but I thought you were nuts."

The room in question, Jim's Moorish Room, was a bit unusual. The walls and ceiling were black, and a brass chandelier hung over the bed, which was raised on a pedestal. There was silk gauze over the windows, and all sorts of filigree, highlighted by a remarkable grillwork over the bottom sashes, a sort of chain mail that Jim had asked his girl friends to assemble, a link at a time, with pliers. The walls were decorated with fragments of colored glass embedded in an adhesive. And on the far wall, Jim had erected a sort of throne, from which one could observe what was going on in bed.

Needless to say, when I mentioned Jim Moran to Mother in my letters, I left out the Moorish Room. I wrote about his African masks or about his antique grand piano, a gilded, rococo treasure that had once belonged to Mozart or somebody. (Mother spent many happy hours at her own piano, practicing the Chopin "Preludes," Beethoven's "Moonlight Sonata," and "Claire de Lune."

Aside from the fact that I was willing to paint walls for him, Jim saw in me a quality lacking in the erotic butterflies he kept about him. Jacque remembers asking Jim, "Don't you think the fact that Terry is so superorganized and efficient might turn men off?" Jim did, apparently. My skills were the seat-of-the-pants kind he detested—writing releases, making phone calls, planning itineraries—but Jim was just enough of a businessman to concede that a company—even a company that marketed craziness—needed a few disciplined employees. He began to use my organizational skills for some of his stunts.

As a fledgling publicist, I never actually created a stunt. Jim was the brains of the organization, and he favored promotions that were disruptive and colorful. For David Merrick's production of *The World of Suzie Wong*, Jim staged a subway-ricksha race in midtown Manhattan. (The ricksha won.) To promote Brooklyn's St. George Hotel, Jim sent a mounted knight wielding a lance into Brooklyn's rush-hour traffic with directions to "joust with something." For the movie *Myra Breckenridge*, Jim purchased an enormous and garish cowgirl statue that had been a sign on Sunset Boulevard in Hollywood (and which figured in Gore Vidal's novel) and hauled it across the country on a flatbed truck. In every city and town he would trundle the cowgirl up to City Hall and present it to the mayor, to be displayed permanently as an object of civic pride "on the order of the Statue of Liberty," as Jim put it. The mayors always refused Jim's gift, but Jim invariably got interviewed by all the local newspapers and radio-TV outlets, giving *Myra* a badly needed boost.

Jim's right-hand man, Desmond Slattery, did some clever things, too. Desmond was a very colorful character, a publicist and part-time actor who was a dead ringer for Errol Flynn and who had lived with Jim back in the crazy Hollywood days. When I met him, Desmond was selling crickets in cricket cages. He then began importing Mexican jumping beans, claiming that he owned a jumping bean field down in Mexico, but you couldn't believe everything Desmond said. He loved Jim, but he thought him a bit impractical sometimes. "Ideas are a dime a dozen," he used to say. "The idea is maybe ten percent of the thing. The rest is putting it together."

I enjoyed all this stuff, but my role was "putting it together," the 90 percent. For the movie *What's New, Pussycat?,* I was the traffic cop for what we called the Great Pussycat Caper. From an office command post filled with ringing telephones, I dispatched "pussycats"—young women in leotard costumes with tails and ears (Jacque was one!)—to radio stations, newspaper offices, restaurants, or wherever, with clever, personalized messages. Like most of Jim's stunts, the pussycats were mildly disruptive and incongruous enough to get onlookers to scratching their heads and laughing, "What the—?" Word of mouth was excellent, and *What's New, Pussycat?* did a strong first week of business.

Jim brooded, though, because few of his stunts had the impact of his pioneering efforts in Hollywood. Newspapers no longer gobbled up staged happenings and goofy stunts—journalistic standards were changing. Jim had to *trick* newspeople now, or create stunts so disruptive that they couldn't be ignored. That was often expensive, and if a stunt didn't work, the money was wasted. Television commercials and print ads, by comparison, were a sure thing.

The publicity stunt was on the endangered species list. I loved working as a publicist for Jim, and I still wanted to write plays, but I wanted to eat, too. Jim sympathized. He had a client at the time, an obscure Manhattan book publisher, who had an opening for a full-time book publicist.

"Terry would be perfect for that," Jacque told Jim.

"I guess she would," Jim allowed.

2

*L*yle Stuart was not a gentleman publisher.

His offices were on Park Avenue, but Park Avenue *South*, about Twentieth Street. The building looked like a tenement, an old wooden structure several stories high housing warehouse space and a few commercial tenants. When I worked there I was always terrified of being trapped in it in a fire. The creaky elevator moved both passengers and freight, and visitors getting off the elevator were met by no real reception area, but by a little window with sliding glass doors where customers occasionally came to purchase a book.

Lyle had a reputation for publishing interesting muckraking books. But there was also a line of erotica, with which I was not involved, that was not a part of his regular publishing company, which he sold by mail order as the Rory John Catalog. There was a clear distinction between the catalog and Lyle Stuart, Inc.—Rory John consisted of things that Lyle gathered in Europe, sex magazines, sex toys, and the like. The shipping department for both lines was in the same building. All I knew about the catalog line was that it was very profitable.

Lyle did not believe in decor. People talk about how the old newspaper offices looked so ratty, but they looked like they had been decorated by Billy Baldwin compared to Lyle's offices. Lyle did not believe in privacy either, so his employees worked at battered desks in a big open room with plank flooring and a perpetually sooty atmosphere. Lyle liked to watch everyone through his open office door. Not even his officers got private offices—not even his *bookkeeper,* who really needed more quiet to work—which lent a Dickensian flavor to operations. Lyle had his finger in every pie, knew everyone's job down to the smallest detail. When I worked there as publicity director, I had a desk on the side of the room across from the windows that overlooked the street. It was a noisy office, and I often had trouble talking on the phone, with other phones ringing and typewriters clacking all around me. It was a far cry from my fantasy of a publishing house as a carpeted, walnut-paneled place in which editors sat in wing chairs, surrounded by leather-bound books, smoking pipes and discussing new projects with the great authors.

Lyle was nothing like that. He was a gambler. A high-stakes gambler at that, whose ten-thousand-dollar-a-night limit at Las Vegas casinos dazzled employees who accompanied him on company junkets to Nevada. He could be quite charming and forceful when he chose to be, especially in the days when I worked for him. His wife, Mary Louise, was a lovely lady from Ohio, very attractive, very nice, very bright. She was Lyle's chief editor and shared his office as well as his home. They lived together in a modern co-op building in a very dangerous section of Brooklyn, a neighborhood with one of the highest crime rates in America. Equally odd was the fact that Lyle, a high roller and a very large man, drove to work in tiny little cars.

Lyle could be very unreasonable. I once sent a review copy

of a Lyle Stuart book to *Time* magazine, and although they did not initially review it, with insistent prodding from me they finally relented and decided to review the book after all. The original review copy had long since disappeared, so they asked Lyle for another review copy. He refused! He told them to go out and buy a copy if they wanted one. *Time* said, "Forget it"; and the book never got reviewed.

I had worked very hard to get *Time* to reconsider that book, so I was crushed. It wasn't an isolated instance, either. Before long, I found *myself* buying copies to give to reviewers. Which was crazy. I didn't make that kind of money.

Lyle was also perverse with regard to his editorial policies. Most publishers consider a staff of capable, well-paid editors essential to successful book publishing, but Lyle entrusted his manuscripts to his family. The books that Mary Louise couldn't edit, her sister, Eileen Brand, handled. Eileen— later one of my closest friends—came to New York two or three times a year, but she lived in Gainesville, Florida, where Lyle mailed her manuscripts for editing. Eileen was paid by the hour, and she was usually told how many hours she could put in on a manuscript. She was a fine editor, but Lyle rarely gave her the time to do her best work on a manuscript. Of course, the fine points of editing did not interest Lyle. He rarely read the books he published, a fact that he not only did not conceal but about which he boasted.

Lyle wasn't cheap about everything, though. His company junkets were the envy of the publishing industry. Every year, he closed down the offices for about a week and took everybody on vacation with him—twenty-odd people, the shipping room, accounting, everybody. I hadn't been with the company a full year in November 1966, but Lyle still allowed me to go on that year's junket to Jamaica. It was wonderful. Eileen and I shared a room, and we all swam together and went sightseeing and partied at night. I loved the feeling of "family" in that organization.

The trouble with "families," though, is that sometimes

they won't let you grow up. As I learned more and more about book publicity, I wanted the freedom to run my operation the way I thought it needed to be run. Lyle watched over everything, which bugged me. Also, Lyle's world was the daily press, the newspapers, but I came from a different generation and saw that TV and radio were becoming the main arenas for promoting books and authors. Lyle acknowledged that, but his heart was still with the newspaperpeople and columnists. He wanted me to spend all my time trying to write things to feed the New York columnists, even though I didn't have those contacts.

Lyle worked with me. He always said that I couldn't write, but he never seemed to tire of teaching me. In particular, he pressured me to get something in John Crosby's column in the *Herald Tribune*. I worked for weeks and wrote many clever things, but John Crosby never used them. I was getting ulcers until some kind soul told me, "Don't you know? Crosby and Lyle have feuded for years. Crosby hates Lyle's guts." In fact, Crosby had reportedly vowed that there would *never* be a reference to Lyle Stuart or a Lyle Stuart book in his column!

When I heard that, I was angry.

Lyle never liked my press releases, or the fact that I got too many personal phone calls at the office. But he did respect my radio-TV work, even though he often groused, "You spend too much time on it." Actually, I gave hours of my own time, coaching authors for their promotional appearances, accompanying them to talk shows, establishing valuable contacts at all levels of broadcasting. I was also fairly accomplished at staging publicity stunts, having learned so much from Jim Moran.

Lyle liked stunts. He hired Jim to come up with one to publicize a book by Frank Edwards, *Flying Saucers—Serious Business,* and Jim proposed flying a kite with running lights in Central Park late at night to provoke a rash of UFO sightings. Lyle, Jim, and I tested the kite one day on the beach at Fire Island, running up and down the sand, laughing and then groaning every time the kite crashed under the weight of the lights. Instead of the kite, Lyle finally accepted another idea, which was to dress up two midgets and a mature child (there was a shortage of available midgets that week in New York) in silver space suits and have them picket the United Nations with signs reading FLYING SAUCERS ARE SERIOUS BUSINESS. We got wonderful coverage in the New York papers with that one, and the wire services picked up the photo and carried it across the country.

Lyle was shocked when I quit. I had warned him, though. One afternoon in his office, I told him, "We're working at cross-purposes. You're putting unreasonable pressures on me by demanding that I get you into columns that have banned you and withholding review copies from magazines and shows, then insulting them on the telephone when their people call. I've begun to dread coming to work. If I can't have more control over the way I do my job, I'll have to quit. I don't want to, but I will."

I don't think he took me seriously. As far as I know no one who had become a real member of the Lyle Stuart "family" had ever quit, and since I was female, he wasn't impressed with my challenge to his authority. If a man had warned him, he might have listened.

Anyway, I had decided that Lyle was not going to change and *I* was not going to change, so I hunted around and got two jobs in one. I signed on as a specialist in TV and radio promotion, shared by two book publishers, Simon and Schuster and Cornerstone Library (which was distributed by S&S). I would even be getting more money.

When I told Lyle, he was very upset, taking my move as a betrayal. (Mary Louise never said what *she* thought, but I felt she understood.) He didn't stay angry long, though. He was constantly on the phone to me, encouraging me to marry one of his best friends, the late-night radio talk king, WNBC's Long John Nebel. And one year later, when I started my own book publicity firm, Terry Garrity Publicity, Lyle Stuart was one of my first clients.

On reflection, those were the happiest years of my life. My work as a book publicist introduced me to new ideas and dozens of fascinating people. I was very much into cooking at the time, and I often had small, rather elegant dinner parties at my little apartment on East Forty-ninth Street. The apartment was wonderful, a narrow, brick-walled studio on the ground floor of a renovated building a few blocks from the East River and the United Nations. In the rear I had a tiny balcony that overlooked a sunken garden. When I opened the door to the balcony I could smell the tantalizing smells from the chic restaurant next door, hear the kitchen sounds, and watch the cats who sunned on my balcony leap from railing to fence to ground, stalking food scraps. I was blessed, as well, with a wonderful neighbor, who rented the apartment on the other side of my brick wall. He was a very tall young actor with a charming smile, a passion for baseball, and a never-ending stream of girl friends.

His name was David Hartman.

Years later, when David became host of *Good Morning America,* I sometimes heard the criticism that he appeared "too nice to be believable." As his neighbor for five years, I knew better. David is as kind and sincere as any person you'll meet. He was just getting started when I met him, starring in Rheingold Beer commercials and playing small roles on and off Broadway. I can't think back to my happy time in that apartment without remembering the way David used to enter the building—singing in a rich, operatic baritone—and how I could follow his voice, through the wall, from his front door out to his balcony, where he serenaded the cats and the restaurant workers next door. A few people complained, but I loved to hear David sing. He worked very hard on his voice. In fact, he was always learning something new, polishing his skills, learning to play the guitar, whatever. He was such a happy person, and always falling in love. All his furniture came from the Salvation Army, except for his bed, I guess, which was oversized to accommodate his tall frame. When my brother Johnny, who is six feet six inches himself, came to visit me, David cheerfully dragged a mattress into my apartment for him. Another time, he let my mother stay in his apartment while he was away.

I would return these favors by remembering David when I had my dinner parties. We had only half-size refrigerators, too small to store leftovers, so I would set out late-night snacks for David, who would return the dishes the next day. He used to come home quite late when he played the role of Oscar in *Hello, Dolly*.

My memories of that apartment are of laughter and singing and sunshine. Is it possible? Were there really fewer clouds then? Longer springs? More music? Rainbows over Manhattan?

It started with a taxi ride.

On a cold, gray day in October 1968, I was plucking corroded paper clips out of a pile of good ones in a glass bowl on my desk, pondering the fact that the bigger and richer my clients were, the slower they paid, when the phone rang.

"Terry Garrity Publicity," I answered. "May I help you?"

It was Lyle. "Terry, I've got an idea that will change your life," he said. "I'm on my way to my attorney's office, but I'll pick you up and tell you my idea while we're going across town. You can drop me off and then take the cab to wherever you'd like to go."

I wasn't finished with the paper clips, but Lyle sounded excited, so I agreed.

A few minutes later, I was standing on the curb in front of

my little apartment, wondering how Lyle planned to change my life. When his cab pulled up, I hopped in and we bounced across midtown Manhattan while Lyle, a heavy man with a dark beard just starting to gray, told me his idea. "Terry, I want you to write a book," he said.

I admit I was surprised, although my jaw probably dropped only a foot, not two feet, as Lyle later claimed.

"There has never been a sex book written *by* a woman *for* women," he continued. "This is the time for it, and I think you can do it."

I was tempted to laugh. "Lyle, don't you remember? You think I'm a lousy writer. I'm the woman you said couldn't write press releases. Besides, I'm not a doctor. How could I get away with writing a sex book?"

Neither point seemed to faze him. "The kind of book I have in mind won't be hard to write. All you have to do is line up all the sex and marriage manuals that have sold well and rewrite what they say from the woman's point of view. You don't have to be a doctor to do that."

"True . . ." I hesitated. "But it wouldn't be very original, either."

Lyle looked at me irritably. He knew that my new publicity company was struggling to survive, and he thought I should be jumping for joy at his idea. "Terry," he said earnestly, "you told me you barely have your apartment's rent."

I laughed. "That's true."

"Come in with a chapter and an outline. If we like it, we'll give you an advance. This is a chance for you to make some money."

We had pulled up in front of a downtown office building.

"All right, I'll think about it," I promised.

And I did think about it. I discarded the idea of cribbing other people's work and decided that trying to pass myself off as a doctor was unethical. Also, although I had a tremendous intellectual interest in the subject, I had no more desire to write a sex book than I had to get into a rocket ship and go to the moon. I was still struggling to be a playwright. I wanted to write children's books. I wanted to sell a story to *The New Yorker*.

But Lyle was right about one thing: There were no sex books written by women for women. It was time to change this, and suddenly I knew that there was a sex book I would *love* to write, a book where I wouldn't have to pretend to be something I wasn't. A book I could care about. A book that could help women who had some of the same sex problems I had had and overcome. But did I have the courage to write a book that frank and explicit? Because to do it right, it would have to be the most outspoken and graphic how-to book ever published. Was America ready to read about how to masturbate, how to perform oral sex, *exactly* how to be a more creative lover?

I sat down at my desk and began to write an outline. For Chapter 1 I wrote down, "Sex—Why It's Even Ahead of Horse Racing as the Nation's Number One Sport." For Chapter 2, I again wrote, "Sex—" and followed it with, "It's All in Your Head: You Can Learn to Be Sensuous."

For Chapter 3, the shocker: "Masturbation." I had achieved my first orgasm through masturbation, and I believed it to be the key to fulfillment for nonorgasmic women. I wrote down subheadings for vibrators and water manipulation and chuckled to myself.

All of a sudden, my thinking was very clear. I hurriedly wrote, "The *Single* Woman: Does She or Doesn't She?" "How to Give to Your Favorite Charity—You." "How to Drive a Man to Ecstasy." The whole outpouring took less than an hour, and not one word was ever changed. I now felt the excitement that had been missing in the cab ride with Lyle. I suddenly wanted to write *my* book.

I grabbed the phone and called up my lover, Len Forman, at Simon and Schuster, the book publishers, where he was vice-president in charge of publicity and promotion. "Len, love," I laughed. "I need a title for a book. It's a how-to book."

"How-to what?" he asked.

"Sex!" I said.

"Wait a minute." There was a moment of silence while Len got up from his desk and went to close his office door.

He came back laughing. "Are you serious?"

"Yes, I am!"

I read him some of the chapter titles, and for the next minute or so we threw book titles back and forth.

"Uh, *The Woman's Guide to Sexuality?*"

"Mmmmmm . . . not bad," I said, "but a little formal."

"The Woman's Guide to Sensuality."

"Better. I like that word." I broke it down into three sultry syllables: *"Sennnn*-suuu-alll." I pondered. "Maybe a little blatant. How about *The Woman's Book of Sexual Fulfillment?* . . . Too formal again? *Sex for the Modern Woman?*" I sighed. "This isn't easy. *Female Sexual Fulfillment . . .*"

"How to Have Orgasms," Len said, and we both laughed.

"Woman . . ."

"Sensual . . ."

"Female . . ."

"Sensuous . . ."

And then Len said it, and we both knew, instantly, that we had found the title. He said, "How about *The Sensuous Woman?*"

"That's it!" I cried. "You're a genius!"

I immediately wrote it down at the top of my legal pad: *The Sensuous Woman.*

I had no inkling of how those three words on the printed page would affect my future and touch the intimate lives of millions of women around the world.

In the years that followed, when I promoted *The Sensuous*

Woman, I learned that many people are less interested in sex than in money. "How much have you made off the book?" was a frequent question when I signed copies at bookstores and department stores. Just as often, people who disliked my book questioned my motives by suggesting I wrote it for "easy money" or "the quick buck."

Any best-selling author has to put up with a certain amount of resentment from wage earners who don't understand the nature of book publishing. Thirty or forty thousand titles are published every year in America. Of these, only a few dozen ever reach the best-seller lists. The vast majority never earn the author more than a modest cash advance for signing a publishing contract. It is a rare author, indeed, who manages to make a living from his writing.

Another popular notion is that sex guarantees big bucks. Not so. Hundreds of "sex books" are published every year, but only a handful have ever been best sellers. I had written another book just before *The Sensuous Woman*—a bargain-hunter's shopping guide called *How to Get the Most for Your Money in New York* (coauthored by Ashbel Green, an editor at Alfred A. Knopf). Nobody believes me, but the cash advance for that book was actually greater than for *The Sensuous Woman.* The truth is, my cash advance for *The Sensuous Woman*—the sum total guaranteed me—was $1,500.

In five installments.

Every time I mailed in a section of the manuscript, Lyle would mail me a check for $300. Accordingly, I was frugal with materials: I wrote the book in longhand with felt pens on the backs of invoice forms I had saved from my tenure at Thompson Newspapers.

I wrote *The Sensuous Woman* at night and on weekends. It went like a streak of lightning because little research was necessary, thanks to those meetings with small groups of women friends where we discussed sexual problems and swapped sexual information and advice. For a nonexpert, I knew an awful lot about female sexuality.

I assumed that Lyle had chosen me for that reason. Actually, I learned later that he had started through his Rolodex wheel looking for "women who wrote," and finding no one in A through F who wanted to change her life, he had called the first G.

Me.

The hardest part was making the writing clear without being simplistic. I had test readers on every chapter, and they kept taking out all my cleverest and witty passages. I followed their advice, cutting and simplifying, cutting and simplifying.

I can thank Norman Monath at Cornerstone Library for teaching me the how-to-book "formula." Cornerstone specialized in how-to and self-help books, and when I worked for Norman I was immersed in titles like *Play the Guitar in Five Minutes, The Magic of Believing, How to Get Rich While You Sleep,* and *How to Play Tennis.* I read self-help books to the point that I flinched when I walked near one.

The "formula," basically, is this: *You tell them you're going to tell them. . . . You tell them. . . . Then you tell them you've told them.* Every chapter follows this structure, with repeated summaries of the previously learned material, which makes it easy for the reader to absorb the crucial messages. I contend that any how-to book that follows the formula will be a success. I know that books that *violate* it usually fail. With *The Sensuous Woman,* I followed the formula to the letter, just as Dale Carnegie did in *How to Win Friends and Influence People,* and Maxwell Maltz did in *Psycho-Cybernetics.* Which is not to say that I *liked* all these books—for one thing, they're all pretty much the same—but I recognized the common denominator for their success.

From the beginning, I had made one thing very clear to Lyle: I did not intend to write the book under my own name.

I suspected that a candid sex book would not endear me to children's book editors, and I felt squeamish about being identified as a "sex book author." (It wasn't the sort of thing one wanted printed in one's hometown newspaper, and I knew all my old schoolmates at Lee's Summit High School didn't miss much that was printed in the Kansas City *Star*.) "Besides," I told Lyle, "a sex book author could attract all kinds of kooks. I don't want the Boston Strangler on my doorstep."

Lyle was unhappy with the idea of a pseudonym. He wanted his author out promoting the book.

"What if I agree to make some promotional appearances under another name?" I offered. "I just don't want anybody to know who I really am."

"I guess so," Lyle said, without enthusiasm.

Later, though, after giving it more thought, I decided that I wanted to be truly anonymous, foregoing any and all promotional appearances. "I don't want my family to know," I explained. "Particularly my mother. She isn't ready; she'll *never* be ready for *The Sensuous Woman!*"

Lyle was again opposed, but gradually he backed off. Mary Louise was on my side, and he always respected her opinion. Finally, he agreed that anonymous authorship might even make the book more mysterious, and therefore more salable: People would think it was more wicked. He gave me his word that my identity would be kept secret. We shook hands on it.

But what pseudonym? We considered a long list of names which I had assembled, and which everyone agreed were terrible. My favorite was Gayle Jaysen, but we kicked around other zippy names as well, such as Mary Smith and Jane Doe.

"Why not a letter?" Lyle said. "Like X or A."

Dr. X had recently written the successful *Intern,* so X was taken, and we all agreed that A, for Anonymous, was overused. Z belonged to Zorro. We rejected G for Garrity and T for Terry. Then I said, "Wait a minute. Joan Theresa Garrity is my legal name. How about J?"

Everybody liked that.

"*The Sensuous Woman* by 'J,'" I said. "Yes, I like that." I was the proud possessor of a pen letter.

During the months I was writing the book, Len and I existed in a sensual haze. *The Sensuous Woman* was our private aphrodisiac. We looked forward each night to testing out such erotic delights as the Silken Swirl, the Hoover, and the Butterfly Flick. We thought, dreamed, acted out, analyzed, and reveled in the many subtle and exquisite gradations of sexual loving.

Would *The Sensuous Woman* have the same impact on readers? Eileen Brand thought so. She inadvertently test-marketed the book in June when she lost the manuscript at the American Booksellers Association convention in Washington, D.C. "I carried it with me into the hotel beauty shop," she told me later, "and somehow I left the manuscript there, on a chair. As soon as I got back to my room, I realized it was missing, and I frantically called down to see if they had it, and yes, they did. So I ran downstairs and burst into the beauty shop, and all these ladies were under the dryers, each with a separate chapter, and they were just buzzing." Eileen was wide-eyed. "They thought *I* was the author! They said, 'Not yet! We haven't finished!'"

Only one other person read the final manuscript: my "little" brother Johnny, who had just arrived in New York with very little money and an unmarketable degree in history from Stanford University. Within a week he had found a job as an assistant editor at a magazine called *High Fidelity Trade News,* but I had him poring over *The Sensuous Woman* before he was even unpacked. I don't remember many of his editorial comments, but I've never forgotten his advice when I asked him, halfway through his reading, if I should tell the rest of our family about my book. He looked up and laughed uneasily, obviously weighing the possible impact on our mother, whose outlook on sexual matters was Victorian. "No," he said firmly. "You hadn't better. I'm not sure even *I* want to know about it."

"Not a word?"

"Not a word," he said. And again we both laughed—nervously.

Personally, I thought my book would be either a big seller or a total failure, and I leaned toward the latter. When I saw the first jacket design, my instincts shouted, "Flop!" Lyle proudly showed me the artwork one day in his office, and I was revolted. The jacket was black and chartreuse and pictured a woman's face with her mouth open in a salacious manner that was obviously meant to suggest fellatio. "Oh, no, Lyle," I pleaded. "You *can't!*"

He was baffled by my outburst. He thought the cover was hot stuff.

"Women won't buy a book with that jacket," I insisted. "It's vile. It's pornographic! Lyle, the cosmetics industry spends millions to find out what women will buy. Why don't we take a look at the cosmetics department of some store?"

Lyle sighed. He didn't look too happy.

Happy or not, he went with me to Bloomingdale's. I walked him through the cosmetics department to show him the kinds of packaging women bought: tasteful, feminine, understated containers with pastel colors, elegant type styles, and soft photography. The soft sell. "We need a jacket that a woman won't be embarrassed by," I insisted. "We're selling sensuousness, not smut. The book should be packaged like a fine French perfume."

I don't know whether Lyle was truly impressed by the cosmetics packages or whether he just wanted to get out of Bloomingdale's. But he agreed to order another jacket design.

I breathed a sigh of relief.

The first copies of *The Sensuous Woman* arrived at the publisher's offices in early December 1969. I hurried down to Park Avenue South to haul away my twenty-five free copies, and was greatly relieved when I saw that the book had a plain jacket. Lyle had added the words *The Way to Become* in small print above the title, and for the first time I saw the quotation marks around J, which the jacket designer had added. The jacket was very plain, very conservative, and featured a quite feminine typeface that would later be much copied.

I opened the book and looked through it, but I couldn't read it. It's very hard to read a book if it exists in your head. I didn't quite know how to feel. The joy for most authors is not really the potential for making money, but the pride of authorship. But so few people knew that I had written this book. It was just beginning to sink in that my anonymity imposed special conditions. What I had written I had written as Terry Garrity, but it was now in print under the authorship of "J."

I began to share the mild curiosity of everyone who first gazed upon that plain jacket with its distinctive type: "Who is 'J'?"

3

*B*ooks were in the stores for Christmas 1969. Piles of books! Usually, when a new author walks into a store to check on how his or her book is selling, he or she finds the bookstore doesn't even have it in stock. *The Sensuous Woman,* to my amazement, was displayed in bookstore windows.

I remember stepping inside Doubleday on Fifth Avenue after work one day and seeing the stacks of my book for the first time. It was a very cold evening, and I was all wrapped up in my usual cocoon of coat, scarves, furry hood, and lined gloves. The store was very hot, and I was about to leave when I saw a man pick up my book and begin turning the pages. I was mesmerized. I pretended to browse, but actually I was watching, with darting eyes, his every move. He was the bookkeeper type, middle class, soberly dressed in coat and tie and a hat. He read slowly and didn't jump around from chapter to chapter as do most book shoppers.

I was sweltering in all my coats and scarves, but I was determined to wait him out. My book purchases mounted—I couldn't just stand there and stare at him, I had to shop—and I began to feel feverish and weak. I looked up at the store clock; I had wasted an entire hour, and my quiet man had read almost the entire book. Finally, he put the book back on the table and left!

I had learned the folly of writing a thin book: You lose half your sales to the bookstore browsers who read standing up. A woman came in a minute later and bought *The Sensuous Woman* without so much as cracking a page, but by then I had nearly passed out from the heat and had spent a fortune on books. I felt rather foolish.

"But it's wonderful, isn't it?" I asked Len back at my apartment. "It's exciting to be published, even if nobody knows it."

I had no time to wallow in self-congratulation. I had "retired" my ailing publicity business and taken over as publicity and promotion director for Meredith Corporation, a publisher on Park Avenue. I was dashing all over town promoting Toots Shore's autobiography, escorting authors to radio and TV shows, and working late into the night on catalog copy for Meredith's fall list.

One morning, the phone rang for what must have been the twentieth time, and I groaned when my secretary told me it was Lyle Stuart. "I'm *never* going to finish this stuff," I sighed, grabbing the phone. "Yes, Lyle?" I said, bright and cheery.

"Terry, could you come by the office this afternoon? It's extremely important."

When Lyle had something interesting to say, he liked to dramatize it, but you could never be sure if he had good news or bad news. "Can't you tell me over the phone?" I asked, looking at the pile of half-written promotion copy on my desk.

"No," he said. "It's very important that you be here in person."

That afternoon, when I got off the rickety old elevator and

entered the offices of Lyle Stuart, everything was just as I remembered it. The phones rang and the typewriters clacked and everything was as noisy and cluttered as usual. Nobody even looked up from his or her desk. It struck me that my former co-workers were intentionally ignoring me. Why?

Lyle spotted me through his open door and waved me into his private office. He tried to maintain a poker face, but a smile was tugging at the corners of his mouth.

"Lyle, what *is* it?" I asked.

"Terry, I've got news for you." The smile broke out. "Today, you're fifty thousand dollars richer than you were yesterday."

I heard the words, but I couldn't absorb them.

"I reached agreement with Dell Publishing this morning," he continued. "They're paying one hundred thousand dollars for the reprint rights to *The Sensuous Woman*."

I was speechless. My contract, which was typical in this respect, stipulated that all reprint income be shared fifty-fifty between the author and the hardcover publisher. I had dared to hope that Lyle might peddle the rights to some paperback house for $20,000, which would have meant a guarantee of $10,000 for me.

"Say it again," I said, my heart racing.

"One hundred thousand dollars."

With big round numbers, the math is easy. I was a *fifty-thousand-aire!*

Suddenly, the rest of the Lyle Stuart family was rushing in the door, crowding around me, congratulating me. It was joyous, exhilarating, a celebration. Carlos Gonzales, the bookkeeper, brought in the company checkbook. No money had actually been received yet from Dell, but Carlos made out a check for $15,000, and Lyle signed it and presented it to me on the spot. Everyone cheered. My hands trembled when I took the check. It was the most money I had ever held in my hands in my life.

I called Len immediately with the exciting news. Then I

went to dinner with Lyle and his son, Rory John. It was a joyous evening; we even sang old songs together. It was late when I got back to my apartment, but I rushed to the phone and called Johnny, who was living in a $4.25-a-day cell at a YMCA hotel on Thirty-fourth Street. "You'll never guess what happened!" I bubbled.

Although never grumpy on the phone, Johnny was not quite awake. "Uhhh—*what?*" Over the phone, I could hear the usual throbbing of the post office trucks beneath his window.

"Johnny, the paperback rights to *The Sensuous Woman* have been sold for a hundred thousand dollars!"

"The—uhh, what?" I could hear him fumbling around for the light switch.

I laughed. "And fifty thousand of it belongs to me!"

There was a moment of silence on the line. "In that case," he mumbled, "could you loan me ten dollars this week instead of five?"

"But of course!" I said blithely. "You shall have champagne and caviar!"

"That's wonderful," he said groggily. And then, "Holy cow."

He was awake.

I thought of that first $15,000 as found money.

"Found money is the unexpected windfall," I explained to a few close friends. "It's the inheritance from the maternal uncle you never met. It's the stock certificates you find in an envelope in the attic that turn out to be worth thousands. It's special." For some reason I felt I had to justify what I was about to do. "I'm going to reward myself with a little shopping spree," I proclaimed.

My old friend, Jacque Thompson, who was now a financial writer, was never shy about money matters. She asked bluntly, "How much are you thinking of spending?"

"Oh, I don't know," I said airily. "A few hundred, a thousand, maybe. Nothing wild."

"A thousand *dollars?*" yelped Jacque. "That's one twelfth of your yearly income!"

"Not anymore. Why, do you realize that I could walk into any store on Fifth Avenue tomorrow and buy almost anything I want?"

Jacque's eyes narrowed. "If you don't watch out, you'll run through all the money and have nothing to show for it."

"I'm only going to buy a few necessities," I protested, "like maybe new shoes and a new nightgown and peignoir. I'll be sensible with the rest of the money. I'll put it in some stodgy, interest-bearing account."

Jacque looked doubtful. I couldn't stop justifying myself, which was probably why she looked doubtful. "Jacque, something like this happens just once in a lifetime. I've got to get some pleasure out of it, don't I?"

"Well, sure," she said.

I was puzzled by Jacque. I thought she knew me better. True, she hadn't known me when I was a struggling actress in Greenwich Village. And she hadn't seen me as the hat-check girl at Lucky Pierre's. She hadn't met me yet when I was still a fumble-fingered puppeteer on that Volkswagen tour of summer camps. But she knew that I had always had to practice thrift. Jacque was impressed by my "envelope budget system," by which I broke my paycheck into weekly cash stipends for groceries, rent, clothes, laundry, and treats.

"Have you ever known me to be foolish with money?"

"Well, no. But you do like beautiful things, and you've never had this much money available to you at one time to play with. You could get carried away."

"Jacque, I'm far too sensible to do that."

"When are you going to do all this shopping? This weekend?"

"No sense in putting it off," I murmured dreamily. "I think I'll start tomorrow."

And I did.

I have always liked to shop. It's a mental distraction, a sensory stimulant, good physical exercise, and, if I buy something desirable, I achieve feelings of pleasure and satiation that stay with me far past the moments of purchase, unwrapping at home, and first using or wearing.

Many women make shopping a recreation or pastime. The only way I felt I differed from the average female shopper was that I rarely could bring myself to purchase anything expensive unless it was on sale or at a discount. And since I didn't have many credit cards, I seldom fell into the trap of impulse buying because of the convenience of being able to use a little rectangle of plastic.

So I wasn't concerned. This would be a brief fling, and then I would go back to "real life."

Throwing away money proved to be exhausting. All morning long I traipsed in and out of shops along Fifth and Madison avenues. B. Altman, Lord & Taylor, Saks, Gucci, Cartier, Tiffany, Bonwit Teller, Bergdorf Goodman.

All I bought was lunch—a cheeseburger at Bun & Burger.

My "found money" was burning a hole in my pocket, but I couldn't bring myself to spend it. I would head for the cash register with, say, a two-hundred-dollar dress, but then I'd think, *No, this isn't a memorable enough purchase,* and put it back on the rack. I was not having fun.

"This is ridiculous," I muttered. "I'm not going home today until I buy something fun and frivolous, something that I would ordinarily never let myself have.

I started again at the top of Fifth Avenue. I looked in Steuben's window. Nothing frivolous there. I crossed the street and eyed a necklace that seemed to be made from crushed aluminum cans in another window. That's *too* frivolous, I thought. *And ugly!*

I walked around for another hour and finally found myself on a side street off Fifth Avenue. Maybe I was just tired, maybe I had walked off my inhibitions. But there in the window of a tiny hat store, perched upon a marble pedestal, my eyes fixed upon something worthy of my quest—a golden sable fur hat. "That's *beautiful*," I said under my breath. It was frivolous but beautiful. (It was also functional—it was cold out.) I went inside and tried the hat on, and it fit my tiny head perfectly. "I love it," I said.

The proprietor, no doubt smelling an easy sale, quickly produced a matching golden sable scarf. "The set is marked down a hundred and sixty dollars," she said in her silkiest voice, "—to only three hundred dollars." That did it! The hat and scarf were not only fun and frivolous . . . they were also a bargain!

Minutes later, I strolled out of the hat shop in my new finery, feeling that I had accomplished something. I had shed a heavy weight, some unaccountable sense of burden. Examining myself in the mirrored wall of a department store, I felt a surge of excitement . . . except that I saw that my navy boots were the wrong color for golden sable. A stop at Mark Cross quickly rectified that problem: I bought a pair of brown leather boots for $75. "Gloves!" I said. It was back to Saks for brown fur-lined gloves at forty-some dollars a pair. Now I was painfully aware that I had to ditch my navy handbag. Luckily, Gucci was able to help me out: I bought a splendid golden beige handbag there for $150. Naturally, I now needed a new coat. I worked my way back down Fifth Avenue, trying on coats, until I reached Lord & Taylor, where I picked out a classic fur-lined coat, on sale, for a mere $250.

The ensemble was complete.

I glided back uptown in a state of euphoria. It was four P.M., but I couldn't wait for evening to have Len see what I had bought. I popped in at Simon and Schuster's offices at Rockefeller Center to see if he approved of my new look.

"You look gorgeous," he raved. "The image of a successful author."

I felt gorgeous. "It was a wonderful experience," I told him. "Everyone should have that experience just once in a lifetime.

I was so elated that neither one of us noticed something odd. Everything I had purchased was either brown or beige. I never wore those colors. They depressed me.

I did not want to let go of the euphoria of that first shopping spree. I wanted—no, I *needed*— to share my good fortune with those I loved. I became Lady Bountiful. I bought a Scandinavian lamp and a gray pin-striped suit for Johnny; a Baccarat Pisces paperweight for Len; black patent-leather shoes from Gucci for Jacque. I showered other friends with crystal squirrels, beautiful linens, and fresh-cut flowers.

My spending spree was going way over budget, but since Lyle had gone back to press with *The Sensuous Woman,* I decided that no harm had been done. I thought I might buy a few more things, "practical" purchases this time. I bought a new Hide-A-Bed couch, one with a more comfortable mattress. Then I bought new wall-to-wall carpeting. I had always had chintzy carpeting over the years, the kind you buy in a big plastic bag. Now I insisted on the deepest and most luxurious green carpet money could buy. It was taller than high grass and wonderful to walk in barefoot. Sometimes I would stretch out on the floor in the narrow space between the couch and my white captain's chest, close my eyes, and concentrate on the soft tickly feel of the carpet pile on my neck and arms and feet. Best of all, it was heavenly to make love on.

I was full of projects. What could be wrong about getting a green-and-white shade custom made for my picture window? Why not a specially designed storage chest to fit into that odd space by the kitchen counter? Why shouldn't I have the newest Sony color TV? ("After all," I rationalized, "I need it for my work.") I surely deserved an occasional treat, too. A few books. A crystal vase for my cut flowers.

I began going to fine picture framers, the best florists, the top fabric stores. I did an awful lot of walking, window-shopping, and decision making, and I found it all exhilarating. I didn't notice that I was no longer purchasing items on sale or discount.

I did notice that buying fine things was complicated. Shopping on a limited budget, I had always gotten to walk out of the shop with some treasure under my arm. But now I was buying things that didn't yet exist, things that had to be manufactured to my specifications. Custom draperies took months. Fine picture framers promised delivery by fall or spring, no sooner. When I ordered my German wall unit, a wonderful white monolith crowded with drawers, cabinets, shelves, and a fold-down desk, Macy's promised delivery within two weeks. They didn't bother to mention that my unit was languishing on a dock somewhere in Belgium, tied up in a longshoreman's strike. Nine months crawled by before I finally got that wall unit, and it was dropped on my doorstep unassembled. It took two earnest men hours to put the thing together. "I love jigsaw puzzles," I told them, "but I never dreamed I would spend two thousand dollars for one."

I was like those 1950's folks who remembered the Great Depression by hoarding meats and vegetables in basement freezers, except that I was stockpiling not groceries but beautiful things, things of lasting value, things I might never be able to afford again.

Finally, I reached shopping satiation. I assessed the damages and, to my relief, found that I had spent only half of my found money. The rest went into an interest-bearing account until I could get my bearings. This money was exciting, but it made me nervous too. I didn't want my life to change radically.

Meredith Corporation had decided to close down its New

York operation, so I had no office to go to anymore. I suddenly had the opportunity, temporarily, to be a lady of leisure, so I spent hours now in the quiet of my tiny apartment, reading, listening to music, cleaning, polishing, reorganizing, and waiting for purchases to be delivered. Perhaps I sensed that I would soon *need* an aesthetically pleasing private nest, a refuge.

It was a strange but cozy sensation to be suspended in time, untouched by the outside world. The phone hardly rang; the mail was pleasant.

Outside, momentum was building to turn *The Sensuous Woman* into a best seller. The jacket copy alone was selling books in many markets, particularly in the South and Midwest. Lyle's newspaper advertising was boosting initially sluggish sales on the West Coast.

But we had competition. After a slow start, Dr. David Reuben's book, *Everything You Always Wanted to Know About Sex but Were Afraid to Ask,* had caught fire. Lyle was worried that Reuben would overshadow *The Sensuous Woman.* The good doctor was doing a terrific job promoting his book on network television, which was having an immediate impact in the bookstores. When Reuben broke onto *The New York Times* best-seller list, Lyle was agitated. "You've got to make promotional appearances," he told me.

"Lyle, I *can't,*" I said. "People who are negative about sex see *The Sensuous Woman* and Dr. Reuben's book as dirty books. I don't want to be harangued by such people. I don't want to be treated like a leper."

Lyle had been publishing "objectionable" books for so long that he couldn't understand my timidity. "What do you care if people call you names?" he said gruffly. "Do you want the book to sell or do you want it to die?"

"What about my mother?" I asked, ignoring his question.

"She doesn't know I've written this book, and I have no intention of telling her."

Lyle couldn't hide his exasperation. "Terry, you won't be appearing as Terry Garrity. You'll be '*J*,' the mystery author."

"I want to *stay* a mystery," I said, a hint of panic in my voice. "That won't be easy if I'm on the eleven o'clock news."

"That won't happen," he scoffed.

"But what if it does?" It bothered me already that Lyle introduced me as "J" to salespeople and publicists at his office, while calling me Terry within earshot of everyone. "No, I can't do it. I just can't risk it."

Gradually, though, Lyle wore me down. He made me feel guilty. Ungrateful. I knew that he worked very hard to promote a best seller. With trepidation, I struck a bargain with Lyle. "I'll do some radio," I said. "No television, no newspapers, no magazines. I'll do radio talk shows as 'J' if . . . *if* . . . you promise to continue to protect my identity."

Lyle agreed.

"J" made her first public appearance after midnight on a freezing February night in 1970. She introduced herself to the night staff of a Boston radio station as "Miss J." She did not volunteer her real name. She dressed primly. Her blond wig was short and turned up under the ears, so that when she smiled she reminded people of a young Carol Channing. "J" was vague about her background and career, but none of the station personnel pressed her. Callers on the all-night talk show were similarly unconcerned with her identity. They played the game; they referred to her simply as "Miss J."

The mysterious blonde did subsequent guest stints on talk shows in New York, Washington, Baltimore, and Philadelphia. Her appearances provoked some controversy. Talk-show hosts had to humor the raspy, angry voices on the phones—frustrated, lonely, alienated voices from somewhere out in the dark—voices angry at "Miss J" for not sharing their outlook on life, angry at her bubbly, enthusiastic voice, angry about sex. But no one seemed to care who she really was.

When "J" returned to her hotel room, the Carol Channing wig came off and "J" was gone. It was Terry Garrity who called room service and ordered diet soft drinks. It was Terry Garrity who checked out the next morning without incident.

Suddenly, *The Sensuous Woman* took New York by storm. New Yorkers were talking about it, buying it, borrowing it, reading it, passing it around. You saw it everywhere, in handbags, in shopping bags, on lunch counters. Receptionists were reading it at their desks. A young woman on a crosstown bus was reading my book so intently one afternoon that she missed her stop and had to jump up and dash out the doors. (I loved that.)

Some women felt the need to disguise the book, either with a brown paper wrapper or with pretty patterns of shelf paper. Still, they carried it around with them. *The Sensuous Woman* was in all the department stores, in bookstore windows; it was referred to in the newspapers, joked about by disc jockeys, mentioned in the "happy talk" of TV news anchors.

"J," whoever she was, was suddenly a celebrity.

"Who could have written this book?" I kept hearing women, strangers, raving about *The Sensuous Woman*. It was the best book they'd ever read, or the wildest, or the most amazing, this or that. "I borrowed it from a friend," they said. "I was tenth on the list."

I confess, I loved it. At cocktail parties and dinner parties, when I heard people talking about *The Sensuous Woman,* I'd sidle up to them to eavesdrop. If someone didn't like something in the book, I could jump in and defend it. That was the best part of being anonymous. I'd say, "I think the author meant *this*." We'd have heated discussions, and I often won over people.

Nobody dreamed that I was "J." My life was like a child's fantasy of coming back from the dead, of attending one's own funeral, of being a ghost. I thought, *They can't see me, but I can see them! Incredible!*

I was invisible.

One night in April, Len came to my apartment to pick me up for dinner, bearing an iced bottle of French champagne. He had a huge smile. "Congratulations!" he said, giving me a big hug.

I was baffled. "For what?"

"You don't know? Your book hits *The New York Times'* best-seller list this week!"

"It *does?*" I felt a surge of glee. *"Ooooh!* Fantastic!" I hugged him back and then dashed about in crazed circles, yelling, "I did it! I can't believe it! I am a best-selling author! My book is on *The New York Times'* best-seller list!"

Len laughed at my antics and then did the practical thing: got out two glasses and opened the champagne. A few gulps of superb bubbly quelled my mania enough for me to cuddle on the couch with Len, a beatific smile on my face. I felt like I was sitting on top of the world.

I should have remembered a law of physics: What goes up must come down. Lyle's phone call came a few days later. "I thought I'd better prepare you," he told me. *"Time* magazine has found out who you are."

I went numb.

"How?" I stammered. "Who could have told them?"

"I don't know."

I felt sick. Unnerved. I was floundering unexpectedly in uncharted waters. The first thing that came to my mind was *Mother!* I was going to have to tell her before the news reached her in Florida. How could I soften the blow for her?

She was so proud of her children. What would she think when she learned that her daughter had authored a best seller describing sex acts in the most graphic and enthusiastic terms? What would she tell her friends?

And Daddy. How would he feel when he heard that his little girl had written a steamy sex manual?

And my brother Tommy, what would he . . . But I had little time to think. The phone rang again.

It was a reporter from *Time* magazine. "We're doing a cover story this week on the sex books," he explained. He was referring to the unprecedented trio of explicit books on the best-seller list: mine, Dr. Reuben's, and Masters and Johnson's *Human Sexual Inadequacy*. *Time* had already prepared most of the issue, apparently, for the story was to run in less than a week. The other "sex authors" had all been interviewed, the photographs were taken, the copy was set in type. The only thing missing was an interview with the mystery author, "J."

Who had betrayed me? "All I can tell you," the *Time* man said, "is that it's somebody you know."

Somehow I stumbled through a short interview—what was the point of being uncooperative now?—and hung up the phone with trembling hands. I had so little time. Less than a week to tell my out-of-town friends, to confess to Mother, to prepare for the cold splash of notoriety. I couldn't keep the thought out of my mind: *Who was the Judas? Who had betrayed me?* "Somebody you know," the man had said.

I wished he hadn't told me that.

I dreaded talking to Mother. I called Len first, and then Johnny, but what could they do for me? It wasn't *their* duty to break the news to her, it was mine. I expressed my trepidation to Johnny with a lot of nervous laughter and joking, but I was not laughing inside. The news was going to disappoint her and hurt her.

Mother had never discussed sex with me. She was a very cosmopolitan, sophisticated woman in most matters, but she had a Victorian moral outlook. The use of words like *masturbation* or *orgasm* made her visibly uncomfortable, and she could only mention something as delicate as menstruation by employing the most convoluted euphemisms.

She was a study in contradictions, really. In West Palm Beach she conducted a "salon" in our living room. Our house was always crowded with creative and outrageous people— dancers, actors, musicians, artists, homosexuals, heterosexuals, anti-sexuals—all sheltered and nourished by Mother. She loved unconventional people and unconventional people loved her. But everybody respected the fact that she was a "lady," and that certain matters had to be treated delicately.

Whatever *The Sensuous Woman* was, I knew it wasn't delicate.

I made the call that night. Mother sounded so cheery when she heard my voice that I couldn't drop it on her all at once. We chatted first. My publicity work. New York friends. The theater. Finally, I came to the point. "Mother, I called to tell you something," I blurted.

"Yes, dear," she said, suddenly concerned. "Is anything wrong?"

"Mother, you'd better sit down. I have something awful to tell you." I shouldn't have said that, for I knew she would jump to some horrifying conclusion—that I had a dread disease, that I was going to die, that I was pregnant, or, if she had misread my nervousness, that I was going to marry someone she disapproved of. "Mother, there's a book that's out on the best-seller lists that a lot of people are talking about. It's called *The Sensuous Woman*. Have you heard of it?"

"I've heard something about it," she said, sounding puzzled. "The women at *The Post-Times* [the newspaper where

Mother was working as an advertising proofreader] have discussed it. . . ."

It was agony for me. "Mother—" I held my breath a moment. "I'm the author. *I* wrote that book. I'm 'J.'"

She was shocked. Speechless.

I tried to fill the void with explanatory chatter: how *Time* was about to reveal my identity to the world; how an unwelcome notoriety was about to descend on the Garritys; how I was earning vast sums of money for the first time in my life; how I had tried to spare her the upset by concealing the facts from her.

When she finally responded, it was with a shaky voice. "I have to think about this, dear," she said. "I can't absorb it all at once."

I was right to have dreaded that moment. She was shaken. Confused. It seemed completely unreal to her. For years, I had hidden a side of my nature from Mother, knowing she would disapprove. I had told myself—in fact, I told everyone—that I was not ashamed of *The Sensuous Woman*. But with Mother? I felt *shame*. I had associated myself with something that was dirty in her eyes.

My own feelings were very confused. I resented her prudishness; I feared her disapproval; I felt sorrow; I felt guilt; I felt anger.

There was no time to send Mother a copy of the book before *Time* hit the newsstands. "I'll go to the bookstore tomorrow and buy a copy," she said, sounding distressed. "I'd better know what it's all about when the phone begins to ring."

That trip to the bookstore must have been very difficult for Mother. I visualize her bicycle on the sidewalk, leaning against a palm tree. I see Mother inside the store, thumbing through the wrong book—the Pablo Casals autobiography or an E. B. White collection—afraid to even glance at the stack of her daughter's books on the best-seller table. I'm sure she was stricken with embarrassment when she timidly handed my lurid volume to the cashier.

I can't imagine what sustained her when she got home that evening and actually read the book. I languished in remorse in New York, waiting for the phone to ring. I imagined Mother's embarrassment as she read my pointers on masturbation; her dismay and horror at the Hoover, the Silken Swirl, and other variations on fellatio; her utter disbelief at my halfhearted endorsement of anal sex. At that moment, I wanted to go out and destroy every copy of my book. I felt bitterness toward the unknown person who had betrayed me to *Time,* but the blame was mine alone. *I* had written the book.

I couldn't have felt much worse. It would be many years before I would be able to shed my remorse at hurting the person who had loved me the longest and best in my life.

Mother called me late the next evening. Her voice was still shaky, but she made an effort to sound cheerful. "I won't pretend that I'm happy that you've done this," she said, "but I'll always love you, dear, and be proud of you. And if you felt you had to do this, I'm proud at least that you did it well."

The unhappiness in her voice was transparent, but I was so relieved that I cried. I'm sure Mother cried some, too, but I should have known that she would stand by me. Mother always did the "right thing." We had battled over that when I was growing up. I was always strong willed, fighting the constraints and obligations of the grown-up world, while Mother always spoke up for "duty."

Well, Mother knew her duty as a mother, and she was determined to be a good mother. She would not chastise me. She would defend me against the world.

And I mean the *world.*

4

The instant *Time* magazine hit the streets, my phone began to ring with calls from the English press, the Australian press, newspapers from all around America, magazines, talk and news shows. Not just the press was after me, either, but strange, weird people, most of them calling long distance, who had phoned all the Garritys in the Manhattan telephone directory trying to find me.

Preachers reviled *The Sensuous Woman* from the pulpit, Bible groups prayed for me, small towns fought over inclusion of my book in the public library.

My mail brought unsolicited sexual fantasies, vile threats, religious tracts.

Madam:
An acquaintance of mine gave me your book as he did not want his wife to know that he'd read it, and I promised to get rid of it for him. It's already in the trash where it belongs. I read it in two hours. It is, without a doubt,

the most boring book I've ever read, and it's infuriating to this reader that, while I struggle to earn $500 a month as a salaried worker, you probably made a packet of money from a worthless piece of rubbish only because the general public is hypnotized these days on anything sexual and they'll buy books like The Sensuous Woman *before realizing that they have made a lousy bargain . . . moneywise. I wouldn't mind so much if you were a real pornographer jumping on the money bandwagon instead of the charlatan that you really are. If you've read this far, you'll realize that my objection to the book stems from the fact that you made a lot of money from a book that is a complete fake; totally devoid of literal style and sensitivity; offers nothing not already known by most people; and geared to a fifteen-year-old female mentality. Your book said very little about love, and I suspect you've not had your fair share of love and that you have compensated for this lack in a most bizarre manner, including the authoring of a very badly written, ill-informed, and utterly stupid book.*

My Christian correspondents, on the other hand, rarely claimed to be bored. That's because they would not admit to having read the book at all.

Mrs. Joan Garrity:
I heard you on NBC News Tuesday and I heard what you said about your filthy book. You should be ashamed of you self spreading evil things in this world. The Good Lord made marriage and sex sacret not to be put into evil things. Someday when you face thee Almighty Father in Heaven you'll see what you have spread all over the world. I will pray for you because you need it bad. A lot of people are against you. Why don't you spread good things, there is enough evil right now, that's why sin of

*the world will destroy it. Its our sins that cause war's and
many more things, so please fall down on your knees and
ask God to forgive you. May God bless you.*

I had more than hate mail to cope with. Lyle had finally
convinced me to go out on a full-scale national promotion
tour. ("I might as well," I agreed. "There's no chance of my
ever regaining my anonymity.") I put away the blond wig
and allowed Lyle's publicity director, Carole Livingston, to
book me on talk shows as Joan Garrity—a shadowy person
halfway between the fictional "J" and the real Terrry Garrity.

The first major show I did was *The David Susskind Show*.
They taped in Philadelphia, so I was picked up at my apartment by a limousine and driven through the Lincoln Tunnel
and out into New Jersey through the desolate industrial
wasteland that surrounds New York. In the limo with me
was another of the show's guests, a Marine just back from
Vietnam. Wearing his full-dress uniform with decorations,
he was going to speak in support of the war. He was very
nice, and we chatted about safe subjects. I was by then
very much against the war, but I didn't want to argue. I was
very nervous about the show, and so was he. "I'm not used to
this," he said.

"I'm sure you'll do nicely," I replied. He smiled in appreciation, but it didn't make him any less nervous. As darkness
fell, and as we hurried in our long, dark limousine through
the mysterious lights bordering the New Jersey freeways, I
appreciated that the strange events which had brought me to
this uncomfortable brink were probably less jarring than my
Marine had experienced. What was the pressure of a nationally syndicated television show, I wondered, next to the
nightmare of the jungles of Vietnam? And yet, he was
scared, too.

The taping took place at the WMAQ studios in Philadelphia, where they usually taped *The Mike Douglas Show*. I had previously met David's producer, Jean Kennedy, a lovely lady, when booking authors on her show, but I had never met David Susskind. Critics sometimes described his on-the-air manner as pompous. I found him anything but that. The moment he heard I was in the studio, he hurried over to welcome me with great warmth. He had fought for my appearance, he told me. Metromedia had balked, fearful of viewer reaction, and some affiliates had threatened not to run the segment.

"I'm going to do it anyway," David said. "This is an important book, and I want people to know about it." I was surprised by his intensity, by the fact that he was willing to risk the disapproval of his stations. It also disarmed me that he seemed so sensitive to my predicament: that I was about to be thrust out under a battery of bright lights to talk about sex and my private life. Jean Kennedy and her staff were just as gracious, and it occurred to me that they must have told David that I was sincere in my advocacy. I felt I was in a safe cocoon. I felt the pressure and I was frightened, but these were the people I had worked with as a book publicist. These were allies.

There was no studio audience for *The David Susskind Show*, just two lonely chairs out in front of the cameras. I had a long wait, since the segment with my Marine friend was taped first; but once I settled into the chair opposite David, with those powerful lights beating down on us, the time passed very quickly. Again, I found David very warm. Fastidious in appearance, yes, but nothing pompous, and with a gentle wit and kind eyes. He did one of the best interviews ever done with me. He disagreed with me on specifics and he was constantly playing the devil's advocate in that perplexed, abashed way of his, but I knew he was on my side. He relaxed me and broke through my emotional defenses so that I was more myself with him than with later interviewers. I told people later that David Susskind was under-estimated.

Our limousine rolled through the deserted streets of Manhattan very late that night, two or three A.M. The driver waited at the curb while I let myself in the front door of my building, and then drove off when I waved to him. I was exhausted, but I was exhilarated, too. David Susskind had given me confidence, which I sorely needed if I were to continue.

I have since wondered what would have happened if my first major television appearance had been with one of the mean-spirited egomaniacs I encountered later. Would I have quit? Said to Lyle, "Kill the book, I don't care"? Probably.

What David Susskind did for me was very simple, really: He treated me with dignity.

As it turned out, *The David Susskind Show* did not get that much flack over my appearance. Not many people wrote or called in to complain, and most of those who did hadn't actually *seen* that segment. What pleased me most was that David's earnestness raised the level of the controversy. He hadn't wasted my time with endless questions about my morals or whether or not *The Sensuous Woman* was a dirty book. He had been willing to talk about female sexuality. He admitted that he was extremely old-fashioned about sex, very conventional and romantic, but he was willing to listen, even if my approach sounded "clinical" to his masculine ear. The fact that the two of us could discuss sex on a national television show without being vulgar or prurient opened the gates for other television bookers, who now saw *The Sensuous Woman* as a safe subject. More importantly, "J" seemed to be a discreet and dependable guest, not some tempestuous sexpot craving publicity and movie roles.

The "road" was a revelation to me. Everyone seemed to have a preconceived notion of what a "sex book author" was like. Dick Spangler, a radio host on a station in California's San Fernando Valley, opened his show with, "Miss 'J,' I know you've been accused of being a nymphomaniac. How would you react to that?"

My eyes must have gotten big. "No, I *haven't* been accused of being a nymphomaniac," I protested. "This is the first time the word has come up!"

Spangler smiled, as if to say, "Let's see you carry the ball, Sweetie."

"To me," I continued, "a nymphomaniac is a woman who jumps from bed partner to bed partner and gets no sexual pleasure. I, on the other hand, am a woman who sticks with the man she loves and gets a good deal of sexual fulfillment." I smiled back. "I don't think that's a nymphomaniac."

Spangler smiled grudgingly.

But he was right: People *were* accusing me of nymphomania. Not to mention pederasty, necrophilia, buggery, adultery, and disrespect for the American flag. Even my "nice" critics suggested that I was "oversexed." ("Compared to some women in America, perhaps I am," I admitted. *"I* don't consider myself oversexed. I consider myself happy.")

I always fielded attacks pleasantly, but sometimes I could feel my smile freezing on my face. I knew I dared not lose control. I kept my voice carefully modulated, even under the worst provocation. If a talk-show host, in an oily, insinuating voice, asked, "How many men have you slept with, Miss 'J' ... *roughly?*" I deflected his boorishness with some quip.

Actually, the hostility hurt me deeply. In the parlance of book publicity, I "did" a city a day, but I often felt that a city had "done" me. More than once, I was close to tears on camera.

"Oh, Len," I sighed when I called him late at night. "Why didn't I write that children's book?" I longed to be back in New York with him again, answering to the name of Terry instead of "Miss J."

The fact that some folks expected—or hoped—for a tramp was apparent. Often, when I waited in a radio or TV studio with the other guests, the host or talent coordinator would fail to pick me out as "J," the author. If there was some blonde there who looked snazzy or sexy—*anybody* else—they always walked over to her, not to Terry, the churchmouse. Who would have guessed that "J" was a Carol Burnett look-alike who dressed like a schoolteacher? (Like schoolteachers used to dress, anyway—all white collars and cuffs, mid-western wholesome.) To a degree, of course, my wardrobe was a symptom of my defensiveness: "At least I can't be attacked for my clothes," I told myself. When Lyle saw me on TV, he thought I didn't look very lively, but I resisted his suggestions to dress more provocatively. I suspected his own taste in women's clothing ran to Frederick's of Hollywood, and he would have thought it wonderful if "J" had dressed like a slut.

"You might like it," I said, "but the women of America would not be charmed."

In a way, I suppose, "the women of America," to me, always meant Mother. It didn't matter, really, what strangers thought of "J," but what Mother thought was vital to my happiness. I spent a lot of quiet time on planes and trains thinking about the mother-daughter relationship.

It was fitting that I did so. For millions of my women readers, *The Sensuous Woman* was a double-edged sword. It expressed their yearnings for sexual fulfillment, but it forced them to question the sexual values with which they were raised. If sex was "all right," if sex was "fun," if sex was "healthy," these women wondered, why did Momma teach me that it was "dirty?" Why do I feel so much guilt? Do I believe "J" or do I believe Mother?

In writing *The Sensuous Woman,* I thought I had declared myself free of those kinds of self-doubt. But I hadn't, obviously. I had groped and stumbled and finally found what I thought was a satisfying and guilt-free sex life, but . . . *but* . . . it shook me when my Mother found out. It *shook* me! I felt like a teen-ager caught necking. I could quote a thousand psychologists and doctors and experts to the effect that my sexual practices were normal and healthy—the fact remained, my mother disapproved.

Her disapproval, however well she masked it, was a heavy burden for me.

Have you ever noticed how when someone dominates your thoughts you often hear from them? I had just gotten back to New York from a swing around the Midwest when I got a call from Mother. She had the worst possible news. "Dear, I'm going into the hospital tomorrow," she said in a trembly voice.

"Mother, why?" I was instantly alarmed.

"Exploratory surgery. They want to look at my right shoulder."

The word jumped into my thoughts: *cancer.* It had been three years since she had had her cancerous lung removed—three healthy, happy years—but doctors didn't pronounce cancer patients "cured" until five years had passed without a recurrence. Neither of us would admit the possibility that the cancer was back—"It's just a routine precaution," Mother said without conviction—but I know we were both thinking it.

I quickly repacked my bags and caught the next flight to West Palm Beach. Mother's sister, Lorry Hubbard, arrived from Minneapolis the next morning, and the two of us began a hospital vigil, waiting for Mother to come out of surgery. We talked for hours about the family. "She's a tough old girl," Lorry assured me. "If anybody can lick this thing, Grace can, don't you worry about that."

Our worst fears were realized. Dr. Robert Diaz told us that Mother's "bursitic" shoulder concealed a cancer that had spread from her lungs to the bone marrow. Dr. Myrl Spivey, our family internist, sat down with Aunt Lorry and me and gave us the prognosis—the expected stages of deterioration, the horror that was to come. I was grateful to him for telling the truth, but it was hard to take. It was a death sentence.

For the next few weeks, I flew regularly to Florida between book appearances. I rented a car and drove Mother to the hospital for her radiation treatments, but we didn't dwell on that unpleasant subject. Instead, we went out to dinner a lot. We went to art galleries. I helped her furnish her new apartment in bright, happy colors, and I bought her the work-saving appliances that she had resisted for many years.

At night, after Mother went to bed, I would take long walks along the quiet streets and beachfront of Palm Beach. *The Sensuous Woman* furor seemed very remote there. The palms rustled; the moon sparkled on the ocean; colored lights made magical shadows in the trees and hedges.

Palm Beach, to me, was not a millionaires' playground, but a comfortable and familiar place. For years, whenever I could hitch a ride, I had fled the cold New York winters for its warm sunshine. Palm Beach had always been my refuge from heartbreak, and Mother, my protector. I found it aesthetically pleasing: towering royal palms, gorgeous plantings, clean streets, endless blue ocean, elegant walled estates. People greeted you with a smile. Crime was nonexistent. The pace was slow, in contrast to New York's frantic life-style.

Best of all, I was Terry there, not "J."

There was a building in Palm Beach that Mother and I had long admired. A famous architect had set it on a block-wide plot of oceanfront property not far from the elegant Breakers hotel. I walked past this building many times on my nightly walks, growing more and more fascinated by the architecture: the white walls, the high, narrow windows, the tall green hedges and chest-high white walls that enclosed private patios. I didn't really expect to buy an apartment there, but I saw no harm in at least looking at one. "If I actually look at an apartment," I told Mother, "I'll probably be disappointed and get the building out of my system."

So I looked.

And I was enraptured.

The staff showed me a spectacular third-floor apartment. It was actually a two-story arrangement with upstairs bedrooms and an outside balcony. I gazed out at the fishing boats bobbing on the blue ocean, and thought, *Here I might be able to return to a normal existence.* Then they showed me two ground-floor apartments, which had private flagstoned patios surrounded by hedges and tropical plantings. The apartments were gorgeous. High ceilings, wonderful natural lighting, a marble-tiled central courtyard, a sheltered swimming pool shadowed by towering palms.

I knew immediately: I had to live there.

My accountant and financial adviser, Arthur Halper, thought I was insane, but the ground-floor apartment I craved, on the ocean side of the building, was only $65,000 in a temporarily depressed market. (Today it's worth perhaps $300,000.) "Arthur," I said in an unusually firm tone of voice, "I *want* it."

Arthur heaved a sigh. The next day he opened negotiations for my Palm Beach apartment.

The wolves continued to howl. The mayor of Clifton, New Jersey, hearing of a planned library acquisition, proclaimed Clifton a "good old-fashioned type of American community" and determined that public funds would not be used for what she called "trash, filth, smut, and pornography." (Meaning, my book.) The Clifton library board supported her stand by a 5 to 4 vote after one councilman testified that certain passages of *The Sensuous Woman* "sickened" him.

I was completely unprepared for the wave of "morality"

that swept America. My midwestern Catholic background had exposed me to Church "positions" on sex, but since adolescence I had viewed them as scare tactics to discourage sexual experimentation by young people. *The Sensuous Woman* was nonjudgmental about common sex practices like cunnilingus, fellatio, masturbation, and even anal sex. "The psychologists say all these acts are quite normal," I told a radio interviewer. "There really isn't that much that's considered *bad* anymore."

I should have known better! People wrote "J" and quoted biblical injunctions that seemed to prohibit all sexual contact between humans, up to and including handshakes. They connected masturbation with venereal disease and madness; told me that oral sex, and not cigars and pipes, caused cancer of the mouth; and suggested that anal sex would result in "intestinal pregnancies" and similar abominations.

My more progressive critics conceded that performing these sexual acts might be acceptable, but *describing* them was not. As one worried radio host put it, "Some of the examples in your book tend to, . . . well, form pictures in the mind that are more than just 'exact,' as you put it. They're straight from the shoulder."

"That's just the point," I explained patiently. "The doctors who write marriage manuals say that these sexual practices are quite normal, but they don't tell you how to *do* them. My feeling is that if the experts approve of these sex practices, it should be acceptable to describe how to do them." I was staggered by America's strange guilt trip, which apparently could accommodate all kinds of sexual behavior, but felt shame about "pictures in the mind."

Nor was I prepared for the beginnings of women's lib.

The women's movement was just getting started in New York, mostly in the Village, and *The Sensuous Woman* was a focal point for its wrath. I considered myself a liberated woman and was an early strong supporter of women's issues, particularly equality of opportunity and equality before the law. I saw nothing in *The Sensuous Woman* that was inconsistent with those ideals, and I touted the book as a blueprint for the attainment of full sexual potential for all women.

Radical women's libbers didn't see it that way. They blasted me for "exploitation of women." My emphasis on fantasy, role playing, and "pleasing" men infuriated the radicals, who denounced "J" for perpetuating the image of women as "mere" (their word, not mine) sex objects.

"We supposedly have all this sexual freedom now," I told my women listeners, "but we're not getting all we want from sex. Is it a put-down to tell a woman she can have a sex life as good or better than a man's?"

My frothy style didn't help any. Most women's libbers were as unbearably grim as the religious moralists. Having grown up in a family that delighted in wit and laughter, I found the slogans and ponderous pronouncements of both sides very dreary. But I was reluctant to do battle with the true believers on either side. I wasn't cut out for controversy.

It seems ridiculous to me now that I was so sensitive to even mild criticism in those first months of notoriety, but thin skins don't thicken overnight. I was most distressed by an ax job on *The Sensuous Woman* that appeared in the August 2, 1970, *New York Times Book Review*. The story was headed PERSONAL PUBLISHING and its author, Marcia Seligson, lionized Lyle Stuart as the "small publisher" with the "Midas touch."

Something that the publishing community has always suspected—that Lyle Stuart has a secret weapon for turning dross into best-seller gold—is being exemplified (some might say with a vengeance) by his current resident on the list, The Sensuous Woman, *number two this week.*

This particular example of the how-to-be-sexy genre, whose author favors the Kafkaesque pseudonym "J," is Stuart's third title to make the list in the past year alone. . . .

The Sensuous Woman *overflows with self-evident or nonsensical tidbits masquerading as cogent how-to's: How to find a lover if you're a married woman ("if you have a large, bare yard, get an estimate from that handsome landscape architect"), how to increase the flexibility of your tongue, how to fake orgasm, and an abjuration to "bathe often." Housewives are advised to spruce up every evening for hubby in a different erotic costume—Monday Roman slave girl, Tuesday gypsy fortune teller. In short,* The Sensuous Woman *tells you nothing you've always wanted to know about anything—with the possible exception of the much-talked about "whipped cream" segment. Fortunately Stuart, who admits, "I never read anything I publish," caught this one in the outline and immediately smelled best-sellerdom.*

Marcia's dumping on *The Sensuous Woman* hurt me. But the real pain was inflicted further down in her story when she identified "J" as "a former Lyle Stuart publicity girl who was fired because she couldn't write releases."

Granted, Lyle had always considered print promotion my weak spot, but he had not fired me for it. I had *quit*. Simon and Schuster had thought I was an excellent release writer, and Meredith Corporation had hired me as its publicity director, which Marcia did not mention.

The crowning insult was Marcia's last paragraph, which cited the sales explosion that followed after Lyle ran a Los Angeles newspaper ad under the headline THE AUTHOR OF THIS BOOK IS NOT PRETTY. Marcia printed that as a testimonial to Lyle's promotional genius, and she was quoting *my* line, lifted from jacket copy *I* had written!

I felt sick. And angry.

The *Times* review contributed to the souring of my professional relationship with Lyle, which was already strained by a growing dispute over the terms of my contract. Like most authors, I had signed a "standard" publishing agreement that specified that the publisher would provide me with twice-yearly accountings for all royalties due me. Since *The Sensuous Woman* was in bookstores before Christmas 1969, and since Lyle had made a sizable paperback rights sale to Dell at about the same time, I thought it reasonable to expect a royalty statement by June or July 1970. But Lyle seemed very vague on this point. His line was, "If you ever need any money, you can ask me for it." As warm and protective as those words may sound, they made me a little uncomfortable. "Why do I have to ask Lyle for money?" I asked my accountant, Arthur Halper. "Doesn't he *owe* it to me?"

Arthur agreed that he did. Arthur also wasn't impressed with Lyle's practice of sending me, at random intervals, what Lyle called advance checks—without an accounting. Whenever Arthur wrote or called the publisher for a royalty statement so that he could file statements with the IRS, he invariably got a carefully reasoned justification for the slowness of accounting. "The computers are tangled up," he was told, or the bookkeeping system was being altered to promote efficiency. I called several times myself and got the same excuses.

This was nine months after the book hit the bookstores; *The Sensuous Woman* was now number one on *The New York Times'* best-seller list.

My interest was not academic. I had put down a deposit of $500 out of my cash on hand to secure my Palm Beach apartment, and when I called Lyle and told him I needed money for the down payment, he was agreeable. "No problem," he said, in effect. But as the closing date approached, no check was forthcoming, and Arthur Halper still had no royalty statements. Arthur was disturbed by stories of Lyle in Las Vegas, dropping tens of thousands of dollars at the blackjack tables and roulette wheels.

I was now physically ill, as well, hemorrhaging from a chronic gynecological condition that needed attention. My new doctor, Dr. George Blinick, was head of the obstetrics/gynecology department at Beth Israel Hospital and the toughest, most skilled, most caring gynecologist I've ever known. "Your uterus is in very bad shape," he told me during an office visit. He described the growths he had found on my uterine walls, confirmed previous diagnoses of adenomyosis and endometriosis, and told me the damage was irreversible. "And your age is more and more a factor," he said. "I'm concerned that any baby you would have might not be normal." He strongly urged me to undergo a hysterectomy.

I left his office in a daze. First I had learned that my mother was dying; now I had learned that I could never have children. On top of that, I had the nation's number-one best seller, but couldn't lay my hands on the money. To make matters worse, I was the target of a witch hunt by fundamentalist Christians on the right and militant women's libbers on the left. Finally, I was bleeding.

"I'm running out of energy," I told Len that night, "and I'm running out of blood."

I was tired of controversy. I was tired of defending myself. I was just plain tired.

I was admitted to Beth Israel Hospital on October 2, 1970.

Everything was done with the utmost secrecy. I called Carole Livingston, Lyle's publicity director, and requested that absolutely no one be informed of my whereabouts. No one was to know that I was undergoing surgery. No calls were to be forwarded. *Nothing.*

Eileen Brand, more aware even than I was that I was an emotional as well as a physical wreck—and knowing that Lyle was unhappy that I was interrupting my publicity tour—added her own privacy request for me.

Carole agreed.

I felt safe. I lay back in my hospital bed in a big private room overlooking one of the uglier stretches of First Avenue and tried to relax. Everything was peaceful. I could smell the flowers and just stare at them for minutes at a time: nice yellow daisies, yellow roses, pink begonias, blood-red and deep-purple anemones, carnations. I could read. Not just snatches of news magazines, but whole books. I had time now to confront my natural fears about the impending surgery—not the most pleasant feelings, certainly, but so very human. It was a relief to feel like a real person again instead of a hounded creature.

I busied myself preparing my will. Arthur Edulian, my longtime friend and a lawyer, was handling the legal language, but I surrounded myself with lists of my possessions and assets, trying to match them with my friends and beloved relatives. My favorite scene in the old movies was always the "reading of the will" scene, in which some rich old codger made his greedy relatives squirm before giving them each a hundred dollars and leaving the bulk of his estate to the prodigal son, the loving orphan, or to his faithful housekeeper. Lyle—who had not sent flowers or a card—was now my equivalent of the unworthy relative. I told Johnny, jokingly, that I planned to disinherit my publisher. "Lyle will not be remembered in this will!" I laughed. It was the most fun I'd had in weeks.

The night before the operation, several close friends gathered at my bedside to witness the signing of the will. Len was there, Eileen, Jack McDonnell, my old friend from summer stock days, and, of course, Arthur Edulian. "I want lots of witnesses," I explained, "so that the most important clause will be carried out." That important clause, the interment provision, read, "I direct that my executor shall cause my earthly remains, either cremated or not, to be buried in the warm waters of the sea, and further that the song 'The Heather on the Hill' from the musical comedy *Brigadoon* be performed at my last rites."

Everyone protested that my fears of not surviving surgery were silly and groundless. I knew they were probably right, but I mulled over every hospital disaster I had ever heard of: too much anesthesia, mistaken identity, the removal of the wrong organ from the patient, the removal of the right organ but from the wrong patient. "It would be irresponsible not to prepare a will," I insisted.

When my friends had gone, I sat up in bed and watched late movies on TV until I finally fell asleep.

I came out of surgery in the intensive-care room, minus one uterus and one ovary. As soon as I was stable they returned me to my private room, where more flowers had bloomed in my absence. I was still too groggy to appreciate them, but I did notice them when my eyes struggled open for a few seconds at a time. I was in pain, but I took comfort in the fact that they wouldn't have to charter that boat quite yet, and no one would have to sing "The Heather on the Hill" over my ashes. I felt quite alone and secret, which is how I wanted to feel in my misery.

I fell in and out of sleep, vaguely aware of the rhythm of the hospital around me, the squeak of carts and equipment outside my door, the distant, hushed conversations, the gentle ring of the elevator bell. I couldn't help thinking of Mother, who had spent so much of her life in hospitals, and whose life was now dwindling and would probably end in a hospital room not unlike mine. The hospital gowns, the plastic wrist tags—they reminded me of the little time she had left. . . .

The sun was streaming in the window the next morning. It was a moment or two before I realized I had been wakened by the telephone ringing on the night table beside my head. I moaned softly and tried to ignore it. Where was my nurse?

The phone kept ringing. I thought: *Len.* Or *Johnny.* Something important, maybe. Or *Mother.* I hadn't talked yet to Mother, although Johnny had called her to tell her the operation was successful. I reached awkwardly for the phone, conscious of the pain and of a sickness in my stomach. "Hello," I said groggily.

The voice was asking for something. I started to panic. It was a voice from outside. It was a reporter's voice. The nightmare of the tour suddenly swept back over me: my defensiveness, the misery, the feeling of having enemies and of being attacked. The voice said she was with *The New York Times;* she wanted an interview. She said Lyle Stuart's office had given her my number. I was trembling. Who had she said she was? Was I dreaming this? The voice said she was Marcia Seligson.

I don't remember what happened next. I went into hysterics, sobbing and shaking. Nurses came running; a doctor rushed in, tried to restrain me, and barked out orders for a strong sedative. I don't know how long I struggled, but finally I felt the needle jabbing my arm; within seconds, I felt my body relaxing; soon, my head fell back and I was again in darkness, safe, alone.

I was unconscious for hours, unaware of the guard that was now posted outside my door. When I finally awoke, I fell into fits of weeping.

I wanted my mother.

5

When I got home from the hospital, Mother was waiting for me. She had taken two weeks' vacation from West Palm Beach's *Post-Times* to fly to New York to take care of me. I lay in bed all day, sipping freshly squeezed fruit juices and taking naps while Mother fussed over me. She said it made her happy to be needed and distracted her from the twinges of pain in her shoulder. Every day, after seeing to my needs, she would wrap up warmly against the chilling autumn winds and walk briskly about the city. She especially loved the Metropolitan Museum of Art. She went back again and again, always returning with some exciting "discovery" to report. Johnny took her to Broadway at night—Bob and Ray for laughs, *Fiddler on the Roof* for tears—and as I got stronger I joined them for dinner at interesting restaurants like the Cafe Argenteuil, The Rainbow Room, Gallagher's Steak House, and Shun Lee Dynasty.

We had to be careful what we said when we were with Mother, for we were keeping secrets from her. It was a "secret" that we knew the seriousness of her shoulder problem.

Johnny's trial in federal court in San Francisco was another secret. While at Stanford University, he had refused the draft as a protest against the war in Vietnam. Mother knew that, but Johnny had not been indicted then. The government and the FBI had made repeated offers to him to change his mind or to apply for conscientious objector status, which he had declined. Finally, he *was* indicted. Now he was risking a substantial prison sentence because, as he put it, "the killing won't stop unless *we* stop it."

Mother supported without reservation Johnny's stand against the Vietnam war, and she admired his courage for what she called "standing up to be counted." But she worried, too, and Johnny didn't want to burden her with the thought of his imprisonment until or if it became necessary. I slipped up one night in an Italian restaurant and blurted something about "Johnny's trial," and a cloud passed over Mother's face. We pretended that Mother had heard it wrong, and went on talking; maybe we convinced her. But I told Johnny afterward that it was a great strain juggling secrets. "I can't remember who knows what. It's unnatural."

I still felt guilty for the embarrassment I had caused Mother, and we rarely discussed *The Sensuous Woman.* We talked about everything associated with my book—the money, the celebrity, my problems with the publisher—but not the contents itself. Mother betrayed her feelings now and then by saying wistfully, "Isn't it a shame it isn't a cookbook?" But mostly she concentrated on my "success." I began showing her a careful selection of letters people had written to "J"—letters from ministers who approved of the book, from doctors and psychologists who were using *The Sensuous Woman* in therapy, from women who had been helped by my program. Those letters relieved her mind. They validated *The Sensuous Woman,* for Mother was a great believer in worthy deeds.

She also approved of my eagerness to learn all I could

about my subject. I had begun reading every book I could find on the psychology and physiology of sex. I was wading through medical journals and psychological abstracts. I recorded doctors and sexologists whenever they appeared on talk shows. My coast-to-coast tour had convinced me that I had to be an expert on sex, even if I disclaimed that expertise. "It isn't enough to tell people that a certain notion about sexuality is a myth," I explained to Mother. "I have to be able to back it up by citing scientific research or solid data." (My schoolteacher clothes were not just "safe" costumes, Len pointed out. There was actually a schoolteacher aspect to my personality.)

In some ways, Mother and I were closer than we had ever been, but I always felt a strain—the strain of my "secrets," the strain of my "J" activities, and, worst of all, the strain of pretending that Mother's cancer was cured. Her arm was out of the sling, yes, and she toured New York with great vigor and enthusiasm, but there was that growing pain in her shoulder. She tried to conceal it, and when she couldn't hide it, she began to complain of "arthritis pains."

The time was short. Mother had always been a rare person in that she knew how to enjoy the little things in life—the song of a bird, the beauty of a sunset, the excitement of a piano concerto. Johnny and I dedicated ourselves to providing her with as many of those moments as we could in the time she had remaining.

When we put Mother on the plane back to Florida, Johnny and I knew it was the last time she would ever travel. But Mother was adamant: "I'll be back to see spring in New York."

One communication from Lyle came not by post or by phone, but in the form of an advertisement on the book review page of the Wednesday, October 28, 1970, *New York Times*. Headlined OPEN LETTER TO AN AUTHOR, it was a facsimile of Lyle's letterhead, signed by Lyle, with the salutation, "Dear J":

You asked me how your book The Sensuous Woman *is doing. Here is how it is.* The Sensuous Woman *has sold more than 500,000 copies and is selling at the rate of* about 5,000 copies a day. . . . *(It is, in case you haven't realized it, the largest selling nonfiction best seller written by a woman ever to be published in the USA!)*

The Sensuous Woman *is* not *available and* will not be available *through any book club. It is too important a book to be one of those "6 for a dollar" items.*

The Sensuous Woman is *being published in England, Norway, Sweden, Denmark, Finland, France, Germany, Japan, Italy, Holland, and Brazil. (The censor won't permit its publication in Spain.)*

The Sensuous Woman *is #1 on major best-selling lists!* (New York Times; Time; Book World; Publishers Weekly; *etc.) It is the winner and new champion . . . and there are no serious contenders on the horizon!*

You ask me who is buying it. Women. Women. Women. And men. Men are buying it for their wives and sweethearts. Women are buying it for themselves and for their friends.

The Sensuous Woman *has not only changed the ways in which a million women make love, but it has changed the ways they think about themselves. It has, we believe, brought joy and new happiness into thousands of lives.*

You haven't just written a book, baby. You've caused a love revolution! (And one in which everybody* wins!) Thought you'd like to know.

Your devoted publisher,
Lyle Stuart

You haven't done badly yourself! Your estimated earn-ings on The Sensuous Woman *have now passed the half a million mark!*

L.

Half a million dollars? Even allowing for exaggeration—you can't believe any publisher's sales claims—I wasn't seeing anywhere near that kind of money. I showed the ad to Arthur Halper and to Len, and they both suggested that I see a lawyer. "Lyle never returns my calls," Arthur said. "He ignores my letters. Maybe it takes a lawyer to get his atten-tion."

Len suggested Don Engel, a well-known New York copy-right attorney. Engel was Len's personal attorney and he also served occasionally as corporate counsel to Simon and Schuster and other top publishers. "You won't find a better publishing attorney," Len said.

"I bet he's expensive."

"Yes, but you can't afford not to have the best," Len said.

So Len and I met one afternoon at Don's offices on Madison Avenue. Don Engel was a tall, athletic-looking, trim man with a lot of nervous energy. He wore aviator-style glasses, which were new then, and I told Len afterward that Engel looked like he had jumped out of the pages of *Gentlemen's Quarterly.*

Len and I told Don about Lyle's seeming reluctance to pro-vide me with a royalty statement. Don simply nodded and asked a few questions. Finally, he said, "It may *be* a com-puter problem. Why don't you try one more time? Drop him a line, or have your accountant write him again. If that doesn't work then I'll give Lyle a call and see if that does the trick."

That was it. No complicated proposals, no legal talk. Don just said, "If nothing happens, I'll call him."

Still, when Len and I left his office, I felt much better about everything. "I feel like a real burden has been lifted from my shoulders," I told Len. "I don't like to talk to people about money."

Len gave me a hug. "That's what Don Engel is for."

When I had something to tell Lyle, I told Eileen instead, and she passed on the message. Or he and I wrote each other letters. "Dear Lyle—I gather Eileen gave you the doctor's verdict. I can't make any appearances for three months. This is for two reasons: (1) my operation and (2) my ulcer. I will be in great shape and ready for the rat race again in February. . . ."

The real race wasn't with the rats. As early as April 1970 I had realized that the success of *The Sensuous Woman* was going to inspire sequels and imitations. I had heard that a book called *The Sensuous Couple* was already in the works, and figured that some publishing genius was undoubtedly hatching the most obvious sequel, *The Sensuous Man*. The latter possibility alarmed me, because I was afraid somebody would publish a truly vulgar *Man* and my readers would mistake it for the companion volume to *The Sensuous Woman*.

The solution to this dilemma, Lyle and I had decided, was to rush ahead with *The Sensuous Man* ourselves. By writing it myself, I could control its content and protect what was left of my "good name."

I had signed the contract in June, but of course there was no way I could have written the book right then. I was touring, jetting from city to city, hotel to hotel, studio to studio, with no time for research or reflection, much less the actual writing.

There was yet another obstacle in the way of my writing a successful *Sensuous Man*.

I wasn't a man.

It wasn't until I wrote the outline for *The Sensuous Man* that I began to appreciate that my way of looking at the sexual relationship was unalterably feminine. And my writing style! When I showed a few pages of preliminary *Sensuous Man* manuscript to Johnny, who was now a book editor at Simon and Schuster, he frowned over it and clucked his tongue. "It's too cute," he said. "Too gushy." He pointed out my flights of hyperbole, my forest of exclamation points, my critical harpooning of what I considered to be failings in masculine sexual behavior. Pointing to a passage where I had followed an account of a sex technique with "Yummmmm!" he said, "That's not a man's word. This was obviously written by a woman. You're still writing as 'J.'"

Conceding my shortcomings as a writer of male-oriented nonfiction, I decided that I would write the book, but that Johnny would take the manuscript and "punch up" the maleness by editing out my feminisms and inserting whatever peculiarly masculine concerns occurred to him. "I'll do the actual writing in the fall," I told him. The fall seemed far away.

Of course, in early October I found myself in a hospital room on the Lower East Side, under sedation and with a guard posted at the door to keep out unwelcome visitors. Nothing was yet written, and I was quite incapable of writing.

One night, when I mentioned for the fiftieth time that I really had to get to work on *The Sensuous Man,* Len asked, "What is Lyle advancing you, anyway?"

"The same as *The Sensuous Woman,"* I replied. "Fifteen hundred dollars."

Len's jaw fell. "You've got a number-one best seller!" Then his eyes shot sparks. "He should give you fifty thousand for *The Sensuous Man.* It can't miss!" Len went on to call Lyle a few choice names, prompting me to remark, "Are you sure you aren't part-Irish?"

I really didn't care about the advance. As long as I got my *Sensuous Woman* royalties I was well fixed, and I was sure that *Man* would make lots of money, regardless of how the book turned out. "A chimpanzee could write this one and have a best seller," I told Len. "My only concern is that I won't get well and somebody—some other chimp—will beat me to it."

Nonetheless, deep down I must have thought of *The Sensuous Man* as a $1,500 book, because I wasn't unduly worried about the delay caused by my surgery. That changed, however, the day that Eileen brought me some staggering news: Dell Publishing had bought the reprint rights to *The Sensuous Man,* sight unseen, for $400,000!

I nearly had a relapse. Four times the advance for *Woman!* I could not believe, after years of nickel and diming my way around New York, that I could suddenly command $200,000—my share—for just a *title.*

"My God, Eileen, do they know that there's no book?"

Eileen laughed, but she warned me that I would be under deadline pressure. "Lyle has to have a completed manuscript in his hands by no later than December first."

"December first?" I fumbled for my date book and studied the calendar, feeling panicky.

"Johnny can help," Eileen said.

Sure, but Johnny had a full-time job. He also had his draft case coming up in San Francisco. "He may be in *prison* by December first," I muttered.

Obviously, we needed help, another collaborator. A man, preferably.

I turned to Len. He was not a writer, but he knew the publishing business and he knew what would sell. We spent all our free time together anyway, and he *was,* after all, an authentic sensuous man. "You and I and Johnny," I urged him. "We'll share equally."

Len was excited by the idea, but he had one reservation. "My role would have to be kept a secret."

Len was concerned about his reputation at Simon and Schuster, but he was not alone in demanding anonymity. Johnny feared exposure because he thought association with a "sex book" would undermine his credibility as a free-lance journalist. And I, of course, had to remain a secret because the mystery author had to have a convincingly male aura.

We went to my attorney Don Engel, therefore, to sign a second *Sensuous Man* contract. It called for Terry Garrity, John Garrity, and Len Forman to share equally in all revenues derived from the book *The Sensuous Man* by "M." Engel felt I was being way too generous, since I had the name, track record, and contract, but I didn't have money on my mind. I loved Len and was eager to share my financial success with him in a way that wouldn't hurt his pride. I also thought it was a good way to provide Johnny with some financial security.

The contract made one further stipulation: that none of us could reveal his authorship to any person other than a wife, husband, or a professional with a code of confidentiality, such as an attorney, accountant, or priest. "A priest?" I asked.

"That's just an example," Don said.

As we left the building, I said to Len, "It seemed like a funny example. I would have thought a psychiatrist." We both laughed.

The Sensuous Man was written in a week.

Certain writers of genre fiction write that fast—writers of mysteries and romances who dictate their work or furnish their publishers with sparse but publishable first drafts. But I doubt if a number-one nonfiction best seller of 253 pages had ever been written in just one week.

It wasn't easy.

For an evening or two we tried to work at Len's apartment on the Upper East Side, but Len had cable TV in his bedroom and he kept disappearing to watch the Knicks play basketball. Len had a sorrowfully short attention span. When I assigned him a chapter to write, he busied himself for a few minutes at his dining-room table, composing six or eight lines. Then he would push it across the table, saying, "Well, here it is!"

"No, no," I would say firmly. *"Expand* your thoughts." Len would look hurt and confused and would return to his chapter with a heavy heart, no doubt thinking of the joy in the hearts of Manhattan moviegoers and partygoers who didn't have books to write.

So we moved everything to my little apartment, where the Knicks were strangers and where only the bathroom and a closet afforded hiding places. It was more efficient, anyway. My apartment was where my supplies were stored—reams of paper, boxes of paper clips, stacks of legal pads and file folders, quivers full of felt pens. "Supplies are the most important part of writing," I assured Len, my tongue in cheek. (It worried me that he didn't argue this point.)

We all had different ideas of who "M" was. In my mind he was Paul Newman or Burt Reynolds. Len was trying for a Steve McQueen brand of machismo, but kept lapsing into his own persona, which meant that "M" golfed at a Long Island country club and read the Sunday *New York Times* in bed.

We could never pin down Johnny on his image of "M." He originally claimed it was bespectacled Wally Cox. "Wally Cox in his early, heroic role as Hiram Holiday," Johnny hastened to add, "not the Wally Cox of Mr. Peepers fame." Johnny wanted "M" to carry an umbrella everywhere and to collect butterflies.

The "M" that emerged was a truly remarkable man: jumping fences on a motorcycle one day, piloting a golf cart the next; drinking Manhattans at the Tavern on the Green, then cheering the Rolling Stones at a rock concert. You might find "M" shopping for groceries in the local A & P, clinching a major business deal with a transatlantic phone call, writing love poems to his mistress, or picking up girls at church functions. He was detached and yet committed; traditional and yet "liberated"; all man, and yet sensitive.

(When he was asked who "M" was, Lyle's strategy was to deny that it was somebody. Robert Redford, say. Lyle's denial planted the idea that it maybe *was* Redford, or somebody like him. Clint Eastwood? Jon Voight? Peter Fonda? Peter Lorre? Lyle issued denials for them all. The crazy part was, Lyle didn't *know* who "M" was, he just thought he did. Because of the secrecy provisions of my contract with Johnny and Len, Len's role as author was known only to ourselves and to a few people in Don Engel's office.)

Going in, I questioned if I had regained enough stamina to work again. Len seemed to have his doubts—he had seen me shuffling around the apartment in a daze for weeks—and I think Johnny suspected that his big sister was going to be dead weight. To everyone's surprise except my own, the reverse occurred. I always respond to dramatic deadlines with a sharper mind, a great burst of energy. I behaved like a general at a field command post, issuing directives, handling logistics, rallying the troops. The card table, the kitchen counter, the captain's chest, and the floor were strewn with manuscript, some of it typed, some of it in my felt-tipped longhand, and some of it in Johnny's unbelievably tiny print, which made his pages resemble an embroidery turned inside out. I brought in two typewriter tables. The refrigerator was stocked with soft drinks and boxes of Russell Stover chocolates. "This is a working environment!" I exulted.

Len looked about as comfortable as a teetotaler in a drunk tank. At Simon and Schuster, he was an idea man. An executive. He was used to giving orders and having them carried out by the pretty young things who worked under him. Whenever he turned mutinous, I had to coo, "Remember the money, dearest." That usually brought him to his senses. He would sigh deeply and go back to work.

Johnny, whose editorial load was heavy, was no happier. He left from time to time with a folder of material, claiming that he worked much better across town in the solitude of his

Hell's Kitchen apartment. We suspected that he was catching catnaps there, but we didn't really mind because he was the fastest worker of the three of us. When he was with us, he made no secret of his fatigue. He got up from his work every half hour or so and walked around the room breathing deeply and opening his eyes as wide as possible. Sometimes, when he was at the typewriter, he slapped himself in the face and muttered, "Wake up. Wake up."

Len was less animated. When he began to wear out, his eyes just got glassy, he stopped moving, and that was that.

"I don't know what's wrong with you two," I said cheerfully. "I'm not tired," I lied. They both gave me glances that Jimmy Hatlo used to caption, "If looks could kill."

Eileen was helping with the typing, and when we had both typewriters going she edited the pages as fast as we turned them out. Even so, we despaired of meeting our deadline. After Day Five we lost Johnny, who had to fly to San Francisco for a court appearance. (Prison was starting to look good to him.) Len was burned out, and I, too, finally faded; I slept all day after the fourth night.

We began to entertain ideas of getting a deadline extension. "Just a *week*," I told Eileen. "Otherwise, the manuscript will read like it actually *was* written by chimps."

Eileen called back with bad news. "No extension," she said. "Lyle has this elaborate machinery set up to print the book the minute he gets the manuscript on Sunday. It can't be put off."

I groaned.

Still, with two days left we faced only the sex technique chapters, plus a few loose ends. One of the loose ends was Len's concluding chapter, "Love as an Aphrodisiac," which seemed to defy conversion into "M"s style. The chapter opened with the Elizabeth Barrett Browning sonnet, "How do I love thee? Let me count the ways." Len, who was intensely romantic, had picked up where Elizabeth left off.

"You can love many times," he wrote, "but rarely are you 'in love.' It is a time of erotic feeling beyond the limits of imagination. Her eyes are stars, her lips are petals. Her neck is swanlike, her breasts are mounds of pure alabaster pliant to your touch, her waist is a wisp of flesh warm and smooth, her buttocks are solid to the pressure of your hand, and her cunt is the altar at which you pray. . . ."

When she read over this material, Eileen shook her head. "This chapter is written in a wholly different style. Everyone will know that more than one writer was involved." Johnny made the same point before he left. No one would believe that this was the same "M" who had warned, earlier in the book, that the worst consequence of masturbation was "crusty little stains on your sheets, your toilet seat, or your catcher's mitt."

"It's a case of Lord Byron meets *Portnoy's Complaint*."

Unfortunately, by the end of Night Five, Len was exhausted. I hated to make him revise his best effort. Besides, I loved romantic stuff. "I think we should leave the chapter just as it is," I told Eileen.

(Len's love chapter went into *The Sensuous Man* just as he wrote it. People commented to me later that the love chapter seemed sort of . . . well, "different"—as if not a ghost writer, but a guest writer had showed up. On the other hand, when *Cosmopolitan* printed excerpts from the book, it chose Len's chapter.)

Our one other major disagreement came over a chapter I had written cataloging what women didn't like about men. Both Johnny and Len were offended. "*The Sensuous Woman* didn't have a comparable chapter upbraiding women for their shortcomings," Len pointed out. "You're destroying 'M''s credibility."

"I concur," Johnny said.

I would not yield. Perhaps it was unfair to use "M" as a vehicle for the expression of women's concerns, but I wanted

"M," for all his goofiness, to be in step with the changing sex roles in America. He was not a cocksman. He saw women as equals and decried the double standard, the madonna complex and the Don Juan syndrome. No male-oriented sex manual had ever gone so far in conceding sexual equality to women. Johnny was all for the antichauvinist stance, Len a little less so, but I was adamant on that point. "It needs the woman's touch," I said.

The last two days of writing were a blur. Len and I finished *The Sensuous Man* at dawn on December first. Eileen took the last pages to Lyle Stuart, to be rushed to the typesetter. Len dragged himself to work, exhausted and relieved that his ordeal was over.

And I crashed into a twenty-four-hour recuperative sleep; but just before I lost consciousness, I congratulated myself: *I'm still able to pull off the marathon project efficiently. I can still make the adrenaline flow and meet impossible deadlines.* I hadn't lost the knack of pulling the rabbit out of the hat at the last minute. With this talent, I would always be able to survive in the world of writing, with its crazy pressures and beat-the-clock projects.

6

By spring 1971, Mother was too ill to leave her apartment by herself. I hired nurses for her so she could stay in her own apartment, as she wished. I bought her a tiny television set that she could keep beside her on the bed. The people at Dell were kind enough to schedule my paperback book tour in short spurts, which allowed me to be at her side most of the time.

Her courageous smile could not conceal the fact that she knew she was failing and was afraid. When I drove her to Good Samaritan Hospital for her radiation therapy, she would fall silent. While we waited at stoplights, she would watch the sailboats and yachts cruising the choppy waters of Lake Worth, her eyes filling with tears. She stared longingly at the bicycle trail and beautiful, landscaped estates across the water in Palm Beach.

Johnny remembered being with her three years earlier, when Dr. Spivey had told her she had a cancerous lung from over thirty years of cigarette smoking. "She was in the kitchen that afternoon," Johnny said, "and she began to cry. She said she couldn't face another operation." (She'd had twenty-six major operations since childhood, starting with peritonitis from a burst appendix.) "She said, 'I just want to get on my bicycle and ride off into the sunset.'"

Now I noticed that she always looked longingly at the Lake Trail on the opposite shore. It was her favorite bicycle path, winding in and out of lovely estates, shadowed by cavernous, overhanging Banyan trees.

When you see someone you love suffering excruciating, unending pain, you understand "mercy killing." Mother's bones were disintegrating, slowly turning to powder. Chemotherapy proved ineffective. Radiation helped some—by destroying some of the spreading carcinoma—but high dosages of painkillers at best made her groggy and at worst sucked her down into a smothering spiral of anesthesia and nightmares. Without the painkillers, a gentle jostling of the bed, the slightest movement of an afflicted body part, could trigger heart-stopping stabs of pain.

Mother lay on her back all the time now, her body bolstered by an intricate pattern of protecting pillows in different sizes and shapes. The poinciana trees outside her window were beginning to bloom. Her bedroom was like a treehouse, with birds chirping, butterflies floating by, and the sun filtering through the leaves. Her soft brown eyes turned often to the serene view. It nourished her flagging spirit.

"J"'s life was more upbeat, a whirlwind of travel and media attention. The success of *The Sensuous Woman* and *The Sensuous Man* had made "sensuousness" a satirical target for cartoonists and columnists, and a selling point for Madison Avenue copywriters. Datsun advertised its 240-Z as "The Sensuous Car, by 'D.'" The Hilton hotel chain promoted "The Sensuous Inn, by 'H.'" The resort town of Killington, Vermont, offered skiers "The Sensuous Vacation" and called itself "K." The *Sensuous Woman* type style," as it was now called, was reproduced faithfully in most ads, and each use was a free advertisement for *The Sensuous Woman.*

"J" was on all the television talk shows, promoting female orgasm with Phil Donahue, Dick Cavett, Virginia Graham, Dinah Shore, David Susskind, Mike Douglas, Steve Allen, and a dozen other witty hosts. The print media caught the bandwagon. *Newsday,* the Long Island newspaper, ran a clever parody of *The Sensuous Woman.* Russell Baker and Art Buchwald wrote columns about "J." Political cartoonists jumped on the news that Martha Mitchell, the colorful wife of the United States attorney general, kept *The Sensuous Woman* on her night table. *The New Yorker* ran a Charles Addams cartoon depicting a hairy, troll-like creature standing beside a book display, browsing through a book called *The Sensuous Thing.*

Sensuous was the word of the year for 1971.

Sequels and rip-offs flooded the market in the weeks after the appearance of *The Sensuous Man: The Sensuous Couple, The Sensuous Child, The Sensuous Grandparent, The Sensuous Mouth, The Sensuous Dog, The Sensuous Cat,* and *The Sensuous Dirty Old Man.* (This last title, by "Dr. A," was all the more intriguing when it was revealed that "A" was Isaac Asimov, the unbearably prolific science writer.)

Dirty Old Man and the other "sensuous" books exploited my success, but I was more amused than angered. I did resent the more blatant rip-offs, paperback titles like *The Sensual Woman* and *The Sensuous Female,* which imitated *The Sensuous Woman* jacket design and type style with the clear intent to deceive. Dell drove some of these pirates off the racks with litigation.

I seemed to be on the verge of litigation of my own. On December 1, 1970—the day after Night Seven of *The Sensuous Man* marathon—Lyle wrote me an angry letter. "Today, an attorney phoned," he fumed, making no mention of my letter of November 24 asking for the long-awaited royalty statement. He blasted me for ingratitude, argued that he had been holding my money back because he thought I wanted him to, and that he was so insulted that he was going to hold my next royalty check until after January 1, rather than pay me in December, as promised.

The phone call, of course, had come from Don Engel, acting on my behalf. Don had succeeded where all others had failed—Lyle enclosed the June statement, along with a check for $25,640.02—but my "power play" enraged Lyle. "To say that you are not as popular here as you were before that phone call," he wrote, "would be something of a gracious understatement. I hope you act less foolishly with your money than you have acted with this very sorry human relationship foul-up." I might have shed a tear or two if I hadn't let my eyes fall upon the royalty statement that accompanied Lyle's check. More than half the sales to the trade had been made, it claimed, at a 50 percent discount rather than the usual 46 or 48 percent. That struck me as a little odd, but I wasn't knowledgeable about book distribution. What caught my eye was a line that said Lyle had cut my royalties in *half* for those sales. Instead of 12½ percent for those books, I was getting 6¼ percent.

I was bewildered. "The computer must still be out of whack," I told myself. I called Arthur Halper and Don Engel, and they both shared my surprise. "That can't be right," Don said. "I don't remember any clause in your contract that would allow Stuart to deny you half your royalties while the book was actually on the best-seller list and still in its initial distribution. Why don't you send over the royalty statement and I will review it against your contract?"

I did. And then I grabbed my suitcases and hit the road again.

When I was at home in Florida, I sometimes handled one

of the nursing shifts, but I was not a very good nurse for Mother. I took the midnight-to-eight shift, sitting at the foot of her bed, tensely watching and listening. Time after time, I thought her breathing had stopped, and I panicked. I didn't feel competent to handle any real emergency.

We never discussed her dying. It bothered me that I was afraid to talk with her about death, but I see now that she made it very difficult for me by not accepting herself that she was dying. She had been saved from death so many times before that she still believed a miracle could happen. I should have said, "Mother, let go," but I didn't know how. I chattered about inane things, and she talked very little herself, since waves of nausea hit her when she tried to use her vocal cords. I didn't share enough of my feelings with her. We were a family that had difficulty with that.

During the day, when her friends visited her and comforted her, I bought groceries and fed the nurses and kept things running. I found Mother a nice bed tray; I had special pillows made for her; I bought her lovely sheets. I made sure she had her favorite pictures and books in her bedroom. She was determined to keep her mind sharp, and I supplied her with new books and current magazines.

Now and then, the nausea let up and Mother talked. She talked a lot about Johnny: how proud she was of him, but how worried she was about the possibility of his going to prison. "What will he eat?" she fretted, but underneath her concern about his diet was her fear about prison brutality. Johnny had sent her a book, *War Resisters in Prison,* and she read from it often—mostly for reassurance that a young man's ideals were sufficient to sustain him through such trials. She was a registered Republican, but she had refused to vote for Richard Nixon because she distrusted him, and she referred to Vietnam as "that evil war." I had always thought of her as a Victorian because of her sexual prudishness, but Mother also had that Victorian belief in the perfectibility of man—an optimism that was abused by "that evil war," but never snuffed out. It was no accident, I think, that as she neared death she was reading Norman Mailer's book about the *Apollo 11* moon landing, *Of a Fire on the Moon.* She wanted desperately to believe that Johnny's generation would make better choices than hers had.

You wait and you wait—fiddling, organizing, anticipating how to handle the inevitable moment of emergency—and when it finally comes, you find you are not prepared at all.

Mother went to the hospital in mid-June with an intestinal blockage. The same condition had almost taken her life in 1960; I remembered Mother clinging to life at the Mayo Clinic in Rochester, Minnesota, her body packed in ice to combat a raging fever. That time she had beaten the odds, but now when I called Aunt Lorry in Minneapolis, Lorry agreed with me that this was the final crisis. She caught the next plane to Palm Beach.

Mother had an elegant room at Good Samaritan Hospital, but she was far too ill to appreciate the view from her window. The colorful sailboats and graceful yachts on Lake Worth might as well have been a dime-store print in a cheap frame. She was lucid sometimes, but she didn't talk much. We could see that she had finally given up. She was unconscious most of the time, and when awake she was in agony. We had prayed that the cancer would find and destroy some vital organ, ending her suffering, and now that was happening: It had reached her brain. But she was still being tortured. I complained, "Why don't the shots of morphine work?"

Lorry and I took turns at the hospital. Mother's good friend Dr. Joe Doane came by every time he made his rounds and sat quietly with her for a few moments, gently squeezing her hand. The hospital's registered nurses were with us at night, and Mother's private nurse, a wonderful, warm Irish woman named Mrs. Murphy, stayed with her during the day. Tommy arrived from Gainesville, Florida, and shared the vigil. Johnny was at a week-long retreat for nonviolent activists at Struggle Mountain, California, and could not be reached, but I tried repeatedly. We were determined not to let Mother be alone at the moment of death, which could come any hour, any day, any week—we didn't know.

Mother went in and out of a coma. I would sit on the rigid hospital chair facing her bed, lost in a swirl of conflicting emotions and prayers. *Go, go. Hurry, hurry, God, and put her out of her misery. Stay, stay. You can't leave us now when we still have so much to share. You have to be here to see Johnny's books published, to walk the first golf course that Tommy designs, to hold another grandchild in your arms, to see me happily married, to make more plants flourish, to cook more superb meals, to be there—always loving, always supporting—when we need you.*

We waited.

On June 21, Lorry took the first shift. I was home writing Mother's obituary. When I had finished, Tommy and I drove over to relieve Lorry, but she wouldn't leave. "No, I'm staying," Lorry said, "and I think you should, too."

Several hours passed. Tommy had walked down the hall to the nursing station to see if Mother's painkiller had been increased, leaving Lorry and me and Mrs. Murphy in the room. Suddenly, Mother's face became contorted and a horrifying sound came from her throat. "Call out to her!" Mrs. Murphy cried. "Tell her you love her! Call to her!"

Lorry was calling, "God bless you, Grace," and "We love you, Grace," and I held Mother's hand and cried, "I love you! I love you!" and then our voices faded. She was gone.

"I love you," I repeated weakly.

I had been strong through Mother's illness; I assumed I

would stay together after her death. Instead, I was paralyzed with grief. Dr. Spivey had to give me a tranquilizer, and Aunt Lorry pushed me toward my bedroom to "rest" every time I crumpled into inconsolable sobs. I had always had trouble crying; now I couldn't stop.

Tommy took over the funeral arrangements, firmly honoring Mother's wish to be cremated in a modest casket. Johnny flew in from California and we held a quiet memorial gathering at the funeral home. It was attended by dozens of Mother's friends, who loved her for her wit, her kindness, her humanity, and her boundless interest and curiosity about people.

Lorry and I went to Mother's apartment a few days after her death. As we sorted through Mother's things, I felt stabs of loss with every little discovery—the green-handled bottle opener that had been in the family for decades, the old black flatiron that I had painted up for her as a doorstop when I was at Palm Beach Junior College, the rings she wore, her favorite records.

I was in the linen closet when I discovered something solid wrapped in a pale yellow towel. "What is this?" I wondered. I unwrapped it and found Mother's copy of *The Sensuous Woman*.

I didn't know whether to laugh or cry. From where I stood, I could see her copy of my bargain-shopping guide displayed proudly on the coffee table.

"Victorian to the end," I murmured with grudging admiration.

In hindsight, it is easy to see the forest *and* the trees, but that summer of 1971 all I could make out were the trees.

Stress experts now warn that even a *good* life change, if it is a major one, can precipitate life-threatening physical disease and/or mental breakdown. I had had an impressive collection of major stresses hit me in a short period of time: an enormous change in income level; a radical departure in occupation, from quiet, private person, to embattled, controversial public figure; the death of my mother; a new residence; I had undergone major surgery; acquired the classic stress illness—ulcers; had had the dream of having a baby permanently denied; and had a major lawsuit brewing.

There had been no time for me to properly live through and come to terms with any of these changes and stresses. What I should have done then was say, "Stop the world. I'm getting off for a while until I can absorb all that's happened to me." I needed to grieve for the loss of my mother, the children I would never give birth to; I needed to ease into my new life-style and simply be Terry again in her comfortable daily routine.

Instead, I did what I thought was the right thing to do—I got on with my life. There were obligations to be met, and wasn't work the most effective panacea for all ills?

PART
TWO

PALM BEACH, 1978

The door to the master bedroom was closed. No light showed beneath it, no sound was heard within.

Suddenly, at five minutes to four A.M., a muffled bell sounded and continued to ring for about two minutes until it wound down and gave out with a weak chirp.

All was again silent.

At one minute to four, a rude buzz could be heard inside, joined a minute later by a melodious chiming of bells, followed almost instantly by another metallic alarm, and then by a sudden swell of mood music, something with strings and a harp. . . .

The chimes stopped.

The ringing died a minute or two later.

The music stopped a half hour later, at 4:35.

And then there was just that annoying, insistent buzz, like a panicky insect, which went on and on and on and on . . .

Until 4:52, when it stopped.

All was silent again. No light showed beneath the door.

7

Two weeks after my mother's death, I hopped back on the roller coaster, selling *The Sensuous Woman* from coast to coast, giving interviews, making bookstore appearances, speaking to women's groups, negotiating the cable-strewn floors of network TV shows.

I expected to break down. Instead I soared.

I was taping *The Phil Donahue Show* one morning in 1971, in Dayton, Ohio, leaning back in my chair during a commercial break, when it suddenly struck me: *I had changed.* The shy, mousy book publicist had metamorphosed into a confident public woman. She appeared relaxed under the batteries of hot lights, unperturbed by unflattering cameras and often hostile interviewers. *How very clever of me,* I thought. *"J" isn't real. She can't be bruised. She can't be traumatized.*

I had split in two: Terry Garrity, confused, insecure, clinging to the safe and familiar world of family and friends, and "J," outgoing, authoritative, relishing the limelight. "J" parried and thrust with the press and public; Terry quietly savored the roses Dell Publishing ordered for "J"'s hotel suites. "J" signed aerosol cans of whipped cream that male fans thrust at her at bookstore appearances; Terry would have blushed and fled.

Terry wasn't complaining. She sipped champagne in "J"'s first-class seat on transcontinental jets. She allowed "J"'s suitors to take her to expensive restaurants. She bought beautiful clothes and objets d'art with the money "J" was making hand over fist.

Irwin Zucker, the Hollywood-based book publicist who handled my California promotion tours, noticed that Miss "J" was different when she hit Los Angeles this time. "What happened?" Irwin asked. "You can handle anything tossed at you now. It doesn't bother you like it used to."

"I'm just toughening up, I suppose," I laughed. Actually, I was turning my "J" on and off like a light.

Somehow, on the West Coast, promoting *The Sensuous Woman* was kookier, a little less earnest. I still got my message across, but there was more laughter and less resistance. People on the Coast approved of orgasms.

The real difference on my western swings, though, was Irwin. Irwin's motto was "Promotion in Motion," and he lived up to his billing. He was a trim, energetic man with wavy brown hair and a big smile. He usually wore a patterned shirt and a flashy tie, and he seemed to enjoy a passing acquaintanceship with about every third person in the Los Angeles area. If you were being driven somewhere by Irwin, you got used to his spotting people on the sidewalk, in passing cars, or through the windows of restaurants. He'd suddenly swerve to the curb, jump out of the car, and duck in some doorway for a moment to drop off a book or plug an author. An instant later, he'd be back in the driver's seat, picking up the conversation as if he had no more than sneezed.

Irwin believed in the saturation approach, so if you had an hour between Dinah Shore's show and your Los Angeles *Times* interview, Irwin would bring in the high school newspapers. He'd serve you up to the ten-watt radio stations, to the nervous interviewer with the borrowed tape recorder that never worked, to the little newspaper out in the Valley with a circulation of 600, to the senior citizen columnist for a community center newsletter. Irwin had developed these contacts because he was constantly promoting impossible books by unknown authors, many of them self-published and "vanity press" efforts. Irwin was determined to give those authors the same ego gratification that the celebrity authors got. "The unknown author will drive a hundred miles to a ten-watt station to be on the air," Irwin explained. "He'll submit to an interview with a weekly shopping guide and go home happy. So I cultivate the small contacts."

I loved that about Irwin. When he had a giant book like *The Sensuous Woman* or *Sex and the Single Girl,* he didn't forget the small contacts. He rewarded them with celebrity press conferences and short but exclusive interviews. (He didn't neglect his "minor" clients, either. It was odd to feel yourself caught up in Irwin's whirlwind when he was promoting books like *Farewell to Pimples,* or that classic from a chiropractor client, *To Thine Own Spine Be True.*)

Irwin was an important contact for people who trafficked in printable anecdotes about celebrities. He got me mentions on Rona Barrett's national television segments, which had tremendous impact on book sales. One afternoon, Irwin took me to lunch at a drive-in Arby's, and as we pulled into the parking lot he exclaimed, "Rona's here!"

Sure enough, Irwin wheeled into an empty space, and there was Rona in her car with a mouth full of roast beef. Irwin jumped out and raced to her window with gobs of his literature. "Rona, this is Miss 'J!'" he crowed. He then performed effusively on behalf of five other clients, offering

Rona tidbits from books on incest, divorce, billiards, and the Tate–La Bianca murders. "I've even got a cookbook here full of California dried fig recipes," he exulted. Rona disclaimed interest in any of these items, but Irwin made her laugh, and, yes, *The Sensuous Woman* got another mention from Rona that week on network TV.

I promoted the Dell paperback of *The Sensuous Woman* with an efficiency that made my Lyle Stuart tours look inept. I had an escort in each city—usually a local salesperson for Dell—someone who knew the city like a native and who shared my interest in promoting the book. I no longer had to fumble around for cabs or waste precious time asking directions. The Dell representative simply whisked me in and out of studios by saying, "Joan, we're due at KGO in ten minutes," and dragging me out while I made my smiling apologies and waved good-bye.

I made dozens of bookstore visits. If we were passing a shopping center and we had fifteen free minutes, we'd park the car and pop into the Walden Book Store or B. Dalton's, or whatever. The salespeople would introduce me, saying, "This is 'J,' who's written *The Sensuous Woman*," and the clerks and managers would beam and tell us how well the book was selling. I would shake hands all around and sign autographs and talk to passersby, and then we'd stroll back to the car and drive on. I don't know if these visits sold more copies of *my* book, but I know they helped sell the whole Dell line.

Another promotion technique was unfamiliar and baffled me at first. Dell wanted me to get up early in the morning in some cities to talk to truck drivers.

I thought, "Truck drivers?"

"These are the people who actually put your book on the racks," somebody at Dell told me. I knew that the paperback racks at drug stores, newsstands, and department stores were usually serviced by magazine distributors, but I assumed that the truck drivers were without influence. Dell corrected me: "Their support is *crucial*."

It had never occurred to me that a truck driver could put my book on the very bottom rack in the airport newsstand in Phoenix if, for some reason, he didn't approve of me or my book. Or that, heaven forbid, he might forget to take it off the truck, period! And so, starting in Washington, D.C., I began frequenting the warehouse districts at seven o'clock in the morning, giving little pep talks to groups of Teamsters, like a bomber wing commander briefing his pilots before a predawn air attack.

I was warned not to expect an always polite audience: The drivers sometimes walked out on authors, I was told, or sat on folding chairs, looking bored.

Luckily, they were polite with me. I was no dynamo in my presentations, but they seemed to think my book was interesting. *The Sensuous Woman* got terrific rack display every place I went, and Dell attributed that partly to my willingness to brief the truckers at dawn.

On the other hand, it was in these warehouses that I saw the big shredding machines that chewed up unsold paperbacks and magazines. "They wouldn't do that to *my* book, would they?" I asked.

"It doesn't read 'em, lady," a gruff trucker told me. "It just eats 'em."

Actually, it was America that was gobbling up *The Sensuous Woman*. My book had made waves in America, waves that sometimes frightened me. Strangers with emotion in their voices called me on radio shows to tell me that *The Sensuous Woman* was altering their lives. "My wife and I are using your book to try to save our marriage," a man would tell me, and I felt a mixture of pride and worry—the worry owing to the responsibility I now felt and didn't really want. My mail contained many pathetic letters like this one from a woman in Minneapolis:

Dearest "J,"
    I have a problem. The reason I'm telling you is because

I feel that you could help. It's between me, my boyfriend and SEX! I have read your book (The Sensuous Woman) *two times. The first time I read it and tried everything on him it worked just beautiful. Then he went on a trip to South Dakota. Well, during the time he was gone I read your book again. The day he got back I thought I was going to surprise him. I did everything on him like the Silken Swirl, and the Hoover. That did ok but when we made love he just went for about 15 min. I felt real bad about the whole thing and could of just cried. I asked him what was wrong. He said nothing was, but I could tell something was. Then he said maybe it was because he was sick. I just don't know what happened because before we used to go for a long time. Like one time we went for about 2 hours and 45 minutes. That's the reason I'm telling you this. I really want to know because if there's anything wrong with him or me I would like to know. I do love him and care about him and don't want to lose him, so please help.*
PLEASE!!!!!!
Sign,
Jill
P.S. I need to know right away before I lose him.

My usual disclaimer when I made appearances took on a more emphatic tone: "I am not a doctor, I am not a psychiatrist or psychologist," I said. "I am *not* an expert. I'm just a woman." Women's libbers didn't like my using the word *just* that way, but I wanted my readers to understand that I was not "better" than they were, or "smarter." I wanted them to learn from my experience and to enjoy sex fully, but I didn't want to be their guru, or a "Dear Abby." I found myself soft-pedaling my book's shock value, too. "When *Sex and the Single Girl* came out," I reminded audiences, "it was a shocking book for its time. Now, of course, it seems rather quaint. I think *The Sensuous Woman* is going to be that kind of book for the seventies. Today, it's outspoken, but by 1980 it may actually seem old-fashioned." (A prophesy that proved accurate, judging from the strings of books that followed, all advertised with the line, "Makes *The Sensuous Woman* read like *Rebecca of Sunnybrook Farm!*")

While attacks on "J" no longer bothered me, attacks on Terry stung as much as ever. Friends told me there was a whispering campaign against me, that someone was spreading rumors that I was a whore and a slut, that I hopped into bed with producers and talk-show hosts, that I was temperamental and crazed by success. The story was circulating that I wasn't even the author of *The Sensuous Woman,* that Lyle Stuart had hired Terry Garrity as a figurehead to promote the book, and that Carole Livingston, in his office, was the real author.

Lyle ignored my written requests that my mail, royalty statements, and monies be forwarded to my attorney, Don Engel. He sent everything by registered mail to my long-vacated apartment on East Forty-ninth Street, which meant that it was held as undeliverable at the post office branch at Forty-fourth Street and Lexington Avenue. I had to fly to New York and appear personally to claim my mail.

There was still the matter of the $125,000 in royalties withheld from my semiannual statement. When my accountant went to the Lyle Stuart offices to check the royalty statement on my behalf, as provided for in my contract, he was denied access to the key documents.

The litany of harassments grew. A letter from Lyle to Leon Shimkin, president of Simon and Schuster, attacked Len's reputation. Lyle refused to forward my *Sensuous Woman* mail to me. (I had been answering every letter from readers, admiring or not; now I worried that people seeking advice or support would think me too callous to reply.) To top it all, I learned that Stuart had written a column for *Screw* magazine, something mentioning me in language so vile that Len and others warned me that I must never read it.

"J" shrugged off these attacks, but Terry was shaken.

The last straw for me was a conversation I had with a free-lance publicist who had worked for Lyle on *The Sensuous Woman*. This man shocked me by confessing that he was the person who had given my name to *Time* magazine. "I didn't want to do it," he said sheepishly, "and I argued against it in a meeting with Lyle. But Lyle insisted that I give them your name. He wanted that story."

I finally knew. Lyle Stuart was the Judas who had betrayed me.

I forgave the publicist, but I couldn't forgive Lyle. On October 14, 1971, Don Engel and I sent out a press release that we had written together. It was headlined SENSUOUS WOMAN SUES LYLE STUART FOR OVER $1,000,000. My suit charged Lyle Stuart with grossly understating royalties due me, harassment, dissemination of false information about the origin of the book, fraudulently attempting to appropriate the copyright of *The Sensuous Woman,* issuing fraudulent royalty statements, and disposing of subsidiary rights without adequate safeguards against misuse.

Of particular importance was my claim that Stuart broke from book-industry practice by not paying me the full royalty on all copies sold to the trade in the normal course of business (as called for in my contract). Instead he "embarked upon a scheme to secure more money for himself by making 'special' sales although the book was in great demand and on the best-seller lists," thereby enriching himself at my expense.

More than my own rights and moneys were involved in my suit. If I should lose, it would mean that all authors except the giants, who could negotiate spectacular contracts because of their best-selling track records, would possibly lose half of their hardcover book royalties. I later met Jim Bouton, the baseball pitcher who wrote *Ball Four* with Leonard Schecter. His publisher, World, had done exactly the same thing, taken off one-half of his royalties for a substantial portion of his sales while the book was in its major, general distribution. Bouton and Schecter talked to Don, who told them frankly that their legal fees, which would not be recoverable as damages in a lawsuit, would probably far exceed the amount of money they could recover. Reluctantly, they decided not to pursue the case. Similarly, I learned of several Lyle Stuart authors who had suffered losses between $10,000 and $30,000—big money to a writer, but not enough to justify lengthy litigation against a powerful adversary. I seemed to be the only author with enough money to finance this plea for justice. What Lyle Stuart had done in 1970 was not industry practice, but if the courts failed to uphold industry practice, then other publishers, eager for increased revenues, would undoubtedly do what Stuart and Bouton's publisher had done, on the grounds that the law condoned such an act. The authors most in need of full royalties would be the most hurt, so Don and I had a grave responsibility.

I began to have nightmares. I was afraid to fall asleep alone. In one recurring dream, I was sucked up into the funnel of a tornado.

I knew the source of this dream: a family legend. Around the turn of the century, one of my father's uncles, a lawyer and Greek scholar, looked out his office window in the small Irish town of New Richmond, Wisconsin, and saw a great summer storm approaching. With a sudden premonition of tragedy, he raced to the schoolhouse in the rain to get his two sons. He was running home with the boys, down the middle of the main street, holding each one by the hand, when a funnel cloud descended from the wind-whipped rain and plucked one of the two boys out of his protective grasp and sucked him up into the swirling gray unknown. The other child and his father were left stunned but safe in the muddy street. The tornado was gone, and with it the child. The little boy was never found.

Seventy years later—in a New York high-rise apartment, in the safety of my lover's arms—I dreamed I was being sucked up into that New Richmond tornado. The darkness, the swirling motion, and the roaring wind wakened me with a shudder and a short cry.

There were other nightmares. I reexperienced, night after night, my mother's dying moments. I dreamed I was running from Nazis through a brutalized, war-torn landscape. I dreamed I was awake and that a dark, unseen presence was trying to smother me with a pillow while I lay paralyzed.

I would wake in a sweat.

Awake, "J" continued to function effortlessly in her role of controversial sex author. But Terry was less bubbly and outgoing. She now feared that her phone number or address would be discovered by strangers. She approached few tasks with enthusiasm, but felt "driven."

She was also preoccupied by an increasingly bitter dispute she was having with her lover over money.

In January 1970, Len had foreseen that *The Sensuous Woman* would be a blockbuster best seller. When we got the staggering news of my $100,000 paperback advance, Len had offered a practical suggestion. He proposed that he should take a percentage of my newfound riches and spend the money on glamorous trips for the two of us. Paris. China. Tahiti.

I immediately signed a paper giving Len 10 percent of all *Sensuous Woman* royalties as an agent's commission. Len hadn't been the agent for *The Sensuous Woman,* of course; no one had. But that hadn't bothered me; it was just legal language. (*Improper* language, I realized later.)

What did disturb and frustrate me, as the months went by, was that we didn't take any of those romantic trips. Len now contended that he had *earned* that 10 percent of my book because he had thought up the title and had been supportive of me while I was writing.

"I'm supportive of you in *your* job," I countered, "but that doesn't give me the right to take ten percent of your Simon and Schuster salary!"

Angered by my "stubbornness," he began summoning up all the wonderful things he had done for me over the years. "I took you to Don Engel," he said, looking pained. "He put you in good investments. He saved you from losing royalties that are rightly yours."

"Oh?" I was ready to cry. "I thought you did that because you loved me. If you were sick, I'd try to find the best doctor in the world for you. I certainly wouldn't charge you ten percent of your income for that!"

The wrangling went on, casting a cloud over our increasingly fragile relationship. I felt betrayed. It seemed to me that Len had taken advantage of me, knowing that I was financially naive and trusted him completely.

What did Len feel? I wasn't sure. He was irritable and defensive. He was honestly convinced that he was entitled to the thousands and thousands of dollars he was receiving from my book. He said my accusations of unethical conduct on his part were unfounded, that I didn't understand the world of business. It was only right that he be financially rewarded for helping and caring for me.

Len maintained a surface show of loving me, but I felt in many little ways he had moved away from me, from us. The spark, the fire, the trust, the loyalty, the laughter—they were all dying. He was by nature a wheeler-dealer, at ease in a world of rough and tumble deals and ephemeral loyalties. That hadn't stopped us from loving, caring, and savoring a glorious romance, but . . .

"J" continued to preach the joys of sexuality; Terry began sleeping alone.

8

*I*f anyone doubted that I wanted to shed "J" for a while, my next book should have convinced them. It was called *The Golfer's Guide to Florida Courses,* and I wrote it as J. T. Garrity. Lyle was convinced that it was a phony book, and he turned it down as his last option book under the original contract. He wanted another sex book, a book by "J."

"I want to write something harmless," I told Don Engel. "I *need* to write something harmless. I didn't set out to be controversial. I want to get my life back in balance."

The appeal of the golf book, in addition to its "safety," was that it could be a family project. My brother Tommy had finished his graduate work at the University of Florida and was an accredited golf course architect in Daytona Beach; he became my technical consultant. My father had moved to Gainesville, Florida, where he worked in the pro shop at the University Golf Club; I assigned him the job of mailing out questionnaires to all the golf courses and evaluating some of the courses in northern Florida. Johnny was editor of the book.

The change of topics was a restorative. "What a pleasure it will be," I told everybody, "to play all those wonderful courses. By the time I'm through with this book I should have the best golf game of my life!" I polished my clubs, studied the golf tips in back issues of *Golf Digest* and *Golf,* and purchased a new wardrobe of golf clothes and accessories. (The purchase that got the most wear was the golf umbrella, for it poured rain anytime I stepped on a golf course.) I had a wonderful time walking the lush, green courses, alone or with Tommy, studying the layouts and design. I loved the springy grass, the beautiful plantings, the absolute quiet (except for the occasional song of a bird and the muffled sounds of woods and irons connecting with balls). I felt serene and whole again on these walks.

My good friend Norman Monath, president of Cornerstone Library, said he would like to bid on *The Golfer's Guide to Florida Courses* if Lyle Stuart rejected the manuscript. Lyle did reject it, and in the end, Cornerstone got it.

Lyle countered by deducting $45,000 from a royalty statement "against legal expenses according to contract." His "legal expenses" were not those legally chargeable to an author. Thus Lyle Stuart was illegally withholding *my* royalties in an attempt to charge *me* for suing him to collect my own moneys owed me under *The Sensuous Woman* contract! He was trying to get me to pay *his* legal fees to defend himself against my charges.

After a flurry of demands for the illegally withheld $45,000 failed to budge Lyle from his position, Don informed me that my only recourse under my contract agreement was arbitration. Now I had two separate litigations going against Lyle Stuart.

"You're a red-hot commodity right now, Terry. You should strike with a big new book while you're still a household name," Don Engel advised me.

I forbore to ask him what that name was.

"Do you have any ideas?"

"Not really. But I'll start thinking."

Between legal skirmishes Don Engel began looking for another hardcover publisher for me. Most of the publishers were receptive. Mark Jaffee at Bantam Books surprised me by suggesting that I might want to write a novel or a biography. "I would love to," I said. "But I don't know if I could pull it off. I'm a writer, but I'm not, you know—" I laughed. "I'm not a *real* writer. I write how-to books, not literary ones."

I wasn't feigning modesty; despite the fact that I was at that moment the all-time best-selling female author of a nonfiction book, I felt insecure about my writing. I agreed with those critics who had thought "J"'s style was too cute, too syrupy. And I wanted the chance to prove that I had other writing styles and a modicum of talent. "For my next book I want a great editor along the lines of Maxwell Perkins, someone who can guide me, show me how to become a better writer."

Don suggested Michael Korda, the flamboyant author and editor in chief at Simon and Schuster.

Korda was Lyle Stuart's opposite in every way. Korda wore jodhpurs. Korda smoked a pipe. Korda looked good in tweeds and called S. J. Perelman "Sid." He was, in other words, what I thought an editor should be.

Since Don had once served as legal counsel to Simon and Schuster, and since he had a social relationship with S&S president Dick Snyder, it didn't take him long to report back to me that they were interested in striking a deal with me. I could expect a cash advance, Don said, of around $200,000— $198,500 more than Stuart had advanced me for *The Sensuous Woman*.

"But they don't want a Terry Garrity-style book," he said. "They want more of "J.""

The subject was to be romantic love, in a how-to format. The working title was *The Love Book*.

*   *   *

There were men, men everywhere in 1973. I'd never been surrounded by so many enticing males in my life. But as much as I longed to be half of a loving couple again, I avoided intimacy. Terry did so because she was newly aware that men who love you can also hurt. "J" was having different problems. She found herself desired not for her body or mind or heart or personality . . . but for her *initial*. Terry was amused by this phenomenon; as a separate entity she didn't have to take it personally, but "J" deeply resented the many men who tried to get her into the bedroom for the sole reason that she was "J." Even the fact that "J" now had braces on her teeth and was fifteen pounds overweight didn't deter "admirers" from pursuing their goal of bedding her down so they could brag about having made it with *The Sensuous Woman*. In self-defense, "J" rejected the attentions of all men who took an overt sexual interest in her.

Except for Ed.

But then he met Terry, not "J." In an elevator in LaGuardia Airport.

Ed was not subtle. He had been standing behind me in line at the National Airlines counter and heard that I was booked on the same delayed flight from New York to Palm Beach as he. In the elevator to the restaurant where National had arranged for ticket holders to have drinks and dinner, Ed struck up a conversation about the overdue flight. Upstairs, he invited me to have a drink with him. I looked up at the tall, robust, silver-haired man in the conservative suit and hesitated. He didn't *look* like an ax murderer. And with his good ol' boy southern accent and self-confidence he didn't *act* like an ax murderer. We talked. We had another drink. Talked some more. Had dinner.

I liked Ed and was attracted to him. He was both dashing and respectable, highly intelligent and business-smart. And an achiever . . . nationally prominent in his field. And *he didn't know who I was*. He was interested in *me,* Terry. Four hours later when we boarded the plane, we sat together.

When the plane landed in Palm Beach, Ed, who was ticketed to the next city, walked me to my car and kissed me.

The plane, his jacket, and his luggage left without him.

But how to tell him I was "J"? That weekend when I finally got up my courage and told him I was the Sensuous Woman, he had the most heartwarming reaction possible. He was scared to death of me!

Ed did manage to overcome his nervousness at being involved with a female "Good God, sex expert," and courted me with awesome amounts of high energy and zest. There was only one problem. Ed had a terror of emotional commitment and he liked it that way. And, while I was finding it hard to face the truth, I was going through a period of fear of loving myself. This was undoubtedly part of the reason we were drawn to each other. We continued to accept and enjoy each other on our own limited terms.

Maybe the research I was doing on *The Love Book* would make it clear to me why, although there were men, men everywhere, I wasn't finding one to love.

9

_T_ he early symptoms of mental disintegration are often so
subtle that even experts can miss them, so it's not surprising that neither I nor those around me noticed the first
signs that my thinking, perceptual abilities, and behavior
were altering that spring of 1974.

I settled in to write _The Love Book_ with the optimism and
enthusiasm I usually feel at the start of a book project, but
my brain couldn't seem to come to grips with the subject. I'm
one of those writers who has to have a clear-cut picture of
how the book will be styled and a detailed outline on paper
before I can begin the writing. I couldn't visualize this book.
Maybe what's wrong is my thinking hasn't jelled, I hypoth-
esized. _I might as well run out and get a few things done
while my subconscious is completing the organization of_ The
Love Book.

A month passed pleasantly: daily tennis lessons, a little
recreational shopping, a trip to New York to have the shiny
new braces on my teeth checked and my hair cut by scissors

genius Robert Pearson, some light reading (so that my brain wouldn't be too burdened to complete its work).

Month Two: "Maybe it would be a good idea to develop a little filler material on love." I clipped out "love quotes" from magazines and newspapers, any little item from a celebrity or a doctor or a psychologist—even the pope—that had the remotest connection with love. *Fine,* I thought. *But what does it mean to me? What is it that I am supposed to tell my readers?* I thought my subconscious was shirking its responsibilities. Perhaps freedom from distractions and a change of scenery would charge up my desultory mental processes. I island-hopped to Antigua.

Month Three: Don Engel called to ask how the book was coming along. "A little slowly," I admitted. "Love is a much more complex subject than sex, you know. But I don't see any serious problems on the horizon."

I was still on the phone when it finally struck me: *I was in way over my head.* I didn't know the first thing about love!

After I hung up the phone I walked across the street to the ocean in vain hopes that staring at the hypnotic in and out patterns of the surf would ease my panic. *I've signed a major contract for a book on a subject I know absolutely nothing about.* I had already accepted the first $50,000 of the advance (with another $50,000 to come in six months upon completion of the manuscript, and the rest on a fixed schedule). What was I going to do? The monumental task ahead of me made me want to run to a safe place and hide. Somehow I had to research one of the most mysterious and complex subjects known to man, master that subject, and turn out a whole book on that subject in nine (now six) months. How could I have gotten myself into this jam? It was the success game. I had signed that contract simply because it was time, according to my career expert advisers, to write another book. Does anybody *not* write another book?

Well, I would just have to learn what romantic love was,

just as I had tackled orgasm. The next day I began a marathon research project. I waded through medical, psychological, and sociological journals. I read books, interviewed individuals who were succeeding at love (and those who were failing), and questioned newlyweds, divorced men and women, couples who were still together after many years of marriage, and doctors.

Month Four. Digging and hunting for information wasn't presenting any frustrations. But unlike my previous projects, getting words down on paper was. The thoughts were there in my head, but something was interfering with the transmission of those thoughts into written words. To a degree, I was like a stroke victim who has lost her power of speech: Thinking was unimpaired, the mode of transmission was.

And Michael Korda wanted to see some manuscript.

I had no manuscript yet. Just fragments of chapters and little piles of paper marked "junked," "still interviewing," "still researching," and "in rough." I polished up a few of these fragments and sent them off to Michael for his guidance. He called me from New York.

"What do you think?" I asked timorously.

He said, "Well—that's not ex-*actly* what I want."

"I see," I said, my spirits falling. "Tell me what to do and I'll do it. What *do* you want?"

"I don't know, but this isn't it. I'll know it when I see it."

I sent him more fragments, each in a different style. None matched his inner vision. "Maybe you should forget about writing about love," he said gloomily, "and write about sex."

"But, Michael," I protested, "the book is *about* love. How do you leave out the main subject?"

"Maybe that was a mistake," he said.

So I wrote a sex chapter and sent it off to him. "No, that's really not quite it."

I felt so frustrated I wanted to scream. The awful part was, Michael was right. My stuff was bad. I wasn't breaking ground, just rehashing all the standard stuff that *Cosmopolitan* and *Ladies' Home Journal* and the pop psychologists had been saying for years. And for some reason, Michael and I couldn't seem to settle on a "voice" for the new book. I wanted to move away from my *Sensuous Woman* style, escape the frothiness, the girlishness, and the cuteness that people ridiculed—to write in a more straight, journalistic style. I was like the sexpot actress with the big breasts and big eyes and little girl voice who complains that no one respects her "acting." But I was too intimidated by the Korda reputation and manner to request concrete editorial guidance. My doubts about my abilities to write a book—any book—that would be acceptable to Michael increased. I began to avoid contacting him. I suspected that the very idea of a "love book" bored him. I felt that he resented any time he had to devote to me, although, heaven knows, he was always polite.

Somehow I would just have to muddle through the writing without editorial help. Once I got the right first few paragraphs down on paper, the right styling, the right rhythms, I would be okay.

I became obsessed with finding my voice, with getting that perfect first paragraph. I sat in my yellow chair in the living room with a felt pen and a legal pad and worked for the opening paragraph for hours on end. I'd scratch out my first sentence and write a new one. I'd draw arrows from one part of the paragraph to another. I'd switch from the first person to the third, then try the second, then end up starting out, "We . . . ," or "One. . . ." I'd quote an expert. I'd quote a friend. I'd throw out the quotes. I would pretend I was talking to a friend, or I would start to write a speech. I would take out all the adjectives.

Nothing seemed to work. I eventually just sat there in the chair, doing nothing, punishing myself with feelings of inadequacy and guilt. Finally, I would give up, exhausted, read

some more research material, eat some Fannie Mae chocolates, watch part of a late-night movie on TV, and go to bed.

Month Five was gone.

I had heard, of course, about writer's block. I had read of
other authors who had gotten tied up in knots after achiev-
ing critical acclaim or financial success. I didn't think I fit
the category. For one thing, I had written two more books
since the success of *The Sensuous Woman,* and with great
efficiency. *The Sensuous Man* was cranked out in record
time. I had written magazine articles. I wasn't always satisfied with the quality of the work, but I had gotten it done.

Still, I wasn't writing. I couldn't concentrate, couldn't
maintain an energy level, couldn't function. If I had been a
computer programmer, a salesperson, or in almost any other
line of work, these symptoms would have been assumed to be
indicative of serious mental difficulty, and I would have been
hauled off to a doctor for diagnosis. But because I was a
writer, family, friends, and business associates did their own
diagnosing when I went to them for advice: (1) writer's block;
(2) stress; and (3) all the money I had made had spoiled me,
taken away my discipline and desire to work. Conclusion:
Stop being so self-indulgent and pull myself together and
meet my obligations.

I went back to the big yellow chair and the blank pads of
paper with an increased sense of isolation and a strong burden of guilt. How dare I talk of my problem, which was ame-
nable to solving if I could just show a little backbone, when
other people in this world were coping with *real* troubles
with grace and efficiency?

The inability to concentrate, feelings of inadequacy, low
work output, and anxiety attacks continued.

My principal relief from the tension was to "relax" and "reward" myself for my suffering by walking over to my neighborhood shopping center, which just happened to be the most
elegant and most expensive street of shops in the world—

Worth Avenue. I carted home a fire-engine-red moiré gown by Bill Blass, Christian Dior negligees and peignoirs, a Baccarat millefiori paperweight, perfumes, a sports watch, gifts for family and friends, Carlin linens. I began trading in redundancies: two travel Water Piks (because "one might break"), four pairs of shoes (exactly alike).

If shopping gave my daytimes a lift, eating consumed my nights. While I struggled with *The Love Book,* I would nibble some all-butter cookies. I would write a few sentences, stare at the shag carpeting, reread a paragraph or two that I'd written the night before, polish off half a Sara Lee fruit pie, put a Stouffer frozen cheese soufflé in the oven, tune in to the *Tomorrow* show with Tom Snyder, eat the soufflé, watch the late, late show, underline a chapter in a reference book, go to the kitchen and eat a few spoonfuls of Howard Johnson's ice cream, sit down again, make some notes about a medical breakthrough, read a *New Yorker* review of a Broadway play I had seen, read the cartoons, read the "newsbreaks" with their funny captions, get up, go to the kitchen, pour myself a Diet Dr. Pepper, sit down, breathe a sigh, get up, turn off the TV, peer out between the curtains at the first light of dawn, put my soft drink back in the refrigerator, turn off the lights, and go to bed.

The pressure mounted. New York was waiting for a book, but I was writing nothing. I was telling Don Engel I was almost done, when in fact I was "almost begun." Anxiety and restlessness made my mind race. "I'm tired of sitting in a chair getting nowhere," I told myself one night. "I'd rather be sitting in a chair getting *somewhere.*"

I pictured myself on a train, looking dreamily out the window at passing small towns, farmland, and prairie grasses. I saw myself as a character in a thirties' movie, one of the faces in the crowd watching Clark Gable and Bing Crosby and Ginger Rogers play wonderful scenes on transcontinental trains, poking their heads from behind the curtains of Pullman berths, cracking jokes with the porters, singing romantic ballads to each other on the rear platform of the club car. I longed to escape.

I looked down at the floor. It was littered with file folders, clippings, magazines. It was so still, so quiet. I felt like a prisoner in my own apartment. I wasn't enjoying my work; I was cut off from friends; I was starved for a pleasurable experience. I knew a retreat into glamour and fantasy at this time was wrong, but the rush of excitement at the possibility of feeling happy again was too seductive to resist. I threw down the pen. "That does it. I'm taking a train trip."

I ran to the bedroom and phoned Jacque in New York. "You must come too," I said emphatically. "Everyone should ride the *Super Chief* at least once in a lifetime."

Jacque was hesitant. She had started research on her book about multimillionaires—*The Very Rich Book: America's Supermillionaires and Their Money—Where They Got It, How They Spend It,* she called it—and she didn't want to put off her research.

I applied pressure. "You have to write about the California rich, don't you?"

"Well, sure," she said.

"You can do your research and have a fun trip, too! The *Super Chief* goes right by the Los Angeles Public Library."

"I doubt that," Jacque said. She added, as if thinking aloud, "I could visit Forest Lawn Cemetery. . . ."

I was startled. "Whatever for?"

"There are a lot of important rich people there," she said. "Of course, they're dead."

"It won't be any fun if I do it alone," I pleaded.

That seemed to do the trick. Jacque agreed to meet me in Kansas City to catch the train.

The *Super Chief* was wonderful. We chugged across all that

rugged desert country that I had never seen before except from a jet thirty thousand feet in the air. Jacque and I sat up in the dome car and looked for buttes and coyotes and tumbleweeds and all the things you don't see in New York's canyons.

"You know what we should do," I told Jacque. "We should organize a whistle-stop author's tour. You'll be a best-selling author and I'll be a best-selling author, and we'll get three or four more authors and we'll travel in a private railroad car! . . . Say!" I had an inspiration. "Maybe one of your millionaires would lend us a private car!"

"Terry—" Jacque gave me a knowing look. "They didn't get to be millionaires by *lending* people things."

As it happened, we were pulling a private car behind us, one full of railroad executives. At Albuquerque, we got out and walked back for a look. We could see glimpses of railroad tycoon decor through the windows: lampshades, bud vases, a private bar. "The trouble is," I said sadly, "the railroads may be gone before I finish *The Love Book*." I felt a sudden stab of anxiety.

We had a wonderful last meal on the train that night: delicious Kansas City steaks with fresh vegetables. It was all served on linen tablecloths with crystal water goblets and slightly tarnished but historic silver. Whenever my unfinished book crowded into my thoughts, I crowded it back out. "Isn't this wonderful?" I asked Jacque.

Everything was "wonderful."

As promised, I accompanied Jacque to Forest Lawn Cemetery in Glendale, where two of her subjects were interred. The time went fast. While Jacque immersed herself in library research and interviewing millionaires, I went shopping on Rodeo Drive.

Jacque may have known millionaires, but I knew a movie star, Burt Reynolds. He had followed me in the drama department at Palm Beach Junior College, and I also had known him during his stint as a struggling New York actor.

Since then, I had bumped into him several times in Florida, and he had offered to give me a tour of a Hollywood movie set if I ever got out his way. And there I was, finally, curious about my visit to the set of his musical, *At Long Last Love.*

Universal Studios is a huge place—whole city blocks of offices, sound stages, and back lots. They let me in the studio gate without any fuss and I was escorted onto a sound stage where Burt was filming a scene with Cybill Shepherd. It was a brief bit of business where Cybill sang "Let's Misbehave" while Burt went around turning on lights she had just turned off. Burt wore a white dinner jacket and sported a Rhett Butler moustache. Cybill was equally striking in a long white gown slit down the back.

Someone got me a high stool, and I sat and watched while they shot the scene. Peter Bogdanovich, the director, looked very Ivy League, his sweater tied around his neck by the sleeves. He was madly in love with Cybill, everyone knew, and he was working very hard that day to get the best of her on celluloid. They shot the tiny scene again and again.

After each take, people would rush out and adjust Cybill's gown and fuss over her makeup and hair. Technicians would make adjustments to lights and microphones. During these breaks, Burt would come over and talk to me. He was almost apologetic. "You can see why we're over budget and behind schedule."

We laughed about a picture of the two of us that was making the rounds of the tabloids with such captions as BURT REYNOLDS DUMPS DINAH FOR SENSUOUS WOMAN and SEX TITANS JOIN FORCES. (Professor Watson B. Duncan III and his wife, Honey, had been artfully cut out of the picture, which was taken in a Palm Beach restaurant.) "People keep asking me what it's like to date Burt Reynolds," I said.

"What do you tell them?" Burt asked, a twinkle in his eye.

"The truth!" I laughed. "That we were actually out with our teacher!"

Burt laughed, too, and then went back to the set to walk

across the room and turn on the lights some more.

Burt introduced me to people. He introduced me to Sidney Lumet, the famous director, who was visiting the set, and, of course, to Cybill, who said, "How do you do?" but was rather remote. And finally he introduced me to Bogdanovich, who started talking about his recent movie, *What's Up, Doc?,* which starred Barbra Streisand and Ryan O'Neal. "Did you see it?" Bogdanovich asked me rather eagerly.

Had I? My mind was blank.

For some unknown reason, I said, "Yes."

Bogdanovich started discussing a scene from that movie, something played by Madeline Kahn. I listened and smiled uneasily. He suddenly asked, "What did you think when you saw your book in the film?"

My smile was frozen on my face.

Peter and Burt gave me long, strange looks. (Months later, when I finally saw *What's Up, Doc?,* I learned why. There is a funny scene in which Madeline Kahn is waiting in bed for Ryan O'Neal, and she's reading *The Sensuous Woman.*)

Peter glossed over my embarrassment, and moments later Burt was back walking across the room and turning on the lights. I went and sat on the high stool, feeling miserable. *Why did I say that?* I agonized. *Why did I lie?* My head began to throb.

They broke for a late lunch, and a gofer came over and told me that Burt had arranged for me to have lunch in his trailer. It was a "wonderful" trailer, a star's trailer, and Burt even had fresh strawberries for me.

At first, we chatted about the movie, but suddenly Burt stopped and gave me a questioning look. "Why did you say you'd seen that movie when you hadn't?" he asked.

I opened my mouth, but for an instant nothing came out. "I don't know why," I said, baffled. "I thought . . . I think I thought I had seen it."

Burt wasn't bawling me out, really. He was just puzzled.

"It would have been better if you'd said nothing. Why did you say that?"

Again, I said, "I don't know. I don't understand why I did it myself. It just isn't like me."

At that moment, something very strange began happening to me. I was suddenly disoriented in time. Everything was in slow motion, as in a dream. Time actually stopped. Neither Burt nor I moved. And then the film would suddenly start up again.

I was too frightened to tell him what was happening to me.

"Am I going to see you while you're here?" Burt asked.

"No!" I said loudly.

He looked startled.

What was wrong with me? I was being rude to an old acquaintance who had gone out of his way to be kind to me.

Burt tried to make normal conversation, but I was still in the grips of that strange time warp. My ears were ringing. He told me how much he wanted to produce and direct movies, how acting wasn't fulfilling—especially in all those "good ol' boy" films. I hardly heard him. I stammered when I tried to speak; I babbled meaningless things. I was in an agony of embarrassment, desperate to escape, but I couldn't seem to stand up.

I don't remember much of what happened after that. Obviously, Burt had to go back to work. Somehow I executed my thank yous and retreated to my car with tears running down my face.

Back at the hotel that night, Jacque tried to cheer me up, but it was useless. "I couldn't do anything right today. I made a total *fool* of myself, and I don't know why." I was anxious for an explanation.

I began pacing the room. "Oh, I just want to crawl under something and hide! Peter Bogdanovich thinks I'm a liar. Burt thinks I'm rude. And weird! It was like a blackout, only I was conscious. I was almost out of my body, an observer.

Oh, how embarrassing!" Suddenly I stopped my tirade, called room service, and ordered extravagantly. Jacque looked on, puzzled. "I probably shouldn't eat anything," I said. "I probably owe this mental confusion to the antihistamines and migraine painkillers I took for the allergic reaction I had to the lemon meringue pie and fried chicken I ate last night."

Jacque sounded rather stern. "Terry, why are you eating so much? Especially foods that make you sick?"

I clutched the receiver and frowned. "I don't know why." I repeated very slowly, "I don't know why."

A shadow had fallen over my life. I don't mean that figuratively; my world was perceptibly, dramatically darker, as if a cloud had passed over me.

The next day I flew home.

Jacque and I talked recently about this trip to California. I asked her the obvious question. "Couldn't you see that I was crazy?"

"I knew you weren't acting like yourself. All that shopping and eating and traveling around when you should have been home working seemed childishly self-indulgent and self-destructive to me. You'd never behaved like that before. And I could see you were really upset and frightened by your experience on the movie set with Burt Reynolds, but I never thought you were crazy. There was a logical explanation for everything, and besides, crazy to me meant *really* crazy, like thinking you were Jesus Christ or Tinker Bell, or giving all your money to strangers. Giving all your money to Gucci's isn't the same thing. That's just stupid. But *you* were the one going crazy. Why didn't *you* know it?"

At the time, I had a limited knowledge of the types and ranges of mental illness. I had learned a little bit about schizophrenia when I did publicity for the book *How to Live with Schizophrenia,* but my idea of mental illness was mostly based on characters in books, plays, and movies, such as

Blanche DuBois, Ophelia, the wife in *Jane Eyre*, Jack the Ripper. *My* behavior was still explainable at this stage—except for the mental blank and time warp, and since they didn't continue to happen, I finally assumed that I had had a bizarre allergic reaction to some food or airborne substance.

Most people who are becoming mentally ill don't know it. We search for a logical explanation in what's going on in our lives at the time. And if you look hard enough you almost always can find something that seems plausible to you. My early symptoms: inability to concentrate; a single incident of mental and perceptual confusion; increased appetite and significant weight gain; loss of energy; feelings of inadequacy; feelings of excessive guilt; anxiety; restlessness; decreased productivity. All these symptoms seemed to me to be "normal" stress reactions to my impending deadline. In retrospect, I know that this wasn't the case and that my confusion with Burt Reynolds was the first overt symptom of a serious and increasingly disturbing descent into mental illness. This was my first intimation that something was happening to me that I didn't understand. My response to Burt's puzzled inquiry was, "I don't *know* why," a response that was to become my only answer as my behavior became more erratic and my emotions more and more confused.

10

As before, I settled into the yellow chair with all my things around me and tried to write. I stayed up all night *determined* to write, forcing myself not to sleep. I went on twenty-four- and thirty-six-hour vigils, yearning to write. I would get a paragraph, at most. Months Six and Seven crawled past.

That Christmas, I lavished presents on my friends, family, and myself. My friends were aghast at my purchases, at my ability to spend hundreds, even thousands of dollars on impulse. Johnny questioned my purchase of a five-hundred-dollar Ming vase lamp because, when I got it home, the forty-five-cent light socket didn't work. (He said, "A five-hundred-dollar lamp should light up when you pull the chain.") Neither was he impressed by my Gucci golf bag, which cost me about six hundred dollars.

Especially since I wasn't playing golf.

Money was draining away in another direction, also. The lawsuit against Lyle Stuart was costing me a staggering sum. I should say lawsuits, plural, because after rejecting my golf book as the final option book under my contract, Lyle had filed scatter-gun litigations against Simon and Schuster, Don, and me, charging that my new publisher had conspired to rob him of his final option book (which he insisted had to be a sex book and not a book like *The Golfer's Guide to Florida Courses*). These charges had to be answered, and Don Engel's expertise did not come cheaply. His monthly statements, which were meticulously prepared, included out-of-pocket expenses for things like travel, telephone, typing and photocopying, depositions, court fees, and a hundred other items that were costing me thousands of dollars a month. In a six-month period, I sometimes paid out more for photocopying alone than the $1,500 I had received as an advance for *The Sensuous Woman*. And there was no end in sight. A suit like mine would normally take two to four years to come to trial, but Lyle's side employed delaying tactics, withholding information from us and forcing us back into court repeatedly to secure discovery orders. On the Long John Nebel show in New York, Lyle stated that he had *never* paid a judgment to anyone and never *would*. He obviously thought I would surrender or go bankrupt before the case ever came to trial.

To keep me afloat, Arthur Halper reluctantly sold some of my stocks and bonds, which he had set up to provide me with a permanent income. I thought him something of a wizard in that every time I ran out of money, he seemed to turn up something I owned that could be sold. But I knew my inability to live within a budget worried him terribly.

I sheepishly asked Don if we couldn't get a partial payment on my next advance from Simon and Schuster. "It's hard to concentrate on writing when I'm so worried about paying my bills," I explained. "The manuscript will be done by February at the latest, barring some catastrophe."

I crossed my fingers and waited anxiously.

I got Don's reply a few days after Christmas. "I am sorry to give you the bad news on this one," he wrote. My heart fell.

"However," he went on, "if you really can get out the first draft sometime in January, as you told me, we can ask them to reevaluate the situation at that time."

I knew I could not make the January deadline, but February seemed attainable.

But I missed the February deadline.

Don began to call more often, inquiring anxiously about the book. The $50,000 that had been due on December 1, he told me, was not going to be paid until I delivered a completed manuscript. He warned that Simon and Schuster might withdraw its $200,000 commitment if we delayed much longer.

"When can you have a manuscript?"

"Three weeks," I said. "A month at the latest."

"All right," he said. "I'll try to stall them."

I went back to the yellow chair and my legal pads, and tried to fight off the panic.

I missed the March deadline. And the April deadline. May. June. Don was beside himself. I began to ignore the telephone when it rang. I didn't want to talk to anybody until I had completed the first draft, and I thought that would come after a week or two of hard work. I was sure I would be productive as soon as I felt better, or as soon as I cleaned up the guest room, or as soon as I finished furnishing the rental apartment I had bought in West Palm Beach; as soon as those mysterious thinking-process circuits in my brain quit crisscrossing, splattering, and shorting out.

These months of my life are still painful to remember. I was like a professional ballplayer with an undetected muscle coordination disease. Unable to explain why his arm has lost its magic power to hit the outside corner of the plate with a slider, he drives himself unmercifully to recover the timing, speed, and control that have mysteriously deserted him. He grabs desperately at tips the coaches give him, practices relentlessly, perhaps drinks or eats too much at night to relax himself for the next day's battle against his unknown foe—a battle he *has* to win to remain in the major leagues. A battle he doesn't know yet he can't win.

Writers tend to think of the ability to connect words and thoughts in the brain in an organized, unique way that can be transferred to paper as a mystery skill that defies analysis. Even the most prolific authors experience ebbs and flows in productivity for no apparent reason, then practice strange little rituals at those ebb times to appease the writing god so that the words and thoughts will connect again and flow onto paper.

Some writers clean and polish their desks and typewriters; others do writing exercises; still others go on a fanatical health and fitness regimen. Since I didn't know a disease, and not the writing god, was blocking my ability to write, I ritualistically chained myself (figuratively) to the yellow chair and pressured my brain to function again. The daily marathon efforts produced a little pile of writing, but it wasn't good, and it wasn't enough.

One day, the phone rang and rang so long that I was afraid not to pick it up. I answered, "Hello," with the false cheeriness that had become habitual.

It was Don. "Simon and Schuster is losing patience," he told me. "Our position is very weak. Would you be open to help from Johnny? He's an editor. You respect his opinion."

"Sure," I said. "But I don't know if he could leave what he's doing in Kansas City and—"

"I've already talked to him," Don said. "He'll be in Palm Beach tomorrow afternoon on Delta flight one-o-three arriving at five-ten."

"Oh," I said, taken aback.

"Terry, I bargained as best I could, and I got Simon and Schuster to agree to wait until August tenth for the manuscript, but they aren't happy about it. If you miss that deadline . . ."

Don did not have to complete the thought.

Johnny brought barbecue in his soft-sided suitcase: three slabs of ribs and a pound of beef from J.B. & Sons Barbecue in Kansas City. "I had a little trouble taking it through the X-ray machine at the airport," he said. "One guy thought I'd put a dead calf on the conveyor."

I unwrapped the foil. The smell of hickory smoke made me nostalgic for Kansas City, for tree-lined streets, for barrels full of burning leaves, for terraced yards and rope swings. It also made me very hungry. "Why didn't you bring more?" I asked.

Johnny started stirring the barbecue sauce. "Seven dollars a slab, that's why."

With Johnny's encouragement, I got some writing done. Not much, but some. "Write anything," he said. "Don't worry if it's good or bad, don't worry if it's even about love, just write stuff. Bad writing we can edit; blank pages we can't."

No matter what I handed him, he was encouraging. "Great," he said, "keep going."

"I don't think it's very good."

"Keep writing." Johnny pulled several tiny stacks together and rifled the pages. "Look, it's growing."

It was disorienting to have my baby brother, the one I worried about and felt responsible for, switching roles. He was now the strong older brother, I the frightened little sister leaning on him for help. When he offered criticisms, they were guarded, because he didn't want to undermine my confidence. "Perhaps this chapter could be cut in two," he would say, or, "It takes you a long time to get to your point here. What do you think about trimming it a little?"

"You can't cut that!" I argued. "That's my best writing!"

"Right," he would sigh. "Keep writing."

During the day, I slept. If I woke up by three or four in the afternoon, I tried to slip out for an hour or so to pick up "essential" items: trivets, kaleidoscopes, needlework kits. Johnny discouraged these excursions. "Your errands are your way of postponing the unpleasantness of writing," he said. "Write first. Shop later."

Johnny flew in several times that July, always with barbecue. He made his last trip on August 3, just one week before my final deadline. I had perhaps a hundred pages of typed manuscript, and maybe fifty more in rough. "I have to show them at least three hundred pages," I told him. "This is going to be hell. I have to write one hundred and fifty pages in seven days."

Johnny looked skeptical. "I'll feel good if you get fifty."

"Fifty is no good. If I don't give them three hundred pages, I'll lose everything!"

He obviously didn't want to argue. "Well, let's get cracking." He cleared away the debris around the typewriter in the guest room. "I'll do the typing," he said. "As fast as you can turn out chapters, I'll type them up in rough. Then I'll edit them and give them back to you for additions and corrections."

"Did you bring any barbecue?" I asked hopefully.

"Not this time," he said. "We'll feed you intravenously."

I settled again into the yellow chair, my legal pad on my lap, my magazines and files around me. Johnny showed his head every hour or so when he took a break from typing the fifty pages I had in rough. "How's it going?" he would ask.

"Slow," I would say in a weak voice. "Very slow."

"Any progress at all?"

"Some," I said.

He shrugged and returned to the typewriter.

The next time he appeared, I was staring blankly across the room. "Looks to me like you've had enough for now," he said.

"I'm very tired," I said slowly.

"Get some sleep."

"Can I?" I looked with misgivings at the file folders strewn about me.

"You have to," Johnny said. "You don't plan to stay awake for a hundred hours, do you?"

"But I have to finish the book."

He turned off the kitchen light. "You won't finish it staring at the wall. I plan to sleep at least once every day, and maybe twice or three times. You'd better do the same."

I nodded gratefully and trudged off to bed. "I won't sleep long," I said. "Just a while."

The next day went the same. I finished up a section, with difficulty, and passed it along to Johnny for typing. "Great," he said. "Take a break, take a walk, maybe."

"I'd like that," I said, "but I'm so sleepy."

"Then take a short nap. I'll wake you."

I took the nap, and it was dark when he called me. "What time is it?" I croaked, padding into the living room in my terry-cloth robe.

"Around nine," he said. "Ready to go some more?"

I nodded groggily.

After midnight, he found me again in the yellow chair, staring blankly across the room. "Stumped?"

"I'll be going along pretty well," I said, "and then suddenly I get to a hard part and I just seem to go blank. I think and think and think, but nothing happens. Look—" I held up my legal pad. "I've got only four pages."

"What's wrong with four pages?" he asked, looking surprised. "A few weeks ago you weren't writing at all."

"Yes, but I need how many pages? One hundred and fifty? And I've got what, five more days? That's thirty pages a day!"

He stood above me and didn't speak for a few moments. "That's why you're staring at the wall," he finally said. "You know you can't write thirty pages a day."

"I have to write thirty pages a day!"

"You can't!" he almost shouted. "Stop punishing yourself."

"I did it for *The Sensuous Man.*"

"No, you didn't." He sounded impatient. *"Three* people did that. If four pages isn't enough, fine—maybe you can do five. Maybe ten. But you'll never do thirty. If you put a gun to my head, maybe I could write thirty pages in one night, but the next night I would fall asleep, and the night after that I would go to the movies."

"The movies!" I said longingly.

"You're still sleepy," he said. "Take another nap."

"I can't take a nap," I insisted. "I have to write."

"Then write. But take it a page at a time."

"I've only got five days!"

He suddenly disappeared into the kitchen. "Do you want anything?" he called.

"Chocolate!" I called back. He brought me a box of Russell Stover candies, and I went back to work. "This writing racket isn't what it's cracked up to be," I muttered.

"I'm taking a nap," Johnny said. "Wake me when you've finished the book." Neither of us laughed.

Johnny didn't have much to do, since he could type up a day's worth of my output in an hour. He poked around in my bookshelves, reading the Eugene O'Neill biography and a golf book by Herbert Warren Wind. I resented his reading for pleasure while I toiled over my manuscript.

Whenever Johnny saw me sitting motionless for a long span of time, he would suddenly announce, "You're asleep. Time to go to bed." I would shuffle off to the bedroom, set my alarm, and fall asleep instantly. When the alarm rang, I would get up, stumble back to the yellow chair, and go back to work. Sometimes Johnny was there already, writing or reading, the sun streaming through the living-room curtains, or darkness showing on the other side of the glass. I never knew which to expect. Or cared.

Sometimes the room was empty, with just one light left on and Johnny gone. It didn't matter anymore. I just moved back and forth from my bedroom to the yellow chair; sleep was no less real than my waking hours. Everything was dreamlike.

I don't know how many pages I actually wrote. Twenty-five? Fifty? At some point I stopped trudging in to the yellow chair, and my papers now were spread around me on my bed. When the hush grew too profound to stand, I turned on my little Sony miniature TV and let it chatter away beside me while I worked. I became less and less animated. I hardly talked to Johnny now. I just sleepwalked around, took naps, and struggled to write.

On the sixth night, Johnny called from outside my bedroom door. "Terry? Terry? Are you awake?" Hearing no reply, he walked down the bedroom hall and found me sitting up in bed, all the lights on, in a state of bewilderment. He told he later he wasn't sure I even recognized him. I looked at one of my clocks. It said two o'clock in the morning. "I've been sitting here for two hours," I whispered. "I haven't moved."

"Go to bed," he said quietly.

"I can't go to bed," I protested. "I have to finish the book tonight."

"Forget it," he said. "You're done."

"I have to keep writing," I insisted.

"Terry, you are *not* going to make the deadline." His voice was that of a concerned parent reasoning with a child. "The deadline is tomorrow. If you had the book completely written, I could not type fast enough to make the deadline. You will not finish the book this week. You might not finish it this *month*. You are exhausted and depressed."

The tears were streaming down my cheeks now, and I was trembling. "Go to sleep," he said, "and don't think about tomorrow. Sleep all day if you want. Sleep two days or three. It doesn't matter now. In a few days, you'll write five more pages. And you'll keep writing five more pages a day until, in a month, you'll be done. By that time, Simon and Schuster may have cut you free, or they may still be arguing about it with Don, or you may have to sell the book to somebody else. But the important thing is, you'll have written the book."

"I never missed a deadline before this book," I choked.

"There's no point in dwelling on it," he said softly. "If you had written as much every week as you wrote this week, you would have finished the book a year ago."

I was inconsolable. "But I failed."

"We'll talk about it after you sleep."

"I'll have to tell Don. He'll be cross with me," I said, wracked with guilt.

"I'll talk to Don. I'll talk to Arthur." Johnny began scooping up the papers on the bed. "I'll take these. They'll be waiting for you when you wake up."

"I'm so tired," I admitted.

"I know," he said. "It was a good try."

"I really did try," I said, still unable to move.

"I know," Johnny said. "Turn out the light."

"Are you sure this is the right thing?"

"I'm sure," he said. He turned out the light on the bedside table, found his way out in the dark, and quietly closed the door behind him.

It was all so bizarre. I was the strong, matriarchal, older sister, yet the baby of the family, whom I'd tucked into bed and told bedtime stories to not so many years before, was now tucking his older sister into bed and telling her a bed-time story: that everything was going to be all right. Our roles were reversed.

I was extremely grateful that Johnny was fending off the ominous people and responsibilities, but he couldn't do this for me forever. It wasn't fair to him. Yet thoughts of being left to deal with my problems on my own sent waves of panic through me. I saw myself . . . ineffectual, dependent; heard myself . . . defensive and pleading for understanding of something I didn't understand myself, and was filled with self-loathing.

I crawled under the covers in the dark and curled up in a ball, like a tiny, furry animal and, for what seemed like the millionth time, asked myself the question, *Why? Why have I disintegrated into a helpless, irresponsible child?*

And for the millionth time the same nonanswer taunted me: "I don't *know* why."

The obvious answer eluded me: I was sick, and sick people of necessity become dependent in many ways and degrees, depending upon the severity of the illness. What I was doing was normal for a sick person.

In recent years, I have talked to other people with my disease, and while they didn't undergo a nightmare marathon in a fruitless attempt to meet a deadline, they all had the same experience of seeing their mental capacities diminish for no discernible reason. They, too, felt guilt, anxiety, feelings of worthlessness and helplessness, and they, too, thought they were just "weak, bad people." The more conscientious and perfectionistic the people were, the more they drove themselves and the more they suffered. All withdrew from the world as much as possible to conceal their inability to function normally.

I was luckier than some, because I had a brother who was glad to step in and do whatever he could to ease me through this time.

11

I think I was one of the few people to believe in astrology and Ralph Nader at the same time.

Maybe there was a connection. Ralph Nader was always telling me that the wheels were going to come off my car or that the coffee maker would blow up in my face. Astrology made the same claims, only it was romance that was going to blow up in my face, or a family tie that would prove defective. The difference was, Ralph Nader always had bad news, while the astrologers sometimes gave you hope. "The time is propitious for a brief but satisfying romantic interlude." That was welcome news, as was, "No clouds on your horizon in the foreseeable future." I always pored over the monthly horoscopes in *Cosmopolitan, Vogue,* and *Harper's* to see what was in store for Capricorns.

The Palm Beach *Daily News,* my favorite newspaper, better known as the Shiny Sheet, also ran an astrology column. In fact, some readers claimed the horoscopes were the closest thing to hard news to be found in its pages, which were devoted to society gatherings, benefits, cocktail parties, balls, and theater first nights. The odd thing was, the Shiny Sheet's horoscopes were quite often accurate for me. I began to look to them for little rays of sunshine, some sign that my fortunes would improve. I wondered who would answer if I called the phone number they gave for "personal horoscopes."

I thought I was a skeptic. Years before, when I dated Long John Nebel, the pioneer king of all-night talk radio, he introduced me to many of the screwballs and frauds behind most matters of the occult and the extraterrestrial. I knew their tricks and their motives. I didn't go to palm readers and faith healers or any of that stuff.

Why, then, did I call the number? I was desperate for a sign that my luck would turn in the immediate future. The call was taken by an answering service, but the astrologer called back promptly. Her name was Georgia, and her price was one hundred dollars for a one-time personal horoscope. "I don't guess I have anything to lose," I said. She asked me all sorts of precise information that astrologers need to know: the date of my birth, the time of day, where I was born (because the stellar gravitational pull is probably different in Minneapolis than in, say, Bogalusa), the birthdates of my mother and father, the birthdates of my two brothers, the birthdates of my most recent lovers, the birthdates of my best friends. (All "experts" seem to need your history, but what Georgia wanted looked like a chart of sunrises and tides instead of the usual record of vaccinations.)

Georgia lived in Delray Beach, but she delivered my horoscope in person. She was young and very pretty, with brown hair scooped back in a chignon. Very Palm Beach-looking. Not the necromancer Johnny had predicted, garbed in long robes and a Merlin hat adorned with half-moons and alchemical symbols. She was very ladylike. And the horoscope was fascinating: neatly typed, illustrated with tables and graphs and cosmic charts that showed which planets would protect me and which would give me grief. She very clearly indicated "legal entanglements" in my future, and since my lawsuits against Lyle were not an item of local interest or knowledge, I was truly impressed. In fact, the next several months went pretty much as Georgia had predicted, so I hired her to do quarterly horoscopes for me. I was starved for good news.

Instead, Georgia's prophesies got worse and worse and worse. They all came in different-colored folders, beautifully typed, but I got more and more depressed with each gloomy prediction. When Georgia moved to a farmhouse somewhere outside Washington, D.C., she used to call me whenever she mailed her latest data, to soften the blow. "I don't want you to get too upset by what you read," she would say. "This is, indeed, a bad cycle, but it can't last." She was always, always apologetic.

Georgia advised me on every major decision I faced for nearly a year. And I have to admit, she was about 90 percent accurate. It wasn't lost on me that Georgia admitted to two or three marriages, which suggested that she didn't do too well reading her own stars, or those of her prospective husbands, but I walked a tightrope of skepticism and true belief that allowed for a fall or two. What I *couldn't* accept was continuing bad news, and finally, like the ancient kings, I got rid of the messenger that brought the evil tidings. "I don't think I can stand to know three months ahead that things will be worse," I wrote her.

Georgia, being a Pisces, understood.

When I went out in public now, "J" always took over. No one guessed my growing bewilderment. I was compulsively upbeat with friends and strangers. I wasn't just fooling them, I was fooling myself. Because I wanted to feel good and normal, I convinced myself that I was really enjoying things, saying, "It was a lovely dinner party," or, "What a wonderful evening," even though I didn't feel it. I just assumed I felt it.

Similarly, the "J" in me still accepted invitations to appear on radio or television as an "expert"—on sex or golf courses or whatever.

Until Miami.

In December, Channel 2, the public broadcasting station in Miami, invited me down for a fund-raising telethon that was to be hosted by David Susskind. The theme was the "Wonders of Florida," and they wanted me to talk about my golf book and its southern Florida theme. I was pleased at the invitation and said yes.

I was embarrassed by my weight—I was up to 150 pounds—but I bought a caftan at Saks that was flattering and drove down to Miami Beach and checked into the Fontainebleau Hotel, which is one of those flamboyant Morris Lapidus buildings modeled after the glamour of the Hollywood of the 1930's. I devoured some beautifully prepared pompano, a candy bar, and some ice cream, changed into the caftan, checked my makeup, and then went down to the Fontainebleau's entrance. A valet fetched my car while I drank in the flapping pennants and the zanily molded concrete canopies of the hotels. I looked around for the flashy tourists with the pink Cadillacs and their white mink stoles and the ladies with platinum hair and monstrous earrings that had peopled Miami Beach in the fifties and sixties. I didn't see any.

I drove to Channel 2 in good spirits. There was no reason, after all, to be apprehensive. I had done hundreds of talk shows by then, and this one was with David Susskind, for whom I had the warmest feelings.

When I entered the studio, I was greeted very cordially by David. "There will be three of you on the panel for this segment," he explained. (One of his guests was an officer from the National Organization for Women, the other represented a neighborhood coalition.)

"Wonderful," I said. "This will be great fun."

David smiled that charming smile of his and went back to his hosting duties.

We were on the air, in the middle of the live interview, when it happened. I was listening to David, listening intently, looking directly at him, when I realized that something was wrong. I was having trouble following his questions. My mind was jumping. I was experiencing blanks of consciousness, similar to my experience with Burt Reynolds in Hollywood.

I suddenly shivered. A feeling of terror enveloped me. Not simple panic, but terror. David was asking me a question about Dinah Shore, who had recently been denied membership at a Los Angeles country club because she was a single woman. I swallowed hard and could barely speak. Normally, I would have responded that single and divorced women were welcome at golf courses in Florida resort towns, but I couldn't dredge this fact out of my mind. I had forgotten everything, even the name of my book. All I could blurt out was something lamebrained like, "That isn't right. Things have to change."

David hesitated for an instant, expecting me to go on.

But I didn't.

As the interview proceeded, I realized that I couldn't follow the conversation of the other guests. I couldn't absorb sentences. It was as if words were missing. If I could have signaled to David or the producer without being seen on camera, I would have tried to escape gracefully. As it was, I listened so hard to David and his guests that I was almost in pain.

When we were finally excused (David stayed on the set to conduct more of the show), I fled to the shadows. I was too rattled to talk to anyone, and I couldn't get to David to apologize for being such a poor interview. I trembled. What was wrong with me? If I couldn't do a simple interview . . . in a nonthreatening environment . . . with a warm host . . . on a familiar subject . . .

I kept thinking, *If . . . if . . . if . . .* , and it finally began to sink in: Something was terribly wrong with me.

"I need a doctor," I murmured to myself.

I spent the evening in my hotel room, painfully depressed. I had known something was wrong for weeks and couldn't face the truth. The time jumps, the mental lapses—I had them at home, too. They came when I was trying to write. They came when I tried to think. I had attributed them to stress, or to writer's block. But what if it were something worse? An illness that was affecting my brain? Or maybe . . . a growth?

When I got home the next morning, I called my family doctor, Myrl Spivey, and made an appointment for a full medical checkup the following week. Two nights later, in my apartment, I was overwhelmed with panic. I was alone, and although normally I had difficulty crying, I had begun to cry—for no discernible reason—then suddenly I began to have trouble breathing. My heart beat frantically and I felt dizzy.

All I could think to do was consult my home medical guides. I looked up heart attacks and I looked up strokes, but I had trouble reading through my tears. Catching my breath began to seem more important than catching up on my reading.

I felt lightheaded. Still wheezing and trembling, I called my mother's dear friend Ruth Menninger, head medical librarian at Good Samaritan Hospital. She rushed over and drove me to the hospital. By the time Ruth got me to the emergency room, I had chest pains. A doctor took me into a little alcove and examined me. He quickly concluded, "Oh, you're hyperventilating." The nurse handed him an aqua-colored plastic container, and he positioned it over my nose and mouth. "Breathe into this," he said. He seemed enthralled with the device. "We used to use brown paper bags," he told me. "This is very nice."

I still thought I was having a heart attack, but as my

breathing became less forced and more rhythmic, my fear receded. "That's fine," he said, as I took a slow, deep breath.

"What did you say I was doing?" I asked through the plastic container.

"You were hyperventilating," he said. "You can go home as soon as you're breathing normally."

"What causes it?"

"You do it to yourself." I must have looked skeptical, because he started talking about the levels of carbon dioxide in the blood. "When you try so hard to breathe, you get too much pure oxygen and not enough CO-two, so you gasp for the missing element. If you breathe into a paper bag, or even into your cupped hands, you rebreathe the trapped carbon dioxide, the blood stabilizes, and you don't have to gasp for breath any longer."

"That's it?" I was amazed. And not a little embarrassed.

"That's it," he said. "If you have another attack, breathe into a paper bag. Or get one of these." He tapped the plastic container. "These are really fine."

I felt cheated. "I thought I was having a heart attack, or at least a stroke," I told Ruth on the drive home. "Now I feel like such a fool."

The next day, I had a visit with Dr. Spivey. His examination revealed nothing extraordinary, but he expressed concern about my hyperventilation, which he attributed to a high degree of anxiety, my inability to concentrate, and increasing depression. "I'm going to put you on Tofranil, on a trial basis," he told me.

"What's that?" I asked.

"It's an antidepressant," he said. "It should help you get through these next few weeks of pressure by relieving some of your symptoms of anxiety and depression. We'll see. Keep me posted. And when your book is finished, I want you to get on a diet," he grinned. "That's not baby fat jiggling around on you!"

I went home to wait out the two weeks or so the medicine required to be fully effective. I convinced myself I was feeling better. I told myself the dry mouth and sudden sweats—symptoms common to Tofranil—were bearable. I was very jittery.

I went back to work on *The Love Book* (now *Total Loving)*, still feeling frantic and pressured, but suddenly I found myself able to write again. "I don't understand it," I told Johnny over the phone. "The pressure on me is worse than it's ever been, and I don't feel like myself, but I *am* writing again. Ten pages today. Maybe the Tofranil is helping."

As Johnny had predicted, Simon and Schuster had not dropped me, but they had forced a renegotiation of my contract. Simon and Schuster now had total discretion as to revising and editing whatever material I sent them, and they would not advance me anything beyond the $50,000 they had already paid me.

In other words, I had lost $150,000.

I sent in chapters as I completed them. Michael Korda called occasionally from New York to urge me on. He was always hesitant, but in a strong way, tiptoeing around while hitting the jugular vein. "It's not quite right." His key phrase was still, "I don't know exactly what I want, but I'll know it when I see it." I kept changing my style, hoping he would see it. He never did.

Still, the accumulation of pages was comforting. I kept shipping hunks of manuscript to New York in manila envelopes—new chapters, revised chapters, substitutions, addendums, notes to delete chapters—until an unruly pile of typescript littered the office adjoining Michael's. (His own office was as pristene, uncluttered, and dust-free as an Exxon executive's.)

After a while, Michael turned the project over to a senior editor, Joan Sanger, who must have felt like a General Motors plant manager, trying to coordinate raw materials and manufactured parts arriving for assembly. When I had finally shipped all the parts—by the end of February 1976— Joan had enough material to build three cars—or books— and instead of a Chevette she faced a Cadillac with eight wheels, a Buick engine, a Pontiac transmission, and bumper stickers from Carlsbad Caverns. I had to fly to New York to meet with her in her office on March 4—not to edit the manuscript, just to help her sort it out.

I wondered how S&S would deal with the changing voices. "Terry" was represented in the manuscript by a plethora of medical chapters; she was obviously preoccupied with anxieties about her physical well-being, for she included lengthy descriptions of the most obscure female illnesses, which she feared she either had or might get. "J" now had two voices: the old bubbly, exhorting, here's-how "J" of *The Sensuous Woman,* and a new "Expert 'J'" who wrote very seriously and factually, citing studies and surveys and quoting great men of letters. Desperate to produce pages, I had allowed whatever voice was in control at the time to do the writing. I preferred the latter, which was the most dignified voice—but I didn't know which one Michael would choose.

I got my answer in late October 1976, when I received a package and a letter from Simon and Schuster.

Dear Terry,
 Here, at last (sigh), is the edited, final, and superterrific manuscript of Total Loving! *How does it feel to have it done and out of your life?*

I replied on November 4.

Dear Michael,
 If what you sent me is really the 'edited, final, and superterrific' manuscript of Total Loving, *then there has*

been a sudden lapse in your usually impeccable taste and high editorial standards. . . .

Michael had assigned my book to an editor of Gothic fiction (a very good editor of Gothic fiction, I understand), who had rewritten *Total Loving* as a New York Jewish girl's version of *Sex and the Single Girl*. The text was littered with Jewish expressions that I didn't even understand.

The voice in my letter back to Michael was that of "expert 'J,'" but an indignant "expert 'J.'" "My book needed editing," she stormed, "not an arbitrary reshuffling of copy, blurring of the how-to structure, the chopping out of major points while leaving less important material untouched, cuts inadequately bridged, the leaving in of a number of references to material that was taken out, the insertion of fake people's quotes, the ill-concealed addition of another writing style, etc.

"In fairness"—Terry suddenly cut in—"I must say that some of the editing is very good. But the original weaknesses in my manuscript weren't touched, and now a whole new batch of flaws has been piled on top of the original ones. I'm very sorry to have to say this, Michael, but if my book goes to press in its present condition, it will be impossible for me to go out and personally endorse and sell the book to the public. I tell you this now not to pressure you, but because I feel it would be unethical of me to conceal my feelings and conclusions about the manuscript and then drop a 'no appearances' bomb on you at publication time."

I then asked either for more time to put the book in shape—"a few days," I estimated—or the return of my rights to the book so that I might seek another publisher.

My letter to Michael should have killed the book. He was sure he had *Total Loving* out of his hair, and here it was boomeranging back on him, accompanied by *threats,* yet. Fortunately, Don got Michael on the phone and prevailed upon him to at least read the manuscript to see if my complaints had any validity at all.

Michael read it and conceded that they did.

Enter Pat Meehan, the last editor of *Total Loving*. Pat was nothing like Michael. She was a line-by-line editor and questioned every line I wrote. Some of her changes were really good, and some I fought, but we got along well. Except for one thing. I said, "Look, there are two styles in this book, the journalistic style and the *Sensuous Woman* style. It's got to be either/or. I don't care at this point. Pick one."

She never did.

I now wanted to tear the book apart and rewrite it as a simple how-to book. Of course, no one else wanted that. (Having waited three and a half years, that seemed to S&S like making a molehill out of a mountain.) By the time I saw Pat Meehan off on a flight to New York, the edited manuscript tucked away safely in her briefcase, I felt the same way. I had to let the book go. I didn't know if I had succeeded or failed.

Bone tired and brain tired, I put away the legal pads and paper clips and felt pens. I took all the magazine articles and research materials that were spread around the yellow chair on the floor in the living room and stuck them in shopping bags. *I finished it,* I told myself, but I didn't feel very exuberant. I wanted to sleep for a week. I turned off the phone, turned off the lights, and turned off "J."

It was time to take care of Terry.

I really meant to go back to Dr. Spivey, but after *Total Loving* was out of my life, my anxiety and depression melted away. I stopped taking the Tofranil and enjoyed a nearly normal December and January; then, for no reason that I could fathom, the dark cloud began to hover over me in February. I started binging on sweets and refined carbohydrates again. I avoided social activities because they were "too much effort." I slept fifteen—sixteen—hours a day, and when I was up I felt so tired I could barely drag around, except for periods of restlessness, when I shopped, which would give me temporary feelings of energy and accomplishment. Particularly unnerving was the realization that I wasn't feeling sexually responsive: Orgasms were elusive and pleasure stunted. I was filled with self-reproach, oddly indecisive, felt guilty about not being productive, and, worst of all, that old inability to concentrate or think quickly was back. I started taking Tofranil again, but felt no better.

According to the *Diagnostic and Statistical Manual of Mental Disorders,* I met seven out of eight criteria (only four are necessary) for a major affective disorder: a profound disturbance of mood "that is not due to any other physical or mental disorder . . . that colors the whole psychic life."

All I had to do to become a perfect eight on the DSM scale was develop "recurrent thoughts of death, suicidal ideation, wishes to be dead, or suicide attempt."

All in good (or I should say bad) time.

12

*J*une 1977.

I looked in the full-length mirror, something I had been assiduously avoiding for over three years.

I was fat. Twenty-six pounds overweight. My thinning, baby-fine hair draped listlessly around a sallow, sad face. I saw puffy red eyes, tear-stained cheeks, a trembly mouth, and the beginnings of a double chin. The mouth that had been born with laugh lines now stretched mirthlessly across teeth that had missed their three- and six-month cleanings. My skin was dry and scaly. My fingernails and toenails needed cutting. I hadn't shaved my legs or under my arms for at least two weeks. Cellulite on my hips, bottom, and upper legs made me look like I had been rolling around on a waffle iron. My shoulders drooped, my abdomen protruded. There were bruise marks here and there (I had been bumping into things lately).

I studied my eyes. They stared back at me as empty of expression as the button eyes of my growing collection of teddy bears.

Who was this person in the mirror? Terry I knew; "J" I knew; but this visage resembled a bit player from the movie *The Snake Pit.* How could this person be ready in two months to go out on a publicity tour for *Total Loving?*

I faced reality. I needed professional intervention. But for what? Stress? Obesity? Endocrine imbalances? A brain tumor? Mental illness? Was help to be found at the Mayo Clinic? The Menninger Clinic? Duke?

I covered up the awful sight of my body with my old white terry-cloth robe and padded out to the bookcase in the living room.

Books had always given me good answers, but now they failed me. None of the home medical guides had a disease that fit me. I thumbed through *How to Live with Schizophrenia,* by Drs. Humphry Osmond and Abram Hoffer, but I didn't see myself in its pages. I wasn't hearing voices, my food didn't have a metallic taste, my body didn't have a funny odor, and my vision of reality—although interrupted by mental lapses—was not distorted or fanciful.

I picked up Carlton Frederick's book on hypoglycemia, but I had tried the hypoglycemia diet and hadn't noticed any significant changes. The allergy book was of no help; I was already under an allergist's care, had had the desensitization shots, and was avoiding the foods I was allergic to.

My glance fell on a book that I had bought after seeing the author on Phil Donahue's show—*From Sad to Glad: Kline on Depression,* by Dr. Nathan S. Kline. His was the first book for the layman on the history and use of psychotrophic, or mind-acting, drugs in the treatment of long-term depression. The print on the Sad/Glad Scale Test included for readers to take was too small and blurry on my copy for me to take the test, but I read the rest of *From Sad to Glad* in one sitting, interested in the descriptions of the chemical processes of the brain and the function of antidepressant drugs in repairing faulty brain chemistry. I empathized with the women in Dr.

Kline's case histories, but I didn't see myself as kinswoman to their miseries. Those women were often suicidal, unable to function, felt no pleasure in life, couldn't sleep, and suffered a loss of appetite (*that* certainly wasn't me). True, I seemed to be hampered mentally and physically, but that wasn't because of a biochemical imbalance, I was sure. That was from stress.

Or was it? It all seemed so complicated. (Later, I would be baffled at my inability to see myself in *From Sad to Glad*. I was on nearly every page!) But I now realize that by slipping gradually into depression, memories of glad feelings were now hazy. I was accepting gray moods as good. Think for a moment: If someone turned the color down on your TV set just a little bit every week until all color was gone and then left the dial set there, you would be so acclimated to a black-and-white TV world that you wouldn't miss color or report the desire for it.

I stared gloomily at the pile of reference books scattered around me on the floor. The names suddenly leaped out at me: Dr. Abram Hoffer and Dr. Humphry Osmond! Of course! I *knew* these two brilliant psychiatrists—I had done publicity on their book years before. If anyone could figure out what was wrong with me, or refer me to a doctor who could, it was Abram and Humphry, who were pioneers in the biochemical treatment of schizophrenia and other mental illnesses.

I pawed through the shoulder-high mounds of mail on my dining-room table, looking for the notice I had received of a forthcoming national conference of the Huxley Institute for Biosocial Research, a nonprofit institution dedicated to educating doctors and laymen in the nutritional, metabolic, and molecular aspects of mental disorders. Osmond and Hoffer were orthomolecular psychiatrists, a term coined by Nobel Prize winner Dr. Linus Pauling. This psychiatric approach to mental disorders focuses on providing the best chemical environment for the mind by using vitamins, minerals, amino acids, trace elements, and hormones, all chemical substances normally present in the body. If necessary, traditional drug therapy is also used as needed, in conjunction with the orthomolecular approach, to reestablish normal brain-cell function.

I had been a member of Huxley since its inception, although I hadn't been able to get myself together to attend the last few annual conferences. Ah, there was the notice; the symposium was at the end of June in New York City. Wouldn't Abram and Humphry, cofounders of Huxley, have to be at the conference? "This," I told myself, "is the answer."

I didn't call or write. I flew to New York on June 25, checked into the Sheraton-Russell Hotel, and took a cab that evening to the Biltmore Hotel, where the Huxley people were gathering. Eileen Brand went with me.

When we got there, we found hundreds of people milling around the conference area, but I spotted Dr. Hoffer right away. "Terry, how are you?" he smiled.

"Terrible," I said.

"What's wrong?" He wasn't certain if I were joking.

I smiled sheepishly. "Chills, sweats, loss of memory, blackouts, anxiety, scaly skin, loss of hair, crying fits, and writer's block, to name a few."

He looked startled.

"I flew up here to find a doctor," I continued. "Can you recommend one?" I added hastily, "I'll go anywhere in the world."

He smiled. "As a matter of fact, there's a very fine man in Fort Lauderdale."

I was aghast. "Fort Lauderdale, *Florida?*"

"He's just across the room. Come, I'll introduce you."

The man Dr. Hoffer introduced Eileen and me to was a tall, slim, distinguished-looking man in his mid- to late forties. Solid. Pleasant. Dressed meticulously in a navy pin-striped suit, pale blue shirt, and navy paisley tie. His name was Dr. Moke Williams, and Dr. Hoffer introduced him as one of "the most eminent names in orthomolecular psychiatry."

"You must be very good," I said. "Dr. Hoffer does not give out compliments lightly."

Dr. Williams smiled slightly and looked properly modest. I was particularly impressed by Dr. Hoffer's testimonial that Dr. Williams was a great diagnostician. "Maybe you can find out what's wrong with me," I laughed. "I think it's my brain."

Dr. Williams ignored my obvious eagerness to discuss my "case." He took out his wallet and handed me a card. "Call me," he said, "as soon as you get back to Florida. I'll fit you in right away."

Dr. Williams's offices were on the second floor of a professional building in a small Fort Lauderdale shopping center. I was very hungry on my first visit. I had fasted twenty-four hours in preparation for a series of tests that were administered by a laboratory in an adjoining building: urinalysis, blood works, hair analysis, thyroid. The most unpleasant test was the six-hour glucose tolerance test, which required blood sampling throughout the day.

In between blood lettings, I was kept busy upstairs with forms to fill out. I filled out a complete medical history. I listed the foods I ate and all known allergies. I answered, to the best of my limited knowledge, questions about the psychiatric histories of my parents, grandparents, cousins, aunts, uncles, and brothers. Dr. Williams wanted everything, it seemed, short of my astrological data. I was up to my elbows in forms.

I also took written tests, including the MMPI (Minnesota Multiphasic Personality Inventory), the EWI (Experiential World Inventory), and the HOD (Hoffer-Osmond Diagnostic).

In my Lyle Stuart days, Dr. Osmond had visited the offices once and shown his new test to me. I had been fascinated by its success in identifying certain mental diseases, but I never dreamed that I would one day be taking it. Instead of answering questions with a pencil, I was asked to put cards in one pile or another for a true or false answer. "I often hear or have heard voices." That was false (and I assumed it was a diagnostic for schizophrenia). I put the card on the false pile.

"An orange is like a banana because they both have skins rather than because they are fruit." (I guessed that to be a test of my reasoning ability.)

Many of the questions dealt with my perceptions. "People watch me all the time." (False.) "My bones often feel soft." (False.) "People's faces sometimes pulsate as I watch them." (False.) "At times my ideas disappear for a few moments and then reappear." (True.) "Sometimes I feel there is a fog or mist shutting me away from the world." (True.) "Cars seem to move very quickly now. I can't be sure where they are." (I learned later that many schizophrenics answer true; when behind the wheel, they tend to bump into cars ahead of them.)

The tests took most of the day, and when the doctors were through with me, they sent me home.

That night, I reflected on my family history.

"Insanity runs in the family!" That had always been my laughing defense when somebody questioned my eccentricities or my unorthodox life-style. I knew that my unfortunate Grandmother Stuart had been institutionalized, first in a sanitarium and later in a state hospital. Grandmother, in her middle years, was given to alcoholic binges and fits of paranoia which her doctors attributed to schizophrenia. (In those days, unfortunately, most female mental disorders—even postpartum depression—were diagnosed as schizophrenia.) There were no surviving psychiatric records, but I grew up with a sketchy notion of my Grandmother Stuart as a once great beauty who sat around in her bedroom all day eating boxes of chocolate and alternating between hysteria and a drunken stupor. (Mother seldom talked about her mother. She had never gotten over the shock of her last visits, as a teen-ager, to the mental hospital, where her mother lingered as a dazed inmate, unable to recognize her own daughters.)

On my father's side, I recalled the case of one of his cousins, Mary Casey, who had committed suicide in St. Paul by jumping out of a window. "Mary was a very, very attractive girl," Daddy had told me. "She didn't look like she was off her rocker. She was intelligent, very aggressive, very active. But every now and then she would blow her stack and they would put her in Oconomowok, which was a private insane asylum south of Milwaukee. That happened several times. Just as suddenly as she would get sick, she'd get well and they would send her home again. No one seemed to know why."

I was struck by the "coincidence"—that I had a female relative of energy and ability who had suffered mood swings, and finally had committed suicide, but I pushed aside the unthinkable: that I was already insane or about to be, and would end my days like Grandmother Stuart in the back ward of an asylum, or take Mary Casey's route—jump out a window. No, the psychological testing and inquiries into my family history were intellectually interesting, but peripheral to what was going to be discovered was wrong with me. Dr. Williams, I was convinced, was going to find a physiological cause for my inability to think and function normally. A rare endocrine disease, perhaps, or a strange tropical parasite or bacteria that had invaded my nervous system.

13

July 5, 1977, my first appointment with the psychiatrist. Memories of the film *Captain Newman, M.D.*, starring Gregory Peck as the dedicated shrink, flitted through my head as I sat on the plush maroon love seat (one of a pair) opposite Dr. Williams's desk and studied him. He returned the gaze, no doubt studying *me*. Was it my imagination, or did Dr. Williams look something like Gregory Peck, with his dark hair; lean, sensitive face; reserved manner?

"Tell me a little bit about yourself," he requested.

I awkwardly gave a capsule version of the highlights of my young life, mentioning that recent years had been stressful.

Dr. Williams was curious about what these stresses were. I mentioned the traumas of my lawsuits against Lyle Stuart, my mother's death, and my writer's block. It was only when I mentioned my fears of going out on tour again in my jangly, worn-out condition that it suddenly dawned on Dr. Williams who I was.

"I'm sorry. I thought you knew. I'm 'J.' I wrote *The Sensuous Woman*."

Dr. Williams is one of those psychiatrists who can go on forever without showing much expression, but this wasn't one of those times. He was startled.

I know he was startled, because he blinked.

"The thing that worries me," I continued, "is that I have to go back out on tour August seventeenth. That's only a little more than a month away. What happens if I have the black-outs like I did in Miami? What happens if I hyperventilate? How can I appear on camera with my Tofranil side effects, especially the dry mouth and sudden sweats? Can you take me off Tofranil and put me on another medication or vi-tamin-mineral program that will make me feel normal again?" I begged him.

He seemed to give these questions the most sober consider-ation, sitting there silently for a moment, looking out into space, and gently tap, tap, tapping his black-and-gold Paper-mate pen against my file folder. Not wanting to disturb Dr. Williams's reverie, I watched the plant opposite me grow for a while. Eventually he removed his gaze from space and peered out at me intently through his horn-rimmed glasses.

I edged forward on the love seat, eager to hear the name of his instant cure. I would have to wait, it seemed.

"Let's start with your test findings," he said. "You have difficulty in gastrointestinal absorption. Your thyroid is not functioning properly. There is a problem with your pan-creas . . ."

Dr. Williams sounded more like a gastroenterologist than a psychiatrist.

"Can these things cause mental problems?" I asked.

"It's a possibility," he said. "My philosophy is that you can't separate the head from the rest of the body. The brain is an organ that interacts with and affects the rest of the body's organs. And when other organ systems malfunction, they have the potential to influence the brain's ability to function efficiently. A classic example of this is the severe depression some people have experienced following an extremely debilitating bout with the flu. A physical illness has produced mental and emotional side effects. So I don't believe that you can cut off the head, so to speak, and treat it as if it exists on its own.

"For instance, your hair analysis, a test that is a guide to mineral levels in the body, reveals that you are very high in copper and lead. These minerals could possibly impair brain functioning by interfering with cellular function and therefore neurotransmission of nerve impulses, which are necessary to thought processes. So we will work on lowering these levels with zinc, a mineral that counteracts copper and lead.

"Your glucose tolerance test shows that you are a borderline diabetic. Disturbed carbohydrate metabolism can affect energy levels and cause anxiety and depression in some people." Dr. Williams devoted some time to changing my diet drastically, filling me full of nutrients and denying me all sugar, flour, and other attractive substances.

"Can't we make a deal?" I giggled nervously.

He smiled slightly. "No, but this new diet should also help your weight problem. You are, I would guess, about thirty pounds overweight?"

"Uhmmmm."

"And you've listed"—he flipped through my file—"about two pages of symptoms here, so I would like to work on your physical problems first so they can be pinpointed or discarded as sources of your emotional and mental difficulties."

An explanation followed of my pancreatic enzyme dysfunction and how the pancreas, enzymes, stomach, duodenum, etc., function; also, a discussion of what happened to the body when these systems broke down and failed to absorb nutrients. Then Dr. Williams put me on megadoses of several vitamins and minerals and lowered my dosages of estrogen and thyroid medications, which I had been swallowing like candy.

"The fact that your thyroid tests still show you to be low-normal, despite the large quantity you are taking, is, again, possibly indicative of a malabsorption problem. The medication I have prescribed for you to take before meals should allow you to absorb your thyroid medication more efficiently. Also, even a small overdose of thyroid can create feelings of "jangliness," edginess, and being uncomfortably keyed up, all of which you have described to me on your list of symptoms and are demonstrating here today."

This time *I* blinked. I thought I was quite calm.

"I'd like to get to your HOD test results, but we're out of time for today," said Dr. Williams.

"No diagnosis?"

"Not yet," he laughed. He rose from his chair to indicate the hour was over. "Have a pleasant weekend."

I wrinkled my nose at him and left.

Nothing had changed, but I felt exhilarated. If Dr. Williams had thought I had a brain tumor or was insane, he would have said so. My body chemistry just needed re-tuning! I made another appointment, went home, and threw out everything in the kitchen that was on the forbidden list. Then and there I put myself on a diet, got a haircut, and started a "new life." Now it would be only a matter of weeks before I became, as my father always put it, "my old self again."

My next visit to Dr. Williams dispelled my visions of a rapid cure.

Dr. Williams dallied only a moment in small talk. "I need to know a great deal more about you," he said, and began barraging me with long series of questions about my mental, emotional, and physical ups and downs from puberty to the present. Next came probings into my childhood, my parents, my brothers, my religious upbringing—the concerns of traditional psychiatry. My quips, occasional giggles, and flip answers drew only faint smiles, a raised eyebrow, or a quizzical glance from the doctor. I began to feel restless and jumpy again. The immediate future was breathing down my neck, and I didn't have *time* for analysis now. "Moke, this is all very nice, and I appreciate your interest in my background, but my publicity tour for *Total Loving* is imminent. I have to leave for Atlanta and then all the way across the country in less than two weeks. Will I be well enough in time?"

"How do you feel now?"

"Better than I did. Fine. But I don't feel in control. But, yes, lots better."

"Then your good feelings may hold. From what you have told me, you generally feel particularly energized in the fall."

He peered at me through his horn-rimmed glasses. "I'm going to leave you on Tofranil until you finish your traveling . . ."

"Oh, no! You can't. That's what I'm so afraid of—those awful symptoms—perspiring and feeling strange—that Tofranil causes in me!"

"The perspiring could be due to Tofranil," he said, "but the 'strange feelings' may have other sources. Terry, your Hoffer-Osmond Diagnostic test score is high," Dr. Williams continued. "Forty-eight. Thirty is top-normal. The HOD is a test that reveals how you perceive reality. Your scores show disturbances of mood and thought which may be a result of long-term stress coupled with poor physical health . . . or something else. For example, your scores indicating paranoia and depression *could* place you in the realm of schizoid-disordered, or there might be some reality to your feelings of paranoia. You *are* involved in a long-standing, acrimonious lawsuit and are in a real position of being attacked. Your 'paranoia' could be based on reality."

Dr. Williams continued to inform me of what my individual HOD scores meant, talking on in a calm, soothing voice that occasionally dwindled to a patrician mumble. I didn't absorb half of what he was saying. Schizoid? Thought disorder? Paranoia? I grabbed onto his phrases, "could be based on reality," "long-term stress," "poor physical health," like a drowning man reaching for bits of flotsam. No, positively, my troubles would be physical. I forced myself to concentrate once more on Dr. Williams. He was still talking.

"I want to start you out on lithium—"

"Lithium!" I interrupted. "Wonderful!" He was going to give me a wonder drug after all. "But wait . . . isn't that for manic-depressives?"

"Primarily."

I was quiet for a moment, trying to puzzle this out. "Yes, but . . . *I'm* not a manic-depressive."

He smiled at me. "Why do you say that?"

He had me off-balance. "Because . . . because I don't have periods of elation; I don't have highs." I frowned. "Is lithium any use for jangliness and nerves, and is that why you're prescribing it for me?"

"What I was saying, Terry, is that I would *like* to try you out on lithium, but unfortunately I can't do that while you're traveling. Lithium therapy, especially in the early stages, must be monitored very carefully. Blood samples must be taken regularly. That would be impossible on your schedule. That's why I think it would be advisable to leave you on Tofranil temporarily. You will be under stress in these next weeks, and Tofranil may help to keep you emotionally stabilized. It's better than no crutch at all now, isn't it?"

"No," I said stubbornly.

I must have looked very discouraged. "You may be overanticipating trouble," Dr. Williams said sympathetically. "You have lost weight, which should give you new confidence; your diet is under control; you report improved energy levels and feelings of well-being . . ."

I nodded uncertainly. "True."

"And remember," he said, "I'm just a phone call away if you need me."

Maybe I am *overly fearful,* I thought, as I opened my car door and stood aside to avoid the blast of trapped summer heat that had built up in the car during my hour's absence. *The fall is my time of year. I always feel my best and accomplish the most then. I'm high with being alive when the leaves are changing and the air is crisp and the wind blows in wild gusts and swirls.*

Maybe I will *be all right.*

I wasn't nervous during interviews with *The* (West Palm Beach) *Post,* Fort Lauderdale *Sun-Sentinel,* and Miami *Herald.* A day spent with *People* magazine was a delight, thanks in great part to the charm and decency of the reporter and photographer, who I inveigled into regaling me with stories of their past interviews and photo sessions with the world's great figures during their illustrious days on *Life* and other news magazines.

Miami interviews went well. Atlanta whizzed by without incident. Houston was fun—a raspberry soufflé with Simon and Schuster rep Charlie Roberts and his wife, Sally. A little cheating on the diet in Dallas, but back on an even keel in Fort Worth.

But I felt this nagging sense of impending trouble, like when you're driving alone late at night on a deserted back highway and the car suddenly starts making a strange noise. I pushed away the fear and flew to New York for my appearance on ABC-TV's *Good Morning America.*

It seemed success hadn't changed him. My old next-door neighbor from 340 East Forty-ninth Street in New York gave me a big good-morning hug.

"I'm so proud of you, David," I said.

He asked about my Aunt Lorry and Uncle Fran, who had become very fond of David during his days as an actor on

The Bold Ones, when David Hartman had made promotional visits to Uncle Fran's brother Stanley's television station in Minneapolis. "Will they be watching?" he asked.

"You know they will," I laughed. "Especially Uncle Francis."

"Well, Miss 'J,'" David said with a teasing grin, "I liked the book. We could talk on the air about old times if you like, but we've got only a few minutes for the segment. If you'd rather push the book . . ."

"Push the book. By all means, push the book," I teased.

David did a warm, smooth interview, but I couldn't quite click in. I remained nervous, not completely in command of myself. I slunk back to the St. Regis-Sheraton Hotel in a low mood and ordered pancakes and hot chocolate from room service to console myself.

Daddy phoned from Gainesville. He said I was wonderful, but he always said that. "Sweetheart, you were a knockout," he said with his usual Irish emphasis. "I was as impressed as hell. I don't recall ever seeing anyone with your command of your material . . ." He went on and on. I didn't believe it, but I found his words touchingly loyal and soothing.

Jacque Thompson was more direct. "You seemed a little tense," she told me. "You weren't yourself."

That afternoon I prerecorded an interview for NBC's six o'clock news in New York, and again I felt unnaturally nervous. This time, I got to see myself on tape back at the hotel as I packed to leave town. "Oh no," I sighed, "I was even worse than I thought."

What had happened to "J"'s ordinarily cool-looking self? She looked tense, sounded tense, and made nervous facial movements. Her speech was speeded up, her sentences broken, her voice higher pitched than normal.

"Oh, dear God," I prayed. "Terry is already a basket case. Don't let 'J' come apart now."

In Chicago, I had barbecue and ice cream with an old and

dear friend, Orrin Stine. It was comforting to see a familiar, caring face . . . except that, according to Orrin (who is president of Wesley-Jessen, the contact lens company), I wasn't seeing him or anything clearly. "You need glasses," he said bluntly between bites of barbecue.

"That's ridiculous!" I said huffily. "I have eyes like eagles!"

"Is that why you hold your menu at arm's length to read the print?" He frowned. "Also, Terry, you don't look or seem like yourself to me. Have you seen a doctor recently?"

"I've just started going to a very fine one."

Orrin walked me to the elevator of The Ritz-Carlton Hotel and gave me a good-bye hug. "I wouldn't put off getting back to that doctor if I were you," he said in a worried tone. "Please keep me posted. . . . And get yourself some *glasses,* for God's sake!" he yelled as the elevator doors closed.

It rained in Philadelphia. I spent a quiet night at the hotel, resting up for my appearance the next afternoon on *The Mike Douglas Show.* I stared out the window at the steady drizzle. Next door and across the hall from me, I had the Hudson Brothers as neighbors. They were very lively, and I could hear them bouncing up and down the halls and horsing around in their rooms. "I used to be like that," I remembered. But how long ago was it? I gave up searching through emotional time and went back to reading a Regency romance novel. I couldn't concentrate on more serious literature.

I shared the Mike Douglas limousine to the studio with actor James Earl Jones, and on the way I began to feel unnaturally nervous again. "There's no reason not to do a good job," I told myself. I was fully rested; the producers had told me what questions I would be asked; Mike Douglas would be friendly. I had nothing to fear.

But I fretted.

Susan Saint James, that week's cohost, looked tense, too,

but she had reason to be. She had to carry a great part of the
show. I knew her to be an advocate of health foods and vitamins, but I was amused to note that she was smoking ciga-
rettes and drinking beer.

Susan Saint James went on first, to open the show with
Mike, and then the Hudson Brothers went out to play some
rock 'n' roll and do a comedy routine. Robert Klein, one of my
favorite comedians, went next and did several minutes of
classy, funny patter. I waited in the Green Room, growing
more and more frightened. I was always nervous on shows
that had orchestras and show-biz guests, but this was worse,
a fear bordering on panic. I felt like bolting for the door, or
feigning sickness (would I be feigning?).

Suddenly my time had come. They were ushering me out
between dark curtains and over cable-strewn floors, out into
the glare of lights, the swelling applause, the blare of the
studio orchestra. I had done it dozens of times, but this time
my legs almost failed me.

I suddenly realized what was wrong: I wasn't "J." I was
Terry. And Terry couldn't handle *The Mike Douglas Show*,
not in the shape she was in.

I sat down and faced Mike, smiled, and waited for his questions, but the panic would not leave me. Where was "J?"
Why had she deserted me? It was a repeat of my David Susskind fiasco in Miami: nothing spectacular, really, no crying
fits, no explosions, no toppling over in a dead faint. Just a
profound bewilderment. My mind went blank for seconds at
a time, so that Mike's questions came to me as, " . . . woman,
that men . . . threatened . . . these changes . . . used to . . .
doors and buying dinner for . . . wife . . . room for love anymore?" He would flash that sincere smile, his eyes darting
over my shoulder to read the next cue card.

I would begin, "Uhh . . . ," like a phonograph record starting from a dead stop, and babble whatever came into my
head that might answer the question I had not really

grasped. I felt short of breath. I knew my voice was pitched high again, but I could not control it. Neither could I control the rhythm of my speech. Every time Mike turned to involve one of his other guests in the conversation, I prayed that he wouldn't come back to me. My words tumbled out mechanically, like melodies from an unattentive but well-practiced pianist. I didn't know if I had them in the right order: They just rumbled in my head, unnaturally loud, as if I had my fingers in my ears.

I am an unreliable witness to what I was like on the rest of the *Total Loving* tour. If I were doing a free association description today, the words would be *panic, perspiring, planes, chocolate, facade, failure, depression, mental confusion,* and *raspberries.*

Raspberries? They are my favorite food, and I ate them all the way across the country, as if each berry would be the last one I would ever be allowed for the rest of my life.

I can confirm that 1977 was a good year for raspberries: I ate raspberries until I felt sick; I ate raspberries until I had hives. Raspberries and cream, raspberries and ice cream, plain raspberries. At the hotel in San Francisco, I wasn't satisfied with the size of an order of raspberries, and I told room service, "A double order of raspberries . . . no, make that *three* orders of raspberries . . . no, wait, let's have *four* orders of raspberries to be on the safe side."

My strange food odyssey wasn't limited to raspberries.

An unidentifiable demon inside me kept driving me, making me crave sweets. It didn't matter that I wasn't hungry, or that I had no appetite; I *had* to put sugar and refined carbohydrate foods in my mouth again and again.

Columbus: French toast and hot chocolate.

Detroit: chocolates.

Pittsburgh: more chocolates.

Washington: back to the raspberries.

Kansas City: barbecue and caramel corn with Johnny and his fiancée, Pat.

Denver: French cuisine with Simon and Schuster rep Henry Hubert and too many homemade rolls at the Brown Palace Hotel.

Seattle: milk shakes and more raspberries.

Portland: finally, something healthy—fresh broiled salmon steak.

Los Angeles: not a raspberry to be found. I stocked Don and Judy Engel's guest house with The Famous Amos Chocolate Chip Cookie.

San Diego: raspberries and cream.

Palm Beach: Home again. Like a drunk trying to piece together a lost weekend, I struggled to comprehend the whats and whys of the previous few weeks. I didn't come up with any answers. All I knew for sure was that my one strength— my clear, quick, rational mind—was slipping away from me again. Three years had passed since I had uttered my first baffled "I don't know why" to Burt Reynolds, and I still didn't have any answers. I prayed that Dr. Williams and lithium would provide the answers and the solution.

Again, I sat in Dr. Williams's cozy office studying his homey bric-a-brac. The bowl of freshly picked flowers on his desk; the snapshot of his Welsh parents on the bookshelf behind him, his mother swathed in a mink stole looking a bit like a heavier version of my Aunt Lorry, his father staring stolidly at the camera; a picture of a very pretty blond woman up high on the top shelf; several elephants in different sizes and materials; some unidentifiable antique objects in matching red velvet-lined picture boxes; a curious-looking gold filigree tissue box, with goppy cupids attached to all four corners, sitting on the tiny marble-top table beside me.

My savior entered briskly, flashing me a cheerful smile.

Today he was attired in a blue Ultrasuede jacket, gray trousers, and a white shirt. *Very doctorish looking,* I thought.

And I looked very much the patient, I suspected, sitting stiffly upright on the maroon love seat, my fingers interlacing nervously, a fake happy smile plastered on my face.

One glance at me and Moke was instantly sobered. "Tell me how you are feeling," he ordered.

"Brace yourself." I grinned, and pulling out my little green notebook, I began to reel off my symptoms. "Muscle weakness, jerkiness, a feeling of wanting to jump out of my skin, irregular heartbeat, shortness of breath, sleeping all the time, nightmares, hair fallout, dry skin, strange speech patterns, inability to concentrate, nausea, bloated stomach and abdominal cramps"—I skipped any mention of my raspberry binge— "tender scalp, loss of body hair, mastitis, cystitis . . ."

"What kind of strange speech patterns?"

"Oh, talking too fast and with funny hesitations in what I'm saying, and my voice is higher and sort of wavery. . . . And I feel like crying all the time or jumping off a building. Other than that, I feel perfectly fine," I said, flashing Moke a bright smile.

"Hmmmm." Dr. Williams wanted to know, detail by detail, about my deterioration on the tour. He made a few notes, asked me some questions. Made some more notes. Asked more questions. Then silence while he thought.

"But it is over. You're through now with these public appearances?"

"Yes," I said, my voice rising a bit. "But I have the *trial* next."

He looked a bit surprised. Aren't psychiatrists supposed to keep up with their patients' activities? The Lyle Stuart litigation was scheduled to begin shortly.

"When does this trial take place?"

"December fourteenth, in New York."

"Then we better get you on the lithium right away."

"Hooray! At last."

"And I'm going to take you off Tofranil."

"Double hooray." All my troubles would be over.

He handed me the instructions to wean myself from my nemesis: "Take two a day for two days; one a day for three days; one every other day for a week; and then stop. By then the lithium should have started to take effect. During this lithium treatment, Terry, I want you to keep a diary or log of your feelings, emotions, and perceptions of your physical symptoms. Also, since we must be careful not to let lithium levels become too high in your body I want you to have blood tests every seven days. The lab will send the results to me."

I took the prescription gratefully in my clammy little hands and made for the door.

"I want to see you in two weeks," he called out to my departing figure.

On the way home, I stopped at my favorite Dairy Queen and had a soothing root beer float—giant size. "Things will get better now that I'll be taking lithium," I mumbled between spoonfuls of ice cream. Mif nodded his head to show he agreed with me.

Mif was my invisible friend. I didn't remember when he had first appeared in my life, sometime and somewhere during that tour, but we went everywhere together now. No, that wasn't really so; we weren't a togetherness couple. Mif had his own separate life which I wasn't too clear about, and his own tastes and habits. I looked over at Mif sitting there, cool and comfortable in his Irish and English tweeds despite the Florida heat. He reminded me of Dr. Lendon H. Smith, the renowned baby doctor, but I thought there were traces of Sherlock Holmes in him, too, plus a little of Moke Williams.

Mif looked over at me, the concern he felt for my eating habits plain upon his face. They continued to be out of control. "After the trial is over, I'll start eating sensibly again," I promised. "Oh, and after Christmas. No one should be asked to diet during the Christmas holidays. Yes, the first of the year would be a good time to turn over a new, low-calorie leaf."

Mif just arched his eyebrows and responded rather acidly, "I'll believe it when I see it."

I was beginning to find Mif more satisfying than real people, who seemed to be ever at me, giving me bad news and making demands upon me I couldn't meet.

I wondered: If the lithium proved effective, would Mif go away? I quit sucking on the Dairy Queen straw and looked over at Mif. No! I couldn't bear the idea of trying to get through even a single day without him. I knew he was a product of my imagination, but that didn't make him, or my need for him, any less real. I reached over and patted his hand to make it clear that I wasn't going to desert him. He evaporated before my eyes. But I wasn't worried. I knew he would be there when I got home.

And he was. Sitting in his favorite big chair, reading Henry James. After dinner we talked for a while about *The Heiress,* and the difficulties a woman with a great deal of money faces in trusting that she is loved for herself alone. It was a pleasant evening—low key. The kind of evening only Mif was able to provide me of late.

"I wonder why I never had an imaginary friend before?" I asked myself as I drifted off to sleep. "It's so cozy, so *rewarding,* to have an erudite, charming male companion who is sensitive to and supportive of my moods and thoughts but who doesn't drain me with worries and needs of his own." Mif, being perfect, didn't have problems.

I envied him that.

14

In the days of the Hatfields and McCoys, feuds were set-tled with long rifles. The feuders faced each other across rocky creeks and shouted insults from behind rocks and fat trees.

Garrity v. *Stuart* went the modern way and was fought with depositions, exhibits, and notary publics. We shot at each other at point-blank range from across a conference table.

On December 15, 1977—six years after filing my suits against Lyle Stuart—I found myself in New York in a con-ference room, seated at a big table, with Lyle and his allies facing me, and with Justice, in the persons of three arbitra-tors, seated at the head of the table.

It had been seven years since the day I had walked into the Doubleday bookstore and watched, fascinated, as the man in an overcoat read my book and put it back on the shelf. I remembered how cold it had been that evening, and how I had sweltered in my wraps and scarves.

Now it was again bitterly cold outside, and I was again *sweltering*. The thermostat in the American Arbitration Association building was malfunctioning, and the temperature in the hearing room hovered around 95 degrees Fahrenheit. I kept mopping my forehead with tissues, but I couldn't keep dry. Even though I was no longer taking Tofranil, there was still enough in my system to cause drenching sweats.

The lithium, which I had counted on for miracles, seemed to have no effect on me save one: the shakes. I noticed that one of the arbitrators had spotted my trembling hands, so I quickly hid them under the table.

I was terrified that my mind would fail me on some crucial question. Don Engel had spent hours the day before going over my testimony. Not coaching, really, just preparing me for the ordeal. There was so much to remember. Don's office was piled high with thousands of pages of testimony and exhibits from the years of litigation.

"How can I remember every detail of events that happened years ago?" I had asked. "I can't remember what happened *this* year."

I was afraid I was going to make a fool of myself. My original suit for unpaid royalties had been the fuse to a string of suits and countersuits that had gone off like firecrackers— my side charging Lyle Stuart with fraud, breach of contract, harassment, and intimidation; his side countersuing over my alleged refusal to write another sex book for Lyle Stuart under the option clause of my contract (a charge inspired by Lyle's belief that Don Engel had conspired with Len Forman and Simon and Schuster to get me to change publishers). We were asking $223,475 compensatory damages for the half of my royalties Lyle Stuart had kept on hardcover books sold "in the ordinary course of business"; $86,255 compensatory damages for breaches of contract related to accounting; termination of the contract for fraud and deceit, along with reassignment of the copyright to me, the author; and $400,000 compensatory damages "for intentional and willful infliction of mental distress and physical harm from claimant's harassment, coercion, and intimidation."

Hindsight tells me that the legal issues in *Garrity* v. *Stuart* were beyond any layman's comprehension. The arbitrators' 1974 decision awarding me $7,500 in punitive damages and $45,000 in compensatory damages had been affirmed by the New York State Supreme Court, further affirmed by the New York State Appelate Division of the Supreme Court, and then partially reversed (the punitive damages only) by the New York State Court of Appeals. The case would inspire a thirty-seven page article in the *Cornell Law Review* entitled "Punitive Damages in Arbitration: The Search for a Workable Rule," an article which only a lawyer could fathom. Publishing law was so complex and precedent-bound that only specialists like Don Engel could handle a major case. So complex, in fact, that most publishing disputes, by contractual agreement, were argued before carefully selected "arbitration panels" rather than before judges and juries.

In other words, I needn't have faulted myself for not understanding all the twists and subtleties of this very complicated lawsuit. But I *did* fault myself. I approached this last arbitration with fear; I attributed my confusion solely to my failing faculties.

Six years to get here, I thought, *and I can destroy my case with one mindless remark.*

Lyle testified in the afternoon. I didn't exchange direct glances with him—I found it uncomfortable—but I watched him occasionally out of the corner of my eyes. He wore a beige turtleneck sweater, and his manner was as casual as his attire. Sometimes he looked bored. Other times he got very indignant and muttered audibly while others were speaking. When he wanted to make a point, he sometimes repeated himself. When Allen Schwartz, his attorney, asked him if he had known, back in 1968, that I had written another book, Lyle replied, "She had not written a book. She was not an author. She was a publicist." He looked up and down the table. "She was *not* a writer. She was a *publicist.*"

He honestly believed he had "created" me.

Under cross-examination, Lyle grew annoyed as Don Engel kept probing the tricky wording of the key money clause in my contract, hammering home the fact that I had signed the contract in Lyle's office without benefit of counsel. "I wasn't in the room dancing with Miss Garrity," Lyle cracked. "We weren't singing songs together. We were spending an hour going over the contract."

Don grew impatient with Lyle's imprecise answers. He finally said, "Can't you answer yes or no?"

Lyle glared at him. "The answer is yes."

"I'm asking you—"

"Don't bait me, Mr. Engel." Lyle looked very angry. "Let's not do it today—"

The head arbitrator, Sherman Saxl, jumped in. "Let me interrupt," he said. "We're going to make much more progress if we don't get into—"

"Personalities," Don said, wearily. "I'm trying, sir."

Saxl nodded and settled back in his chair.

Don asked Lyle, "Did her brother tell you she was a nut?"

"Yes, he did," Lyle said.

I sat up straight and looked indignant, but Don motioned for me not to interrupt.

"He told me—again, he didn't use that word. Yes, he did use the word, but he said it in a—" Lyle hesitated. "—not in an unfriendly way. He said that she was acting a little paranoid in the hospital, and I shouldn't take it that seriously. He used the word *paranoid.*"

Don was satisfied with that clarification. "Did you tell anyone that she was a pathological liar?"

"I may have," Lyle said. "Terry does tell a great many lies."

My mouth felt dry, as if it were stuffed with cotton. Don had warned me that the hearing could turn nasty, but I hadn't expected to be called a liar and a nut on the very first day.

Another of Lyle's opinions, one that I found revealing, came in response to Don's inquiry as to why Lyle had refused to cooperate with my auditors when they tried to check his books. "She has received a million and a half dollars by her own admission," Lyle said with annoyance, "and this was made in nine weeks' work. I don't make a million and a half in nine weeks or nine years, and I work pretty hard."

Lyle hadn't answered Don's question, of course. But he had answered one of mine. "Why kill the Golden Goose?" I had asked Len many times. "Why reduce the royalties on a best-seller when you can make a fortune *legally*?" The answer, apparently, lay in the Lyle Stuart work ethic: He didn't think authors *deserved* to get rich off their books.

We adjourned after five o'clock. I was exhausted, and I hadn't even testified. "I must have had every muscle in my body tensed all day," I told Don at dinner. As usual when under stress, I ate too much.

After dinner, I walked up and down Madison Avenue. The boutiques and shops were open late for Christmas, and I bought things, gifts for people back in Palm Beach and things for myself, too. Christmas was a difficult time for me because shopping was "sanctioned" and the streets were full of people buying presents and carrying packages. I felt a palpable hunger to share in that euphoria.

Mif frowned, but didn't say a word.

I couldn't sleep afterward. My hotel room was so ugly that it made my skin crawl. I tried to watch TV, but I kept worrying about my testimony. Lyle's attorney, Schwartz, was a short, dark-haired man with a loud, irritating voice, and I feared that he would try to humiliate or upset me. Could Don wrench the truth out of me when I was so rattled and forgetful that I hardly knew what the truth *was* anymore? The thought kept crossing my mind: *Am I this frightened because I should be frightened? Or am I frightened because I am ill?*

I tossed fitfully until a predawn streak of blue showed through the sooty curtains. Then I got up and groggily prepared for another day of arbitration.

I wasn't asked to testify in the morning. Stuart's side called Bernie Geis, a well-known book packager and agent, as an expert witness, and Don answered with Anthony Schulte, vice-president for trade publishing at Random House. They gave conflicting pictures of what was common "trade practice" in the publishing industry regarding the calculation of authors' royalties. The testimony was technical, but tempers got raw.

The arbitrators could not conceal their weariness of the bickering. After lunch, arbitrator Jacques Barzun politely scolded both counsels. "I feel bound to remark that there is a growing tendency to give us everything twice over," he said. "I have heard nothing in the last ten minutes that I did not know very clearly yesterday, and at that rate I do not know whether we will ever end. The Congressional Statutory Retirement Law will apply and I will disappear."

I smiled at that. Barzun was a distinguished writer and scholar from Columbia University, and I was surprised that a man of such stature was hearing my case. He didn't say much, but his aristocratic bearing impressed me.

With the expert witnesses dismissed, Don went back to cross-examining Lyle. Don's personal grievances came to the fore again. "Isn't it true, Mr. Stuart, that because of your animosity and malice toward Miss Garrity you have actually directed that at persons associated with her?"

"No," Lyle said.

"On the record"—Don looked at his notes—"you said that I seem to be a 'two-bit Disraeli with a cash register in each nostril.'"

Lyle shrugged. "I think that is a valid description."

Don ignored Lyle's remark and studied a deposition. "I quote an answer of Mr. Stuart's: 'Well, in my correspondence with you on the telephone, you sounded like a shit.'"

I almost groaned out loud because we were back to the Lyle Stuart-Don Engel feud. Only later would I realize that Don was baiting Lyle, working towards something more important. "Do you have any personal animosity toward Miss Garrity?"

"I don't think so now. You are asking me today?" Lyle shook his head. "No."

"Did you ever have personal animosity toward Miss Garrity?"

"I was very disappointed in her, and I suppose there were times when I was angry with her, yes."

"When was that?"

"At various times. After all, she sued me, she libeled me, she brought suits which were obviously an attempt to harass my company and delay our public offering."

"So you did act with malice toward Miss Garrity?"

Lyle was too smart to fall into that trap. "No, I never acted with malice toward Miss Garrity. I never said an unkind word to her. We never had a quarrel."

Don looked up. "You have never spoken to her since December 1970?"

Lyle nodded. "That is true."

Don pulled the next document out of his folder, a photostat of a magazine article. He looked at Lyle. "Did you write a column that mentioned Miss Garrity for *Screw* magazine?"

Lyle acted bored. "I don't recall. I may have."

Schwartz looked unhappy. "Show him the column," he said.

Don handed the page across the table to Lyle. "Mr. Stuart, did you write this column?"

Lyle looked at it. "Yes."

"Is there something in there about Miss Garrity?"

"Yes. There seems to be a paragraph about her."

I began to feel very nervous. Don had warned me that he might have to read the column out loud. Friends had told me that it was awful, but I had no notion of its actual content. I began daubing the perspiration on my forehead with soggy tissues. The heat seemed almost unbearable.

"May I ask you something?" Don stared at Lyle. "This is a magazine that is sold to the public, is it not? A newspaper or magazine? What did this appear in? Do you remember?"

"In Al Goldstein's *Screw*," Lyle said.

Don looked at his own copy of the column. "Mr. Stuart, didn't you write what you wrote about Miss Garrity in here—'Terry Garrity is suing me as a woman scorned'— didn't you write that out of malice?"

Lyle shook his head. "No. This is humor." He smiled. "Half the magazine is humor."

Don looked shocked. "This column was attacking all your enemies?"

"This is all humor, of course," Lyle insisted.

Schwartz, to my surprise, suddenly interrupted. "Don't read it, please," he said. "Spare us."

Don turned to the chairman. "May I have this introduced in evidence?"

Schwartz jumped up again. "I object to this. I object to it. It pertains to all kinds of things and is entirely irrelevant to Terry Garrity, and in truth you are not offering it for—"

Saxl interrupted. "Why don't we read into the record that portion of the article which pertains to Terry Garrity."

While the attorneys squabbled, I leaned over and looked at Don's copy of the exhibit. It was headlined LYLE STUART: STRICTLY BETWEEN US. The blood must have drained out of my face as I read the opening paragraphs:

Al Goldstein, who can't locate his limp cock even when

he uses both hands, has appealed to my prurient interest to write a column for Screw. *Circulation has sunk to 11½ copies an issue, and if Willie Cahn is dropped from the Mafia pad in Nassau County and has to cancel his own two subscriptions,* Screw *is in serious trouble.*

Goldstein offered me everything (including himself) if only I would contribute an occasional piece for him. I settled for two nights with Heidi Handman for each column I write. It isn't that I don't have problems of my own. The pissed-off mob of lynch-ready men and women who kept converging on my Park Avenue South office to demand the next issue of my own paper (The Independent) *forced me to move our offices to Seacaucus, New Jersey. (The paper has started to come like Goldstein—about once every six months.)*

My eyes jumped ahead to a paragraph further down, which began, "Terry Garrity is suing me as a woman scorned. . . . I asked her to write a book that would make cocksucking respectable in America, and we published *The Sensuous Woman.* I've paid her more than $700,000. . . ."

But Don was now starting to read aloud from the column. "You'll have to excuse the language," he said. "I am going to read the last sentence in the paragraph. . . ."

Don read, "'But the sudden riches seem to have frightened away all the fellows she used to blow, and now she's hysterical because with nothing but bananas and overcooked frankfurters to suck on, her buck teeth are threatening to fall out.'"

The arbitrators must have seen me blanch. There was a heavy, embarrassed silence.

Don had prepared me for the *Screw* column, warning me it would be unpleasant. But it was far worse than I had imagined. I kept my eyes glued on my hands in my lap. I couldn't look at anyone. I felt nauseous and tears were welling up in my eyes. I felt that I was a party to some uncontrollable ugliness, that I was mired in muck and would never be clean again.

"I wrote that," Lyle volunteered testily, "in the context of *Screw,* which lampoons and satirizes everything."

"Mr. Chairman," Don said, very quietly, very distinctly, "it is our contention that the column is a vicious diatribe against all Mr. Stuart's enemies, and I introduce it for the purpose of the quoted portions so that the arbitrators themselves can determine exactly what the impact of this article in a magazine of general circulation might be upon my client, who will testify to it."

When Chairman Saxl finally announced, "We will adjourn for lunch," I rose from my chair and edged around behind Don, using his body as a shield from Lyle and the arbitrators. I wanted desperately out of that room, out of that smothering heat and stale air, but I stood there, behind Don, until the other side had left.

I didn't want to talk to anybody.

"The *Screw* article was a turning point," Don whispered to me the next day, just before I testified. He was trying to calm me down. I was drenched with sweat. My hands were trembling badly.

Part of our case, of course, was that Lyle, over the years of litigation, had turned me into a quivering idiot. (Don had a letter from Dr. Williams testifying that, over time, the stress of Lyle's badgering and harassment had triggered my clinical depression.) But Don feared that my lithium shakes would be misinterpreted, or that I would break down under questioning.

The session of December 16 did not begin until after noon. Don opened his examination of me by finally referring to what must have been obvious to everyone in the room: that I was not well. "Was there any particular reason why the manuscript of *Total Loving* was three years late?" he asked.

"Yes," I said. "I was ill."

"This was a period of several years. Would you describe what your problem was during that time?"

"Anxiety," I said. "Severe depression. There were some physical symptoms. Severe weight gain, skin problems." Just talking about it made me nervous, and suddenly I couldn't recall all my symptoms. "I'm trying to remember them all," I apologized. "I didn't know I would have to have them for this." I wanted desperately to be lucid; I tried to summon up the "J" part of my personality. ". . . I had blackouts, inability to concentrate . . . that became more severe with time. . . . Also, there was damage to the pancreas."

"Well, what was causing the anxiety? What precipitated the anxiety?"

"The stress," I said. "My life, what was happening to it. There was a great deal of stress from coping with Lyle Stuart . . . the litigation—"

I wasn't surprised when Schwartz interrupted. "I object to all this," he said, "since she is really not a doctor qualified to do this."

"Objection overruled," Saxl said.

Don surprised me by not really pursuing the medical question. "If this were a knockdown case," he told the panel, "and the whole thing was medical testimony, we might spend five days with medical experts. It is not expedient or practical to do it, though, and the medical part is a very small part of this case. And everything she says is self-serving. I accept that." Don knew that damages for medical problems were rare in cases like mine, and anyway, he couldn't really *prove* that the contract squabble and Lyle's harassment were the legal cause of my ailments.

That did not stop Don from getting my testimony to the effect that I had suffered painful financial losses by battling

Lyle: that I had paid out between $50,000 and $75,000 in legal fees up to Lyle's filing of countersuits against Simon and Schuster and Don, and at least that much since then; and that my earlier court award of the $45,000 illegally withheld me by Lyle had been collected only through a lengthy arbitration, followed by hearings in three other courts up to the Court of Appeals. "It cost me approximately twenty thousand dollars to collect the forty-five," I explained. "So I lost."

Don seemed satisfied with my testimony on those matters, and now he yielded to Schwartz. I braced myself. I knew he would be out to tear me down.

"Miss Garrity"—Schwartz straightened in his chair and looked across the table at me—"you have heard here that Mr. Stuart referred to you in a deposition to your attorney as a pathological liar?"

I felt myself stiffen. "Yes."

"Was it your practice while you were at [Lyle Stuart] to tell tales to the people in the company about yourself?"

I must have looked puzzled. "It was not."

"And that's not a practice of yours in general, to tell tales?"

I didn't really know what he meant by "tales," but I had been warned about asking questions of counsel, so I repeated, "It is not."

"And it is not a practice of yours to tell untruths to people with whom you come in contact for reasons of your own, for your own comfort or convenience or benefit or whatever?"

I was not foolish enough to claim that I had never told a lie in my life. "I have told social lies on occasion, Mr. Schwartz, yes. When you want to avoid going to a party or you don't want to hurt someone's feelings."

Schwartz assumed that look of confidence that lawyers must practice, the look that says, "Now I've got you." "Have you ever been married?"

"I have not."

He nodded. "Were you interviewed by the Los Angeles *Times* on October sixteenth, 1973?"

"I was."

He referred to an exhibit. "Did you ever tell that editor or that author that you were married?"

I didn't even hesitate. "I did not."

Schwartz flashed me a questioning look.

"In fact," I continued, "if you want to take that particular week when I went across the country, you will find me married, engaged, and divorced, depending upon what the writer assumed."

"Did you say, 'He's not a public person, and I don't want him to take all the teasing he would get if people knew that he was my husband'?"

I shook my head. "I did not say that. I said the part about the teasing, but I said my fiancé."

He referred back to his file. "Did you tell different writers across the country that you were married to a man who was playing golf?"

"I never said the word *married*."

"Did you tell the author of the article in the Los Angeles *Times*, 'My husband plays golf, but I am a better putter than he is'?"

I smiled. "I did not."

Schwartz's tone was sarcastic. "None of those quotes are true?"

"Nor did that reporter use a tape recorder, Mr. Schwartz." I gathered up the courage to give him a fairly intense stare of my own. "If you had been interviewed, you will note that you will see quite surprising things in print when they take their notes and then try to transcribe them later."

Schwartz looked directly at me again, this time with a more kindly expression. "Mr. Stuart has a lot of faults, doesn't he?"

I resisted the impulse to look at Lyle. "It has been my observation that he has some flaws, yes."

"Which you recognized while you were at the company?"

"Yes."

"But you also recognized that he was an honest man?"

"I thought he was."

"Straightforward in his dealings with authors and with companies that he dealt with?"

"I didn't have much knowledge of that, but I assumed that he was."

I wasn't sure where Schwartz was headed with his questions, so I was very tense. But apparently all he wanted was my admission that Lyle and I once had been friendly, and that Lyle had not harassed me then. Schwartz placed great emphasis on Lyle's surprise reception for me the day he sold the paperback rights to *The Sensuous Woman*. "Did he have Carlos Gonzales bring you a check for fifteen thousand dollars that day, in advance of the signing of the agreement, there on the premises?"

"Yes," I said.

"Is it fair to say that you were stunned? Overjoyed?"

"An understatement," I said.

"And Mr. Stuart, recognizing that you were in a daze, took you to his home to have dinner that night?"

"Yes, he did."

"And didn't Rory, his son, make a steak dinner for the three of you?"

"Yes."

"And didn't the three of you sit there and sing songs? Do you remember singing those old-time songs?"

I was sticky with perspiration, my head throbbed. What was Schwartz getting at? His style of questioning made the suspense unbearable for me.

"And looked at photographs, yes," I nodded.

Schwartz handed me a picture dated June 2, 1970, from the *New York Post* and asked, "Is that you?"

I looked at it. "Yes."

"Smiling?"

"Smiling," I agreed.

"Thank you."

"Because I smiled for the camera, I couldn't have been unhappy? Is that your suggestion?"

"Miss Garrity"—his eyes narrowed slightly—"is it fair to say that from and after June 1970—I mean, after your name and your picture were publicly credited in newspapers from coast to coast—that you in truth enjoyed the publicity?"

I felt a sudden impulse to laugh, and just as quickly a wave of grief engulfed me. The nightmare image of Mother on her deathbed flashed in my mind, followed by my bloated reflection in my terry-cloth robe, and then the two mixed together in an impression of death and decay.

"Truthfully"—I could barely speak—"I don't think I enjoyed a single minute in the public eye. It was awful." I looked toward the arbitrators. "If I had written another kind of book, I might have enjoyed it. But not as a controversial author." My voice cracked. "It was hell out there."

At four-thirty, the first strains of "Frosty the Snowman" began to filter in from a Christmas party down the hall. The attorneys were now making references to "midnight testimony." After six years of foot-dragging and delay, we were having to crowd our testimony into three or four days of frantic and exhausting hearings.

We took a dinner break, but I was so tense and distracted that I couldn't eat a thing. Don looked very tired; he kept rubbing his forehead wearily. "I don't know how much more of this I can take," I said woodenly.

"It's almost over," he said.

"Are we winning?"

Don allowed himself a thin smile. "Nobody wins in a case like this."

When we resumed, it was dark outside. Lights were on in the offices across the street, but everybody there had gone home. In our own building, the sounds of Christmas revelry in the corridor were now so loud that we were practically having to shout across the table. I was bone weary, and I turned to Don. "This isn't going to go all night, is it?"

"I don't think so," he said.

Lyle's case against me—his countersuit—was based on collusion. From experts Schwartz had accumulated piles of testimony and affidavits that questioned the merits of my golf book as a bona fide option book with Lyle. His witnesses pointed out, quite fairly, that *Total Loving* was ultimately published by Simon and Schuster; that my boyfriend, Len Forman, was an executive at Simon and Schuster; that Cornerstone Library, which published the golf book, rented offices from Simon and Schuster and distributed its books through an exclusive arrangement with Simon and Schuster; and that Don Engel, my attorney, was both Cornerstone's attorney and Len's personal attorney.

I was not surprised, therefore, when Schwartz began to question me about the first meeting that Len and I had with Don Engel in October 1970.

"During the year 1970," Schwartz began, "did you have occasion to meet with Mr. Engel and an employee of Simon and Schuster to review the option clause in your agreement with Mr. Stuart?"

I nodded. "I met with my fiancé and Mr. Engel."

"And who was your fiancé?"

"Leonard Forman." Lyle's eyes seemed to narrow when I spoke Len's name.

Schwartz looked thoughtful. "As early as 1970, you, Mr. Forman, and Mr. Engel were considering the option clause in your agreement with Mr. Stuart's company?"

I gave Don a sideways glance. "Mr. Schwartz, we discussed the whole contract."

"And in fact you discussed whether you still had to submit another book under that option clause?"

I knew I didn't dare make a mistake in this area. "Now, wait a minute." I looked to Don for help. "If I can get this legally right—"

"Objection," Don said. "I object on the grounds of attorney-client privilege." That had a vague Watergate ring to it, but I was glad that Don had come to my rescue.

"Mr. Forman was present," Schwartz noted.

Don looked to the chairman. "Mr. Forman was my client at the time."

"I don't want a speech," Saxl said, "I want an objection."

"The conversation occurred," Don said patiently, "because Mr. Forman referred Miss Garrity to me. Mr. Forman was her fiancé. Mr. Forman was there as a friend."

The chairman wasn't impressed. "Overruled," he said.

I thought the adverse ruling would disturb Don, but he didn't even blink. "All right," he said calmly, "may I make another statement?"

"Yes," the chairman said unenthusiastically.

Don said, without undue emphasis, "Mr. Forman had a financial interest in *The Sensuous Woman*."

Lyle's attorney suddenly threw his hands in the air and roared, "Which I never knew until this second!"

The unexpected outburst made me jump. Schwartz glared angrily at Lyle, and Lyle—I couldn't believe it—looked absolutely bug-eyed. Stunned. *Furious!*

What was happening?

"Of course you didn't," Don was saying calmly, "that's why I hesitate—"

"To this *second!*" Schwartz roared again, slamming the table.

"That's right," Don said. "It was privileged and confidential information which I have been holding."

Chairman Saxl looked almost as shocked as Lyle and his

attorney. "You don't disclose it without the permission of your client?" he asked Don. For an instant, I feared that Don had made some tactical or ethical blunder that had ruined our case.

"I have the permission," Don said, "because the reason for the concealment was his employment by a publishing company, and he is no longer employed at Simon and Schuster. Mr. Forman was my client and had an interest in the book that was financial. And, indeed, I represent him here. He is a silent partner." He turned to Schwartz, who looked mad enough to gnaw on the leg of the table. "There is nothing strange about it, Mr. Schwartz."

I had no idea what had happened. Obviously, something dramatic had been revealed, and whatever it was was good for our side. Lyle had lost all his color, and I thought he was having trouble breathing. He looked like he had been struck by lightning.

The arbitrators were buzzing among themselves. The chairman, trying to restore order, took over the questioning of me.

"Did Mr. Forman also have an interest in *The Sensuous Man?*" he asked, leaning forward.

"Yes, he did."

"And what was his interest?"

"He was a coauthor."

I thought Lyle was going to be sick. I had never seen him look so distressed.

Saxl made some notes and looked up. "There were two clients seeking joint advice," he declared. "They had similar interests, and I think the privilege pertains. And therefore I sustain the objection."

The objection? I couldn't even remember what Don's objection was. It was clear that we had won an important point, but I was totally in the dark. Had I missed something? Was my mind playing tricks on me again?

Schwartz, although no longer pounding the table, was still upset. The purpose of his questioning, he told the arbitrators, was to prove that Len and I had met with Don in a conspiracy to get *Total Loving* for Simon and Schuster.

"I understand that that's your theory," Chairman Saxl said dryly.

It was months before I understood. I had assumed, all those years, that Lyle's claims and countersuits were simply tactics aimed at scaring me away. I had assumed that, by now, Lyle's side knew that Len was coauthor of *The Sensuous Man*. (How long can you keep a secret like that in the gossipy world of publishing?) But they *hadn't* known about Len's role. From their point of view the "collusion theory"—that Len and Simon and Schuster had conspired with Don to steal *Total Loving* away from Lyle Stuart—made sense! They *believed* it! Schwartz's fury was proof of that.

Both sides seemed to have lost their enthusiasm for the hearing. The arbitrators joined in the clock watching, apparently as weary as I, while the two attorneys agreed to a timetable for submitting final arguments.

Down the hall, the Christmas party had ended. The building was silent around us. The windows behind the arbitrators were steamed up like a delicatessen's. The lights in the building across the street had been turned off.

The fight was over.

It was time to go home.

I "won" my lawsuit.

That is to say, I got Jacques Barzun's autograph on a piece of paper dated May 23, 1978, rejecting Lyle Stuart's breach of contract claim against me and awarding me $126,438 in unpaid royalties.

But it was just a piece of paper. Lyle threatened to keep appealing the case, which could have consumed up to two more years and thousands of dollars more in legal fees. I finally had to agree to a settlement—I simply couldn't afford to keep fighting. Lyle ultimately paid us $110,000 in cash, after six more months of haggling. From that amount, Don Engel deducted $63,000 for outstanding legal fees. That left $47,000 to be split up among Johnny, Len, and myself.

When the smoke had cleared, I stood bloodied and triumphant—seven years older, emotionally crippled, a quarter of a million dollars poorer, and clutching $30,000 for my prize—most of which I immediately forfeited to my creditors. "We have really achieved a significant victory," Don wrote to me, "but at significant cost."

PART
THREE

PALM BEACH, 1978

In apartment 2-A, the living-room lights were blazing at three o'clock in the morning. The television was on, a grainy rerun of Herbert Philbrick's I Led Three Lives *series. Clippings and magazines littered the floor around the upholstered armchair opposite the set; an open bottle of Diet Dr. Pepper, wrapped in a napkin, rested on a coaster by the chair.*

The chair was empty.

On an elegant white sofa, surrounded by colorful needlepoint pillows positioned with a decorator's care, a sock-doll monkey in a silk clown costume sat with limp arms and splayed legs.

A lamp was burning on the magnificent red lacquer Chinese Chippendale game table.

The door beside it was dark.

Stacks of magazines, chest high, crowded the dark hallway outside the guest bathroom. The New York *magazines made the tallest pile, with the women's magazines next. One stack was reserved for golf magazines, another for medical journals.*

Rising among the magazines, in one corner, a feather duster flowered like a palm atop an eight-foot bamboo pole.

The only light in the bathroom was a glint reflected off the mirror through the open door.

There were two other doors. The one on the right, to the master bedroom, was closed, with no light shining from beneath.

The door to the left, to the guest room, was open. Narrow wedges of light leaked through the louvers of the closed shutters on the far wall, and one small dim light glowed in the middle of the room. It was a night-light perched on top of a pile of clothes cartons: a tiny honey-colored teddy bear.

The cord disappeared between the cartons and a pile of shopping bags. Shopping bags and boxes, waist high, crowded the floor from wall to wall, creating a shadowy landscape around the beds. Books were everywhere: stacked in the corners, hidden under the beds, teetered precariously atop already jammed bookcases and étagères. Clothes on hangers were piled on the beds and draped over cartons against the walls.

Behind the boxes, amid the pillows and bedclothes, their eyes gleaming in the light from the plastic bear, were arrayed the silent witnesses: a Cat in the Hat doll, a lanky frog, and the four teddy bears.

A note, scrawled in a childish longhand, lay atop a pile of clothes, just within the soft lightfall of the teddy bear light. "I have been dead for quite a while," the note began. "No one has noticed or missed the person that was Terry. It is indescribably painful that the happy, funny, loving parts of me are not mourned, and that all around me settle so contentedly for what is left—a mentally dulled cardboard figure that smiles at the right times and makes appropriate small talk and seems happy enough with her existence. No one sees, or seemingly cares."

A shadow cut across the words at the bottom of the page: "I am alone at my own funeral."

15

*1*978: The year I nearly destroyed myself. The place: Palm Beach, Florida. The weapons: the shopping bag and a happy face. The motive: a desire to experience good feelings again.

The "detective" on my case was having a hard time of it. Lithium had failed to bring about any positive response. The MAO family of antidepressants, monoamine oxidase inhibitors which slow down amine metabolism in the brain by inhibiting the enzyme, thereby heightening emotional and mental response, hadn't worked. The results from tricyclic antidepressants, which differ from MAOs in that they block instead of slow down the re-uptake of amines in brain cells, had only a negligible effect on *my* brain.

The "victim" was stubbornly resisting any investigation of her illness that wasn't strictly physiological. I had gone back to my original suspicion: that I had a brain tumor. Visions of Bette Davis in *Dark Victory* kept floating before my eyes, which, since I hadn't followed Orrin Stine's advice to get an eye examination yet, were giving me increasing trouble. Didn't Bette Davis in the early stages of the movie, before her brain tumor was diagnosed, have headaches and vision problems?

At my prodding, Moke ordered a complete neurological workup, including a brain scan, but the tests failed to produce a brain tumor or any other problem. Was I becoming a hypochondriac? Yes, I can admit now. I was obsessed with my body's minor ailments. And was I becoming delusional? Knickknacks and furniture were in different places every time I visited Dr. Williams's office. The plant stand and bookshelves in the reception room seemed to be migrating to different walls on each of my visits. An Oriental rug suddenly appeared where there had never been one; pictures on the walls came and went. Moke's desk was in a different position. I'd been in and out of his office for months, but didn't remember ever seeing the two persimmon velvet chairs before. Hadn't there been matching maroon love seats in those same spots? Only the goppy gold filigree tissue box remained familiarly in place. Yes, I was going mad.

Moke kept irritating me by bringing up nonsense about manic depression.

And something about compulsive behavior.

And now he was poking around in my *emotions*. My feelings about failure. Inadequacy. Len. Mother's death. Sex. Love.

And I was, for the first time, lying to him. Oh, not outright, but by omission. I thought I knew why I was depressed and panicky. Money. But I was too ashamed of how I was mishandling money to tell Moke about it. He would think I was a bad person, a weak person, and I desperately needed him to like and care about me and my welfare.

So I put on a happy face and, because I *wanted* so terribly to feel good and please him, I convinced myself during several office visits that I *did* feel good. I was Little Mary Sunshine calling on Dr. Albert Schweitzer.

"Terry, you tell me you are anxious and depressed, but you are displaying hyperactive, almost manic behavior. This indicates very strong mood swings. You have heard of manic depression—"

"No, no," I interrupted him. "I don't have highs at all, and when I do have lows it's from *real* reasons. Besides, if I was a manic-depressive I would be outrageously happy—high—and would be able to go without sleep for days and create brilliant work effortlessly and at a tremendous pace. I *never* feel or behave maniacally," I reiterated firmly. "If I did, I would be thrilled to be so productive."

"When you are in the reception room, Terry, you act like a political candidate's wife—charming, gracious, controlled, yet when you walk through the door and sit opposite me all this washes away. Right now you are tense . . . frightened. Is the idea of being mentally ill that terrifying to you?"

"Yes!" I blurted out. "It would mean the end of everything. The end of love. Marriage. No one would marry an insane person. My work. No one would want to publish or read books by a crazy person. Everything that means anything to me would be gone forever. But *I'm not mentally ill!*" I almost shouted at him. And to prove it, I forced myself to be calm and controlled again. "I *know* that I have an oddball physical disease that is causing mental symptoms, and I *know* that with a little more time you will discover what it is."

"And if I don't?"

"But you *will.*"

Moke tap, tap, tapped his pen against his desk top for a couple of minutes and stared myopically at the picture of a Labrador retriever on the wall behind me. Did I detect a slight sigh? I squirmed impatiently.

He returned to the case. "It would be helpful, Terry, if I had a picture from others of what you were like before you wrote *The Sensuous Woman.* Would it be possible to have a few family members and old friends write little personality sketches for me of how they perceived you back then?"

"All right."

Silence. Then, "You're gaining weight."

"Well, yes. I have eaten a few bad foods lately. But I'm going to stop." I didn't see fit to mention to him that I was now downing a Sara Lee frozen fruit pie a day, sweet rolls, and boxes of Pepperidge Farm's Southport cookies. And milkshakes (for my digestion) and doughnuts (for "quick energy").

"Have you been spending an unusual amount of money?"

"No, not at all. Not any more than usual."

"Have you bought anything this week?"

"Groceries. Some books. Those are necessities," I pointed out. "A few nightgowns."

He seemed to think that was interesting enough to write down.

"And elecric can openers." I could see him mentally rejecting a juicy hypothesis about the nightgowns.

"Can openers in the singular or the plural?"

"Only two . . . in case one breaks down."

"Have you purchased anything else recently?"

"Well, let me think. Oh, this lapis-and-gold bracelet is new. I don't usually buy jewelry, but this was rather special, and it *was* on sale."

Moke made a few notations.

"Have your sleeping patterns changed recently?"

"Well, I'm tired all the time, of course, and I'm having my usual trouble waking up. I sleep abnormally deeply and long. I wish you could do something about that," I said expectantly.

"How is your writing coming along?"

"Uhmm. Slowly. I'm still having trouble concentrating, but I'm sure that will pass," I said brightly, "when I'm further into the material."

"What about your sex life?"

"What sex life?" I looked at him blankly. "Oh, it could be

better, but it could be worse." I quickly changed the subject. "Has that lamp always been there on your desk?"

"Yes." Silence. More tap, tap, tapping of the Papermate pen. I wondered if there were little tiny dents in that section of his desk top.

"Why don't we make an agreement together," he said. "I want you to give me your word of honor that you won't buy anything this week."

"Anything?" My eyes must have gotten big.

Moke shrugged. "Food is okay. Necessities like toothpaste and soap. The newspaper. But nothing else."

I hesitated. I seldom gave and never had broken my word of honor. "On my word of honor?"

"That's right," he said.

"Just one week?" I smiled apprehensively.

"One week."

"All right. That shouldn't be too hard," I said, my mind made up. "I'll give you my word of honor."

I had never read anything about compulsive shopping. I knew that buying was an emotional substitute for people with empty lives—I hadn't forgotten the blue-haired "shopping ladies" I had encountered on my first New York spending spree—but I didn't see myself as one of them. "I'm in control," I told myself quite proudly.

Still, I was surprisingly restless the first couple of days. I felt very edgy. It was boring, just sitting around the apartment all day. *It shows how much I've gotten used to buying things,* I thought. I hadn't realized how much of my time was consumed with shopping, with buying, with receiving goods.

On the fifth day, I found myself on Worth Avenue. The sun was shining and the rich tourists in their green slacks and orange sport shirts were window-shopping and smoking cigars. The Rolls-Royces were idling at curbside. And there I was, telling myself that I had to go to the Everglades Pharmacy, at the foot of Worth Avenue, for a necessity: a toothbrush. As I walked, things in the windows would catch my eyes and I would stop to look: a mediocre oil painting, a beautiful blouse, a diamond necklace. Suddenly, I found myself in Elizabeth Arden's, surrounded by lovely things. Things I didn't need, but enticing nevertheless. I was back in that temporary never-never land where things smell good and feel good. I bought something. After Elizabeth Arden's it was some other store, more beautiful things, the same flight from reality, and I bought more things. I kept buying and buying, and before I was through I had spent $1,500.

It didn't hit me until I got home. I piled my purchases on the beds in the guest room, and I felt as guilty as if I had stolen them. I sat down and cried. "This is a disease," I told myself. "I have a *disease*."

Actually, an addiction.

I looked around my beautiful guest room—or what I could see of it. New clothes that I had bought and never worn were draped over the beds. The chairs and table were piled with shopping bags full of items I had never bothered to unwrap after I'd brought them home. Mail-order catalogs and purchases designated as future birthday and Christmas gifts for friends and family clogged the floor between the beds. There was only the narrowest path to my desk through a minefield of Bergdorf Goodman, Bloomingdale's, and Bonwit Teller shopping bags stuffed with old clippings, unopened mail, magazines, and "just things" that hadn't found a place yet.

A horrible thought hit me as I surveyed the pristine bundles and laden hangers. *Could I be a kleptomaniac?* I scrabbled frantically through the boxes and bags. Thank God! There was a sales check for every purchase.

But what was driving me to such self-destructive behavior? I backed out of the room and closed the door behind me. But banishing the horrible sight from my view didn't remove it from my consciousness. My eyes went to the newest stack of unopened bills on the dining-room table. I quickly covered their accusing shapes with a few magazines.

And then I went to the kitchen and ate, standing up, an entire Sara Lee cherry pie that was cooling on top of the stove. "I won't think about this now," I whispered to myself. "Tomorrow, I'll cope with all this."

When I entered the living room, Mif looked up from the book he was reading. "This has been an unnervingly revealing day, hasn't it?"

I nodded.

"Would you like to talk about it?" he asked me, marking his place in his book with a finger.

"No!" I cried. But I didn't want to hurt his feelings. "I love your new tweed jacket," I told him.

Mif smiled and went back to his book. But *Moke* didn't smile when I saw him the following Wednesday.

Telling Moke I had broken my promise was one of the hardest things I had ever had to do. I avoided the subject during the first minutes of our session, but finally I gathered up the courage and confessed. "I've never broken my word of honor before," I stammered.

He looked at me and said, quietly, "I knew you would."

I was dumbfounded. *I* didn't know. How could *he* have known?

"I had you give your word of honor," he explained, "so it would be clear to you that you can't control this compulsion."

Compulsion. There was that word again. "It was just like a magnet," I said. "Something pulled me to Worth Avenue. I didn't know what I was doing. I bought things I can't use."

"You seem to be feeling a great deal of guilt."

"I do. I can identify with the kleptomaniac. I feel like I've been a bad girl."

"Do you think that, or are you afraid that other people will think that?"

I hesitated. "Both, I imagine."

"Are you fearful of criticism?"

I admitted that I was, and Moke nodded. "Of course, you do get criticized a great deal, don't you?" He smiled at me. "Because of your writing? And you know, your need to accomplish things, your perfectionism—these can quickly alienate the average person who cannot keep up with you. You set yourself up for criticism by virtue of who you are. Criticism indeed does enter into the reality of a situation for you."

"But why do I shop?" I implored. "Why do I have to shop?"

In the manner of all trained psychiatrists, he answered, "Why do you think?"

"I don't know!" I wailed. "Nothing I do makes sense to me anymore."

"You have two compulsions, Terry. Eating and shopping. Both are self-indulgent."

"We-l-l . . ."

"They are mechanisms that allow you to reward yourself and to reassure yourself that you are worthwhile; because in depression you feel so worth*less*. Things are so dead inside you that you are trying to find anything that will give you a feeling state again. Depression is so flat, so dead, so dark, that you tend to go in any direction that you might identify as pleasurable or that brings out any kind of feeling, even if it lasts only for a moment. Being presented with a prettily wrapped package, seeing a nice, bubbly cherry pie, takes your mind, temporarily, off the depth of your depression. Your misery. It's like a nice cold beer on a hot day. This is what I think your compulsions are all about."

Knowing that I had a compulsion to shop didn't stop me from doing it. Arthur liquidated more of my dwindling assets to pay for clothes I never unwrapped, shoes that didn't fit me, gifts I never gave. "This is sick," I told myself. "This goes beyond eccentric. This is sick. I have to stop."

But I needed the temporary lift I got at the moment of purchasing each item. I continued to shop.

Often in the next weeks, I went out in search of a specific item, like a pair of sandals, and, after finding them, would still go from store to store, driving up and down the island, shopping for hours and hours, returning home exhausted, the day wasted.

My guest room became my "picture of Dorian Gray": an ugly, festering representation of my disintegrating psyche. Except for the fact that my clutter was mostly new, I was reminded of the famous Collier brothers, the New York pack rats who had died in a brownstone crammed with massive heaps of curios, treasures and outright garbage, all in an undifferentiated mass.

When my guest room held all it could hold, I had to "temporarily" rent a maid's room on the top floor of my building. (Our truly wealthy tenants had live-in help, but I was apparently the only tenant willing to pay one hundred dollars a month for storage with a view.) I transferred what I could to this new cache: more designer clothes, framed pictures, stacks and stacks of magazines, shopping bags full of mail, boxes of stuffed animals.

Soon, even the maid's room couldn't handle the spillover. The clutter crept beyond the guest-room door into the hall closet and the entry hall itself. Shopping bags, books, and packages sprouted under the dining-room table, on the seats of chairs, behind the sofa. I could no longer eat at the table—there was no room. Piles of magazines and notes and needlepoint materials were rising up around my yellow chair in the living room, threatening to overwhelm me.

The only refuge left me in the entire apartment, it seemed, was my bedroom, which I fought to maintain in order. The stacks of magazines were now shoulder high right outside my bedroom door. I was besieged.

And I was about to cut my lifeline.

Moke was on vacation, so there was no one to report my escalating madness to. On the rare occasions that I allowed myself to see friends, I pushed myself to be bubbly, enthusiastic, despite the fact that I didn't feel these emotions. I actually felt empty, gray, ghostlike.

In April, I crashed into terror and despair, but I didn't call Moke. I couldn't face telling him all the bad things I had done—the shopping, the huge bills I had run up that were threatening my continuing existence, the wild eating sprees.

"After I lose a little weight and am coping better, I'll call him," I promised myself.

Mif told me that was wrong, that I was avoiding help when I needed it most just because of foolish pride, but I wouldn't, seemingly *couldn't* listen to reason. Reason meant facing the unbearable—an official diagnosis.

16

I put myself through unnecessary torture during the next
few weeks. Much later, I asked Dr. Williams why I can-
celed my appointments with him at this time. The confronta-
tion where he would give me a name for my disease was
inevitable.

"You were frightened that you had schizophrenia. You had
been exposed to the disease a bit when you did publicity for
How to Live with Schizophrenia, and also through stories
from your childhood of your grandmother's tragic end. As
long as you could avoid the label, you felt you still had a
chance to avoid the disease itself. Also, you were taught to be
heroic and self-sufficient, and that training interfered. You
thought through sheer will that you could fight off the illness, but in actuality, your efforts maintained and acceler-
ated your illness."

For six weeks, I didn't leave the apartment at all. I huddled on the floor of my bedroom in the dark, sobbing. I rocked

back and forth, clutching my knees, the carpet smell strong in my nose. I often fell asleep on the floor, crying.

Day and night ran together. Sometimes I slept for twenty-four or thirty-six hours at a time and woke up with all the lights blazing. I wasn't aware of the outside at all. I kept the draperies pulled. I often could not tell if it were morning or going into evening. I figured out the time and date by checking what was on television against the TV listings.

I couldn't stand sunlight or brightness. I had always loved to look at the palm trees and the sky, but I didn't want them anymore. I never crossed the street to look at the ocean, even when the ocean became the focus of suicidal fantasies. I slept my druglike sleep, rocked in anguish on the floor, or sat curled up in my old white terry-cloth robe, enduring attacks of panic and guilt.

I had nightmares. Terrible nightmares. Normally a happy dreamer, I'd grown fond of certain recurrent dreams, but these were terrifying dreams, lasting for hours.

The night terrors haunted me in my waking hours, as well. I tried to drag myself around the apartment to accomplish simple tasks. Make a phone call. Pay a bill. Where was my energy? It was like the dream where you're trying to run from danger, only your legs are too heavy and you can't. I felt like I was in quicksand. The nightmare followed me everywhere, like a smothering, swirling gray fog.

My mind saw no open doors. Now, every time the phone rang, my heart raced. I felt sick inside. I let the phone ring on and on, praying for it to stop. And when it finally did, the last ring seemed to echo off the walls. I felt even more anxious and agitated than before.

The mail was equally frightening. Boxes of it kept appearing on my kitchen floor. I tried to block out the terrible awareness of what those stacks of envelopes probably contained: lawyers' bills, dunning notices, credit card cancelations. I stuffed them into shopping bags and stacked the bags against the wall.

I tried to fight back. I had to produce something. A book, a play, a magazine article. I tried to write, but couldn't. I tried to organize material for future projects, but couldn't. I tried to conceive of moneymaking ideas, but couldn't.

The loss of my mental capabilities terrified me. Every passing hour taunted me: Another hour lost with nothing accomplished. Whereas earlier I had welcomed sleep as an escape from depression, I now feared sleep. Nothing could be accomplished unless I was awake and functioning. I assigned myself small tasks, like writing a letter, with the idea of denying myself sleep until the task was accomplished. I invariably failed. I would fall asleep and wake up hours later with my note pad on the floor at my feet. Sometimes I would wake up in bed, not remembering having moved from the living room. When drowsiness overwhelmed me, I would avoid the bedroom altogether and allow myself only a short nap on the living-room floor, hoping that the discomfort would cut my nap short. Instead, I would sleep for hours, and when I did awaken, it was always into that swirling gray fog.

In desperation, I made a few panicked trips into the glare of day to buy alarm clocks: a digital alarm clock with an electric buzzer; a little battery-powered clock; a red clock that told the time all around the world; a beautiful antique carriage clock; a Lucite alarm clock. Five, in all. Winding them kept me busy. I would gather them around my bed before risking a short nap, setting them all to go off at the same hour.

Somehow I slept through the alarms, even though my bedroom, at the designated hour, must have resounded with clanging, gonging, and buzzing.

Midnight in a clock shop.

I knew I didn't really want to die; I just wanted relief from the pain.

I didn't have access to a gun, sleeping pills, or "pleasant" poisons, and I didn't feel competent to carry out a violent suicide successfully. I feared that a car crash or a leap from a high place might leave me paralyzed or brain damaged. My suicidal fantasies centered, instead, on the ocean. I envisioned crossing the street and walking into the sea in the moonlight. I thought the ocean would be all velvety. Peaceful . . . dark . . . and private.

The urge to commit suicide ebbed and flowed, but the depression and anxiety did not. I lived each day in a stupor. Only Mif kept me going. He stayed by me, holding me, rocking me, insisting that I could, I *should*, survive. He tucked me into bed, washing away my tears with a cool cloth, handing me one of my teddy bears to cuddle. "Sleep," he said. "I will keep guard over you."

Mif urged me to call Moke, and I finally did make an appointment in a fake, bright cheerful voice, but I overslept on the day. Peggy Johnston, Moke's secretary, gave me a new date a month away. I felt relief, for in my twisted thinking I saw no purpose in taking up the doctor's time. The medication he had prescribed hadn't worked. How could he give me the character and strength to pull myself together? It was up to me to deal with my life. And if I didn't? I clung to the knowledge that I had the means to kill myself, just across the street. "The ocean won't go away," I whispered as I rocked on the floor in the dark.

"No," Mif said softly. "The ocean won't go away."

In June, my prolonged depression was aggravated by an unusually severe summer cold that hung on, settling solidly into my chest. I spent feverish days and nights huddled in my crumpled bed, sure that I had pneumonia, but too weak and miserable to do anything about it. Finally, after a particularly bad night I became alarmed enough to seek medical attention for what I told myself was the cold. But I didn't call Dr. Spivey, my internist. Instead, I made my first gesture of capitulation. I hadn't seen Moke Williams in weeks, but I finally got up the nerve to call his office.

"I have a cold that may be turning into pneumonia, and I'm feeling suicidal," I told Peggy. "I think I can handle it, but I'm not sure."

"You sound terrible, Terry," Peggy said. "Hold on a minute." She was back on the line in seconds. (I didn't realize it, but when a patient says he or she is thinking of suicide, it's like an eight-alarm fire alert in a psychiatrist's office.) "Dr. Williams doesn't want to take any chances. He wants you to check into the hospital down here immediately," she said. She added quickly, "It's not the mental hospital."

"I'm not that sick," I pleaded. "Can't he just see me?"

"Moke wouldn't tell you to go to the hospital unless he thought it was necessary, Terry. So do it." There was an unspoken "or else" in Peggy's command.

I didn't want to go to any hospital, but I felt dangerously ill, so I mumbled a defeated, "All right." I forced myself to dress, packed a few essentials in a shopping bag, and slipped quietly out my front door.

I managed to drive the thirty-five miles to Fort Lauderdale. I don't remember much about getting to the hospitals but I remember the panic when the admissions clerk took my valuables—my wallet, my credit cards, my keys. It was the surrendering of my keys that agitated me. They represented my only means of escape. I looked at them longingly as they went into an envelope to be locked away.

It was a pleasant hospital, posh and private. There were attractively framed pictures on the walls, palm trees outside, a vista of oceanfront buildings. From my room, I had a nice view of the Intracoastal Waterway with boats gliding along under a blue sky. They could have been corpses, for all the pleasure they gave me.

I had barely settled into the bed when Moke came striding

into the room. As always, he was elegantly dressed—a beautiful red tartan jacket, gray flannel slacks, white shirt and tie. He was very reassuring. "You're not in a mental hospital," he said. "You're going to be treated for your severe cold symptoms, and you will be sedated to relieve your anxiety and restlessness." He smiled. "Obviously, you're not doing a very good job of looking after yourself on your own. So we're going to do it for you."

I appreciated the effort he was making, but even I didn't believe in the pneumonia any longer. It was just a "cover" for my hospitalization. Moke was concerned with my suicidal depression. I was under observation.

There wasn't much to observe, really. The sedatives kept me knocked out most of the time, and my waking moments were devoted mostly to crying and sweating, a side effect from yet another antidepressant. I couldn't keep track of the days as they passed.

My friends and family had no idea where I was, but somehow word had circulated around the hospital that "J" was a patient. I would often awake to find strangers peering in at me—nurses, visitors, other patients. "Are you *really* 'J'?" they would ask.

I hated to admit that I was. I had ballooned to 156 pounds. My hair needed shampooing. My face was streaky and puffy from hours of sleeping and weeping. I was ugly, and I didn't want to be pleasant, but people lined up politely to peer at me and ask, "Are you 'J'?" I wasn't "J"—or anyone I knew anymore, but I wasn't capable of explaining this.

So I would croak wearily, "Yes, I'm 'J.'"

And that would satisfy them. They would go away.

I awoke to the sight of Moke sitting in a chair at the foot of my bed going over my charts. He was in surprisingly lively attire, a turquoise-, black-and-white striped jacket that needed only a straw hat and cane to complete the impression that he had just stepped out of the cast of *The Music Man*.

I dredged up a wan smile and a weak hello.

"You look terrible," he said pleasantly.

"I *feel* terrible," I replied, silently cursing the tears that were springing to my eyes. *Please, God, don't let me become a sobby sponge in front of him,* I prayed. *Or he'll think I'm a sniveling fool.*

"Since you feel terrible, why don't you give yourself permission to show it?"

"I do show it . . . when I'm alone," I said defensively.

"Why not with others?"

"Well, I don't really know."

"Yes, you do."

Was this any way to treat a sick person? "I want sympathy and magic medicines, not probes of my psyche," I said belligerently.

"Why don't you allow yourself to show your unhappy emotions to others?"

"Because it isn't nice."

Moke stared at me intently and continued to pursue his quarry. Why was this so important to him?

"It's bad manners to burden others with your personal problems unless they ask you to," I added.

"Who told you that?"

"Mother."

"Is that the only reason you conceal your unhappy emotions?"

"I don't *conceal* them, I just don't expose them. I'm not the flamboyant, volatile type." I took refuge in some nose blowing.

"Terry, you have to quit sparring with yourself and me so we can start dealing with your basic illness."

What was going on here?

"What would happen if you would let all your bad and frightening feelings loose, if you let them explode all over the place?"

"I would be out of control and would fall apart. I have to keep *some* control, Moke, or I couldn't function."

"But *are* you functioning? Terry, what you have been doing is something called masking." He paused to let this sink in.

"Masking?"

"Yes. You're perhaps the cleverest masker I have ever had as a patient. For a while you fooled even me."

"Fooled? I don't understand." I was genuinely puzzled.

"The image you have presented to me has always been a very happy one. You mask your real feelings with a happy face and manner. You submitted yourself for help, but hid your very real symptoms of a serious illness. You were willing to let me see only what you wanted me to see. If you will look back, in every session you have emphasized your depression and your reactions to medications, but resisted giving me any pertinent historical and personal information that could show a dark or flawed side of you and your life. By being unremittingly cheerful when you were really sad, you have suffered unnecessarily."

"But you wouldn't have wanted me to come in whining and complaining about all my nit-picking problems. I couldn't take up your time that way when the hour could be used for a patient who is really sick."

"*You* are really sick. And continuing to hide it from yourself and others won't make it go away," Moke said firmly.

Terror struck at my heart. My worst fear was going to be realized. "You're not going to tell me I'm a schizophrenic like Grandmother Stuart?" I whispered. "Is that why all the furniture in your office keeps appearing and disappearing?"

Moke looked at me blankly for a moment and then burst out laughing. "Did you think you were hallucinating?"

I nodded.

"Furniture actually *has* been going and coming in my offices. I just moved from a large house to an apartment, and I've been trying out some of the leftover pieces of furniture and some pictures from the house to see if they would fit into the office."

"Ohhh." I was greatly relieved. "Then I'm not a schizophrenic?"

"No. You have a cyclical, bipolar illness, with depression being the most severe of your two mood swings," he said gently. "Your high swing is hypomanic rather than hyperactive or manic, and is not a serious problem. Hypomania is similar to, but not as severe as mania, which is a state of exaggerated activity and excitement. When you are in this cycle you feel expansive, energized, particularly productive, gregarious, and overly optimistic, and this is what you have been calling your normal periods.

"Your low swing, your depression, is endogenous, which means it is due to changes in brain chemistry, not life circumstances. Stress can trigger the already existing disease, and does so in your case, but it isn't the *cause* in itself. You were born—genetically programmed—with the predisposition to endogenous depression, Terry. Just like diabetes 'runs' in some families. You can't think yourself in or out of diabetes, and you can't think your way in and out of endogenous depression. You have had mild biochemical mood swings for many years and probably could have gone through your whole life without it becoming a crippling disease, if you hadn't gone through a series of extreme stresses during a compact period of time. This caused your fragile chemistry to 'snap,' or give way, throwing you into a full-blown depressive disease. You will continue to have cycles of these biochemical depressions for the rest of your life."

I felt as if I had been struck across the face with a whip.

"We can't cure endogenous depression, Terry, but we can bring your symptoms under control with medications. As you are well aware, lithium and the various antidepressants we tried did not relieve your recurrent depression, but there is still a good chance we can treat you biochemically with a new drug called Anafranil, which is now being manufactured in Canada. I have it on order, and hope to have it for you within a few weeks."

I nodded again, incapable of speech.

"Anafranil still isn't an approved medication on the market in the United States, but we are obtaining some to see if our findings support Dr. José Yaryura-Tobias's clinical research project. He has evidence that it will help with obsessive-compulsive behavior as well as with depression."

My brain reeled. I was not only a cyclical-bipolar depressive, but an obsessive-compulsive as well?

Moke read my mind. "The shopping and eating, remember? Compulsive behavior can be a symptom as well as a disease in itself."

Moke went on talking soothingly for a while and then took himself off to check on more patients.

I sat in the skinny hospital bed staring dazedly at the identification tag on my left wrist as if it were the most fascinating object I'd ever seen.

I am mentally ill. I am a mental patient. For as long as I live I will carry this stigma. I was branded for life: Terry Garrity, mental patient.

An impenetrable glass wall had crashed down between me and the "normal" people of this world. I could look at them, I could hear them, but I could never break through the wall and join them ever again.

My sense of stigmatization was shattering, an irony that even in that horrible moment did not escape me. There I was, I who had prided myself on my sophistication about mental illness, feeling the very same feelings I had decried in others—shame, contamination. How easy it had been to stand on the outside and mouth well-meant humanistic phrases. I was a bigot: Mental illness was all right for others, but not for me.

I climbed down from the bed and padded into the bathroom to look in the mirror. My own, very familiar face reflected itself back at me. I didn't look any different. No wild eyes, no tics or distorted features, no frothing at the mouth. I couldn't tell by looking at me that I was mentally ill. And I hadn't been behaving like they did in books and movies, talking crazily, throwing glasses against mirrors, crashing vases of roses on the floor, suddenly sweeping everything off tables, going into violent, explosive rages without justification. For one second I thought, *Moke must be wrong in his diagnosis.* But no, I was mentally ill and would have to learn to face it. My medical records and the stigma would follow me as long as I lived, and I was helpless to change that. I watched my image in the mirror dispassionately as the first tears began to spill down my face and drip into the sink.

I just stood there until all the crying was over and then shuffled back to the bed to sit catatonically in the gathering darkness of nightfall. At some point a nurse came by and turned on the bedside lamp, gave me my medications, and took away my untasted food tray.

I turned off the lamp and lay back on the pillows, staring blindly into nowhere until late in the night when the heavy medication sucked me into sleep.

It had taken me a long time to accept the fact that I was mentally ill. Not everyone resists the truth as strongly as I did. Many people with my disease are so relieved to find an answer to their unnerving and crippling depressions that they almost embrace the diagnosis. I wasn't capable of doing that, but I knew my disease and I were going to have to come to terms with each other if we were going to live in the same body. To do that, I would have to learn as much as possible about my enemy.

17

*M*oke discharged me from the hospital a few days later. "Take this," he said, handing me a card with a schedule of future appointments. I looked at it carefully; I was to visit his office every Wednesday at eleven A.M.

"Try not to miss any appointments," he said, "and call me immediately, night or day, if there is any significant deterioration of your mood."

By his tone, I gathered that Moke was reluctant to send me home. He had recommended, more than once, that I wait for the arrival of the Canadian medicine at a nearby psychiatric facility, where I could be monitored around the clock. I had rejected his advice. I wasn't sure if my medical insurance policies covered psychiatric hospitalization. (I was, to be sure, equally concerned about the further stigmatization that would come with admission to a psychiatric hospital.)

"I don't like it that you're living alone with no one to look after you," Moke repeated, "so you'll have to promise me you'll call if there's any change."

"Oh, I will," I assured him.

"And I want you to read a book called *Moodswing* by Dr. Ronald Fieve. It is out in paperback."

"Who's the publisher?" I asked.

Moke smiled at my irrelevant question. "I don't know, but you'll have no problem finding it."

When he had gone, I piled my books and magazines and medications and other odds and ends into my shopping bags and walked, weak-kneed, down the corridors behind a nurse. At the cashier's window, I signed papers acknowledging huge debts to the hospital and to various unknown doctors. Then a clerk gave back my keys and sent me out into the sunshine, a certified mentally ill patient.

I did better at home, for a while. I still confined myself mostly to bed, but I opened the curtains and let the sun shine into my apartment (which was good for my few surviving plants). I called several friends on the telephone, told them the incomplete details of my hospitalization, and received flowers and cards in the mail. (I opened only the envelopes that looked like cards and hid the rest in those ever-present shopping bags.)

Moodswing: The Third Revolution in Psychiatry, the book Moke had recommended, was fascinating. Dr. Fieve was a psychoanalyst who had been unable to relieve the suffering of his manic-depressive patients through classical analysis or talk therapy. Frustrated, he had finally turned to psychopharmacology. He was now a psychiatrist who used drugs to, in his words, "alter or correct abnormal or faulty body chemistry."

Moodswing was filled with case histories of famous people who had endured crippling bouts of depression—Theodore Roosevelt, Abraham Lincoln, Ernest Hemingway, Winston Churchill. I was most deeply moved by theatrical producer Josh Logan's address to an American Medical Association symposium on depression. Logan had told them:

My first impression was that something had sneaked up on me. I had no idea I was depressed, that is, mentally. I knew I felt bad, I knew I felt low. I knew I had no faith in the work I was doing or the people I was working with, but I didn't imagine I was sick. It was a great burden to get up in the morning, and I couldn't wait to go to bed at night, even though I started not sleeping well. But I had no idea I had a treatable depression. I had no idea it was anything like a medical illness. I thought I was well but feeling low because of a hidden personal discouragement of some sort—something I couldn't quite put my finger on. If anyone had told me that I could walk into a hospital and be treated by doctors and nurses and various drugs and be cured, I would have walked in gladly and said, "Take me." But I didn't know such cures existed. I just forced myself to live through a dreary, hopeless existence that lasted for months on end before it switched out of the dark-blue mood and into a brighter color.

The part that really got me was the passage where Logan recalled his irritation with well-meaning friends who told him that he should "buck-up."

It seemed to me that all friends of the average human being in depression only know one cure-all, and that was a slap on the back and "Buck up." It's just about the most futile thing that could happen to you when you're depressed. My friends never even hinted to me that I was really ill. They simply thought that I was low and was being particularly stubborn and difficult about things. If anyone had taken charge and had insisted that I go to a mental hospital, I probably would have gone straight off. Instead, they simply said, "Please don't act that way. Please don't look at your life so pessimistically; it's not

so bad as you think. You'll always get back to it. Just
buck up.

I was amazed. Logan expressed exactly my own feelings of
frustration when well-meaning friends told me to "pull myself together" or exhorted me to "rush on to the end" of some
project or another. My friends, like Logan's, sometimes
thought me "stubborn and difficult about things."

A certain self-fascination replaced my earlier sense of stigmatization. I looked back on my teen-age years, and I saw
now that there was depression in my personality even then,
although the cycles were milder. I had been aware that my
energy levels varied dramatically. During the winter
months, I was more sluggish; tasks took more effort. I would
seek refuge in sleep, which was cavelike or womblike. *I must
have had it then,* I thought.

So what was the straw that broke the camel's back, that
turned my nascent depression into a full-blown, life-threatening mental disease? Was it *The Sensuous Woman,* with its
accompanying exhilaration and overexposure? The personal
trauma of being exposed to the vindictive antagonism of
those threatened by the idea of sexual pleasure? Was it taking these antagonisms personally, trying to please and pla-
cate while standing up for what I believed in? Was it my
mother's death and the feeling that I had disappointed her?
Was it my legal and emotional battles with Lyle Stuart? Was
it the loss of a stable love relationship and my romantic disil-
lusionment? Was it the loss of my capacity to bear children?
Trying to recreate the phenomenal success of *The Sensuous
Woman* by writing *Total Loving*?

There was no way to know, and it matters little now which
of these events broke me, finally. I never took the time to
absorb the effects, to recover; I never considered the possibility of crashing. The important question now was not

which straw broke the camel's back but how to rise up from the crash.

The case histories in *Moodswing*—manic depression and unipolar depression alike—had happy endings, thanks to lithium, the drug Dr. Fieve favored. The problem was—and this was disheartening—I had already tried lithium, and it had not worked for me. I wondered: Would the Canadian wonder drug be different?

"You have to hang on a little longer," Moke told me.

Except for my weekly drives to Fort Lauderdale, I kept to the security of my closed-off apartment. Whereas before I had fought my disability, struggling to write, resisting sleep, I now settled into being sick. The weight of responsibility seemed lifted off me.

I watched a lot of TV. I sat on the floor in front of the TV set and played solitaire for hours at a time. (Superstitiously, I had decided that a run of good luck with the cards would signal an upswing in my overall fortunes, so I played hand after hand at a hypothetical five dollars per card, losing thousands and thousands of imaginary dollars to an imaginary bank.) On the screen, Mike Douglas, Merv Griffin, Phil Donahue, and Dinah Shore interviewed dozens, hundreds, thousands of guests, while I played solitaire in a daze.

Two weeks passed, three weeks, then a month. The medicine from Canada did not arrive.

Every now and then, someone on a talk show would refer to "J" or to *The Sensuous Woman,* and my sense of unreality would deepen. One night, while again playing solitaire, I heard actress Susan Sullivan say something favorable about my book on *The Tonight Show.* That made me cry. Other times, as I watched bleary-eyed, I saw myself featured as an answer on *Hollywood Squares* or *Jeopardy* or one of the other daytime game shows. I took no pleasure in these faint reminders of celebrity. I no longer felt that I was "J." Or even

Terry Garrity. I had become somebody else, a rather grotesque person. I felt Quasimodo-ish—overweight, my hair falling out, heavy spirited . . .

When I passed a mirror, I looked away.

But then, I didn't need a mirror. My apartment was the mirror of my condition. The illness had sapped my organizing energies, and I no longer seemed able to cope with ordinary housecleaning and tidying up.

In the past, my living areas had reflected an almost compulsive neatness. By nature, I was a picture-straightener. For years, everything had its place, and if someone moved one of my knickknacks or a piece of furniture just a fraction of an inch, I could spot it. My tabletops had outlines in the finish where ashtrays, paperweights, and books were carefully repositioned after each dusting.

Now, my rooms were in maddening disarray, and I had ceased caring. I just stepped over and around the debris, putting off cleaning up until the Anafranil arrived, until I was well again. I felt suspended in time, emotion, and action.

I don't recall that anything specific triggered it. But suddenly, one night, I plunged into absolute, total despair. The gray fog collected around me, and the nightmare feeling possessed me. I felt a horrible sense of shame, a conviction that I was a complete failure as a human being.

It was pitch-black in my bedroom, and I was curled up in a ball again on the floor, sobbing and whimpering. I had reached the end of my ability to battle the idea of committing suicide. I felt an overpowering urge to step outside, to cross the street, to drag myself across the narrow strip of beach in the moonlight, and to plunge into the dark ocean, swimming straight out into the night until I was exhausted, and drowned.

Something inside me was still saying no, that I should

live. But I ignored it. If it had been daytime, I might have called Moke, but it was after midnight. The phone was right above me on the bed. There were friends in New York I might call. But I couldn't face them. I had withdrawn from relationships for too long. I truly believed that I was about to die, that the ocean was my only salvation. Miss "J," in 2-A, was checking out.

Why did I leave the bedroom? I don't remember. I must have stumbled through the clutter in the dark, blind and scared, hitting things and making anguished noises in my throat. I must have reached inside the kitchen door and felt for the light switch. There was another phone there, over the kitchen counter. I somehow must have punched up the number from memory, the long-distance number I had called so often late at night, the number of the only person I knew who would probably still be awake at that hour, the one person, other than Moke, I was apparently willing to confess my shame to.

The phone rang several times—I flicked off the light; I panicked; I started to hang up—but finally there was a click on the other end. "Hello?" a sleepy voice said.

"Johnny?" I croaked, using his childhood name, which only the family used. "*Help* me!" I could barely get the words out, between sobs. "I don't think I can go on anymore . . . I need help . . ."

There was a brief silence on the line, and then the rushing noise of a bad connection. It sounded, in my ear, like the pounding of surf.

18

Johnny won't soon forget that night.

It was the night of a great electrical storm that tore through Kansas City, uprooting trees and downing power lines. The storm had passed, but much of the city was without power in the hours after midnight. With no lights or air conditioning in his house, Johnny had given up his stuffy bedroom and was sleeping on the floor by his open front door, trying to catch the feeble breeze. When the phone rang, he had stumbled groggily to the kitchen, bumping into furniture in the darkness, cursing incoherently.

"I didn't recognize your voice," he told me later. "It didn't even sound quite like a voice, just a strangled choking sound. At first, I thought it was a crank call."

I don't remember much about the call, except that Johnny remained very calm, very patient, and very reassuring. "You did exactly the right thing by calling," he said soothingly. "Whatever the problem is, you're going to get help for it. You're not alone, and you must remember that. You've got friends who will be at your side in an instant, if that's what's needed."

I choked and sputtered, trying to explain my breakdown. "Johnny, I—I—I don't think I can hold on . . . any longer. . . . I just want to die . . ." I collapsed into another fit of weeping.

"Slow down," he said. "Try to relax. Take some deep breaths and don't talk for a bit."

I followed his suggestion, and my breathing started to come more evenly. "I've been fighting it for days," I finally said. "I think I'm going to walk into the ocean and drown"—I choked again—"myself."

"Don't," he said simply.

"I don't think I can help myself." I cried in a pinched, little girl's voice.

Johnny had no training in suicide prevention, but instinct told him to keep me talking, to maintain contact with me as long as possible. He kept asking me questions, pumping me for details about my confusion, my compulsions, my financial nightmares, all the frightening shadows that had me crying in the dark like a scared child.

When he had me calmed down enough to listen, he began taking charge. "I'm going to fly down there," he said. "I'll do whatever I can to help you put your life back in order. I'll go through the bills, I'll clear out the guest room, I'll help you simplify things."

"Would you?" I asked weakly. "Oh, thank God."

"Okay, but listen, Terry. I'm not coming today."

I felt a wave of alarm. "But—"

"Let me finish. I'm not coming today because I don't want you sitting there in the dark for ten hours with no one to talk to. I want you to go see your doctor tomorrow. If you can sleep till morning, then sleep. If you can't sleep, then stay by the phone. If you start to panic, if you have to talk to someone, call me. I won't leave the house. I won't go to the airport until I know you're safely in your doctor's hands."

"I don't want to die," I murmured.

"I know you don't."

"I'm so ashamed. I feel so guilty."

"Why?" he asked.

"Because I'm so weak. Because I've made such a botch of my life."

There was a pause. "Terry, are you in the dark?"

"Pardon?"

"I'm standing in my kitchen in the dark and you're standing in your kitchen in the dark. I can't do anything about the darkness at this end, but you might try turning on a light."

I felt around on the wall for the switch. Suddenly, the light came on, and my swollen eyes blinked.

"What do you see?" he asked.

"Bankruptcy," I said with a thin laugh.

"Good," he said.

"Good?" What could be good about bankruptcy?

"You laughed," he explained.

I made it until morning. Moke took me in immediately. I again adamantly refused to be admitted to a psychiatric facility, so he prescribed a heavy sedative to calm me and let me sleep, and sent me back home to wait for Johnny's arrival later that day.

This time Johnny did not bring barbecue. But he didn't bring any painful bromides, either—lines like, "Think of all the people with real problems," or, "Pull yourself together." He was wise enough not to add to my feelings of guilt and inadequacy.

Instead, after consulting with Moke, he began the task of reordering my chaotic environment. I remember—and this is one of my few clear memories of this time—Johnny standing in the doorway of the Dorian Gray Room, awestruck by the boxes, the clothes on hangers, the dozens of stuffed shopping bags that blocked his entry. The bags were overflowing with bills, magazines and catalogs, unanswered letters, and forgotten purchases.

I smiled wanly. "Overwhelming, isn't it?"

He shook his head.

"Leaves you speechless?"

He nodded.

Johnny began clearing a path into the center of the room, piling shopping bag on top of shopping bag. He winced as one whole mound started to slide toward my desk.

"Timmmmm-berrrrr!" I said, trying to be funny.

He seemed uncertain about where to begin. "Do you have any boxes?"

I went to the kitchen and came back with some cardboard cartons that my groceries had been delivered in. "Will these do?"

"Those are perfect," he said, resting them atop a heap of goods.

"Are you sure you wouldn't prefer shopping bags?"

"No, Terry." He grunted as he nearly fell over a bed trying to move a sack full of paperback books. "Shopping bags are the problem."

"That's funny." I frowned. "I thought they were part of the solution."

I watched television or slept while Johnny toiled in the guest room. Every few minutes he would come out with a letter or a legal document or a magazine clipping, asking, "Do you need to save this?"

I would examine the item closely, and then say, "Oh, yes, I was saving that for the book on orthodontics," or, "Yes, that has the wonderful vegetable dicer that looks like a miniature sawmill."

He came staggering into the living room with a pile of mail-order catalogs that reached his chin. "I thought—" he muttered through clenched teeth, "you might—*oooof!*" He lowered the stack to the floor. "Go through these."

"Oh," I said, bemused. "You want me to buy something?"

"No," he said, looking pained. "I want you to throw them out."

He disappeared again.

When he returned, I had gone through most of the pile and was thumbing contentedly through a catalog from the Cheese of the Month Club. "Are those ready to throw out?" he asked, wiping the sweat from his forehead.

"These are," I said, pointing to a small pile at my feet.

"What about those?" Johnny pointed at the more substantial mound beside my chair.

"Those I'm saving."

He did not move, except for his eyes, which darted nervously, and his fingers, which he drummed on his thighs.

"I can't throw away the Horchow catalogs," I pleaded. "They're beautiful."

"But you get a new one every season. And what about these?" He grabbed a handful of another company's catalogs. "And these?"

"Those are for my paperweights," I said. "I *have* to save those. Otherwise I can't keep track of the value of my collection."

Johnny shook his head and returned to the guest room.

Later, I looked up and Johnny was in the kitchen, stuffing things into a plastic garbage bag. "Stop!" I cried. "What are you doing?" I rushed across the room.

He looked up, bewildered.

"That's a shopping bag!"

"This?" He pulled a wrinkled Bloomingdale's bag out of the trash. "It *was* a shopping bag. Now, it's garbage."

"No, it's perfectly good." I took it from him and tried to smooth out the wrinkles. "These are valuable. I never throw them out unless they have holes in them, or spots."

"But, Terry, you've got dozens of shopping bags." His voice rose. "You can't even *walk* around here for the shopping bags."

I took my treasure, the Bloomingdale's bag, to the hall closet and opened the louvered doors. "I'll just put this with the others," I said firmly. I forced it in among the dozens of plastic and lacquered-paper shopping bags I had collected on my travels, bags from Gucci and Bergdorf's, bags from Jordan Marsh and Lord & Taylor and Halls' Crown Center, bags from Elizabeth Arden's, bags which, folded, took up two shelves of closet space and half the floor.

Johnny watched me in dismay. "Terry, not opening your mail because of the bills, I can identify with that. Not answering your phone—hey, I envy you. I can see eating ice cream all day and staying up all night. But not being able to throw away a beat-up old shopping bag?" He shook his head. "I'm sorry, Terry. That's *sick*."

"That's not sick," I said. "It's practical."

Johnny didn't think so. The next day, he began carting material out of the guest room and arranging things in piles on the living-room floor. There were piles for department store bills, piles for credit card receipts, piles for legal memorandums from Don Engel, piles for newspaper clippings about me and my books, piles for things clipped from magazines, and, most of all, piles of magazines. "Terry, how many magazines are you receiving?" Johnny sat on the floor, gazing in awe at the skyline of periodicals he had created at my feet.

"Only those I need," I said, somewhat defensively.

"Are you aware that you subscribe to forty-odd magazines?"

"No!" I was astonished.

"Minimum."

Johnny held up a copy of the *National Review*. "Do you actually read this?"

"Sometimes," I said in a weak voice.

"*Cosmopolitan? Soap Opera Digest? Interview Magazine?*"

"Oh, that's the Andy Warhol paper. It's really strange."

Johnny did some quick figuring in his head. "Terry, do you realize you must be spending, what? Seven hundred? Eight hundred? A thousand dollars a year just for magazines?"

I was shocked. "No, I couldn't be."

"You don't need all these magazines."

"But I do need them. For my research."

"Terry, you don't have to buy all your research materials. Use the library."

I laughed. "Have you ever tried to use the West Palm Beach public library? They don't have anything!"

Johnny suddenly looked very tired. It was obvious that he was frustrated by my combativeness and wished he had started cleaning house when I was still weak and suicidal. "Well," he said. "What can I throw out?"

"Throw out?" I sat bolt upright, as if he had suggested chopping down redwoods or drowning kittens. "You want to throw these *out*?"

The shopping bags and magazines were, of course, symbolic. They reflected my confusion, and they reflected the horrifying degree to which material things had substituted for an emotional life since my breakup with Len.

What really worried Johnny and Moke, though, was my spending. I had left a trail of debts across the continental United States, and the piles of bills on the living-room floor read like a suicide note. "If there is a department store somewhere that you didn't visit," Johnny said, "they must be very hurt."

The beds, too, were covered with invoices, receipts, statements, dunning notices, attorneys' letters. "It's all of a pattern," he said. "In every city you hit the 'name' department store. In San Francisco it was I. Magnin. In Philadelphia it was John Wanamaker's. In Kansas City it was Halls' Crown Center. In Dallas it was Neiman-Marcus. Your purchases ranged from as low as ten dollars to as high as seven hundred dollars, but mostly they were in the two hundred dollar range."

I was dumbfounded.

"Was it fun?" Johnny asked. He sounded genuinely interested, not judgmental at all.

"I don't know," I said. "I don't remember it." I looked at the piles of paper on the bed and swallowed hard. "Do I owe all that?"

"To be honest, I don't know." He shrugged. "I think a lot of these have been paid."

"Who paid them?"

"You did."

"I don't remember paying them." I felt absolutely helpless, like a child. "Am I ruined?"

"Almost," he said.

Johnny remained two weeks, toiling among the artifacts of my crazed past. He was also keeping a discreet eye on me to be sure I didn't become suicidal again. He decamped with great relief when Moke's office called to tell me the good news: that the new antidepressant had finally arrived. "It doesn't look that bad," Johnny said, surveying my apartment one last time before leaving. In truth, my affairs were more orderly than they had been in years: My papers were filed away, the shopping bags were emptied and neatly folded.

Now it was up to Anafranil and Moke Williams to pull me together so that I could take charge of my life again.

"Anafranil," Moke said, handing me a bottle of little yellow pills, "does have some side effects."

"Yes?" I asked apprehensively.

"Notably, increased sweating and drowsiness." He saw me

flinch. "But if it proves effective as an antidepressant, we can begin to return you to some semblance of normalcy."

Some increased sweating and drowsiness? Moke was a master of understatement. Two days after starting Anafranil, I was a walking steam bath. I couldn't put on clothes because they soaked through in minutes. I had to cover my chairs and bed with towels; I wrapped myself in togas improvised from beach towels; I carried towels around the apartment. As for the "drowsiness," I felt like I was under operating room anesthesia. I sweated and slept, sweated and slept, and continued to feel depressed.

I had to call Moke. "I don't think I can stand this," I said, holding the phone with a dry washcloth so that it didn't slip out of my perspiring hand.

The master of understatement pondered. "It's true that not many people have been willing to tolerate the unpleasant side effects of Anafranil," he said. "But, Terry, you have to try. It's all we have for you right now. And the side effects will abate somewhat in a few weeks."

A few weeks! I took a fresh towel and sopped up the perspiration dripping off my hair. Then I fell back into another nightmare-ridden slumber.

Days went into weeks with no change.

Twice a week now, I drove to Fort Lauderdale for sessions at Moke's office. I had to cover the car seat with towels, and I wore a tennis sweatband around my head so the perspiration would not blind me while I drove. I wore driving gloves to make sure my hands would not slip on the wheel.

"You're a writer," Moke pointed out one afternoon. "Since you're having trouble talking to me, why don't you write about what you've experienced?"

I dreaded the idea. I still couldn't string a complete sentence together, and besides, I didn't feel like contemplating my past. "Let me think about that," I said, borrowing time.

With Mif, I was more open. I shared with him my guilt about the responsibilities I had failed to meet; I told him how I had ridden to the brink of financial ruin; how I was still crippled by my past disappointments in love; how I was using food as a substitute for love and sex.

Again, I knew that Mif was imaginary, but I seemed to need a comforting presence, some authoritative figure to assuage my feelings of guilt. Mif sat with me for hours at a stretch, helping me sort through my recriminations and fears. He tried to make me see that much of what had happened to me had not been my fault; that it was the illness that had robbed me of my talents for living, not a hidden self-destructiveness or weakness of character. "But nobody *knows* that," I protested. "People think I'm a bad person. If I say I'm sick, they think I'm just making an excuse. If you've had surgery, they'll listen to the gory details, but no one wants to hear what you're suffering mentally. They like the idea of sending boxes of chocolates, holding hands at the hospital bed, sending flowers, a cheery call or two, and a few get-well cards. But then they want to get *free* of it; they want you to get well and not have to think about you."

"It's human nature," Mif said.

"Yes, but mental illness isn't like having your appendix out. It keeps going on . . . and on . . . and on."

When I took this same complaint to Moke—I finally confessed to anger and resentment because nobody "understood" my problem or did anything to help—he was sympathetic, but not surprised. "Even people who are your closest friends may not be able to do that for you," he said. "They become uncomfortable themselves and pull away. People generally do not know how to help a person who is mentally ill. It is not part of our education, socially, to know how to act."

"If they would only *listen*," I said, "and ask questions, instead of just saying, 'I'm on your side.' If they would only say, 'I may not be able to completely understand what you are going through, but tell me about it.' That would help a lot."

"Have you told them that?"

I pondered. "No. They wouldn't understand."

He smiled. "I've got another patient like you, Terry. He, too, is a great falsifier. He will never let anybody know that he is really depressed. He's going to die rather than let people see he's depressed."

"What good would it do him to moan and groan?" I countered. "Isn't it part of our stoic upbringing to keep these things to ourselves, to keep up appearances? My mother raised me to believe that you don't burden other people with your problems."

Moke stared at me without comment. Finally, I said, "All right. I get your message. I carry it to extremes. What about your other patient? Why does *he* mask his depression?"

He looked thoughtful. "Sometimes there is the identification of someone—family or friend—who suffers from an emotional disturbance. You don't wish to be seen as those people are seen; you have negative recall of those people. You therefore vow not to be 'like my mother' or 'like my father' or your aunt or whomever it may be in the hereditary line."

The image flashed in my mind of Grandmother Stuart—the tipsy autocrat stuffing herself with chocolates and losing touch with reality—and I nodded uncertainly.

"Think about it," Moke said.

When I got home, I did think about it. I tried to forgive my friends for not understanding my illness; I tried to forgive myself for not understanding my friends.

One day, Moke showed me the personality sketch Jacque Thompson had sent him. "Was that me?" I asked in surprise. "Sense of humor? Bubbly? Up personality?"

"Read the whole thing," ordered Moke.

The first impression of Terry I recall was that of an extremely well organized person—frighteningly well organized. I say "frighteningly" because she seemed to or-

ganize everything—emotional, moral, situational, or otherwise. Furthermore, she did not appear to be the kind of person who would be satisfied to merely implement someone else's decisions. She seemed to be itching to be the decision maker herself.

She also struck me as a quick study, in theater terminology; somebody who learns from everyone with whom she comes in contact and eventually outstrips them at their own game, whatever it might be. I could see glimpses of what Terry would become even then.

I remember thinking of Terry as a "solid" person, someone I could introduce to my family without anyone wondering where I'd dug up this weirdo. (Terry and I both knew plenty of people at this point in our lives. In fact, many were mutual friends responsible for our meeting in the first place.) I grew up in a home where the puritan ethic and an absolute, inflexible brand of honesty prevailed. Although Terry didn't have as rigid a definition of honesty as my parents, she was ambitious, hard working and principled. She differed from them in that she was ambitious in a larger cosmos—she was not willing to be a big fish in a small pond, but wanted to be a big fish in a big pond.

Secondly, she tempered her hard work with pleasure and fun: romantic interludes, nutty schemes involving her friends, dinner parties mixing a diverse assortment of people.

Terry always had a tremendous sense of humor and to this day giggles and laughs a lot. I think that ability comes from the fact that Terry has somehow managed to emotionally distance herself from her own life better than the average person. Whether that's good or bad, I don't know. I think at the times when Terry is so distraught that she loses that ability, she hides out, retreats from all contact with others. There are very few times in my rela-

tionship with her—even when she's told me she's de-pressed (I never would have known it from the way she was behaving)—when I have seen her manifest what would generally be accepted as outward symptoms of de-pression and anxiety. She seems to maintain an iron grip on herself most of the time. It's as if she's afraid to appear vulnerable to the world at large. I suspect it is easier for her to show this out-of-control, emotional side to boy-friends than it is to other women, however.

I am not saying that Terry projects a cold, forbidding, and standoffish image. To the contrary, I think most peo-ple would describe her as warm, fun-loving, fast-talking and glib in a very Irish sense, wholesome, and approach-able. I think men may sense her "vulnerability" more than other women, who may have trouble seeing beyond her businesswoman, superefficient persona, at least on first meeting. I think romance and Terry's "vulnerability" are strongly linked in some way. That's why men can manipulate her much better than women. I should qualify that and say "men with whom she is romantically involved" can manipulate her because of the value she places on romance, the almost adolescent "floating on cloud nine" variety. "Chemistry" in her relationship with a man is extremely important to her.

What are Terry's vulnerabilities? That's hard to say even for someone like myself who supposedly knows her well. Her insecurities are something she is extremely suc-cessful at hiding. Even when she is unsure of her ability to perform some function—let's say, give a speech—she has an amazing drive and inner resiliency that (1) forces her to attempt many of the things she feels insecure about and (2) brings her through the ordeal on top. That's one thing that's always astonished me about her. Terry will present a certain stereotype of herself as, for instance, a person who isn't physically coordinated and can't do any sports activity well. The next thing you know, she's gone out and become a tennis player, maybe no Chris Evert, but passable, and certainly not as awful as you would expect from what she'd always told you about herself. In short, I've never seen her fail miserably at anything that involved skills that could be learned, rather than purely emotional "tasks." She has failed at romances, for instance, but never at other types of challenges.

Which brings me, perhaps, to one of the most important ingredients of Terry's makeup: her pragmatism and analytical ability (in my opinion, the two go hand in hand). I really identify with this side of Terry's nature because I'm oriented that way myself.

Terry is fascinated with how things work—whether the "things" are people, situations, or skills. Once she figures out how something works, she immediately moves on to what she is going to do about it. Is she going to step in and try to make the "thing" work better? And she usually can't resist doing this, a trait which many people find annoying to deal with, I dare say. I've found it annoying myself on occasion. Or Terry might take a slightly different tact—How am I going to use this "thing" to my advantage? What use is it? In short, Terry is not a person who can sit back and reflect on something and eventually get her thoughts in order about it and then leave it at that. She has to take the next step and use it in some way. Writing is a good outlet for her in that she can channel many of her practical ideas and observations into self-help "recipes" for others to use to better their lives.

Again, I get back to what is probably a key point: When Terry perceives herself as failing at something, she hides out. Her friends tend to hear about the failure when it's past, something she can talk about in retrospect. If Terry ever discusses her problems mid-disaster, it is usually be-

cause she doesn't perceive the problem as a disaster as yet. She still thinks she has it under control, and possibly she's coming to you for advice on how to handle it.

I think it is only at these times, when she feels she's on shaky ground, that she really takes to heart the advice she solicits from her friends. Normally, Terry is quite independent and makes her own decisions on important personal matters, particularly concerning her love life. Legal, financial, and other technical areas are another matter. In those spheres, she consults "experts."

Again, her reliance on friends' advice has changed somewhat over the years. When I first met Terry—long before her Sensuous Woman celebrityhood—she went to her friends quite frequently for advice and support, but she was always very discriminating in whom she chose. If she had a problem in the emotional sphere, she would pick out the one person, of all her acquaintances, most able to advise her on that particular problem. As she became a celebrity, a supposed "authority" on her subject, sex, she gradually became more of an "authority" about everything, including how to run her own life. This is the only way I think Terry's celebrity status changed her appreciably. The expert, authoritative persona she had to acquire to be an effective saleswoman for her book on talk shows spilled over into her personal life. Even though inside Terry may not have felt any more secure or sure of herself, she certainly gave that appearance to those of us on the outside looking in. Maybe it was just superficial changes that gave me this impression—a better-modulated voice, strong gestures, careful organization of thoughts before she spoke—all skills she had to perfect to be a good guest on talk shows. All I'm saying is, the overall effect was that of a woman who was extremely self-assured and less willing to listen to or even solicit the advice of others.

I think as Terry's celebrity status has become less of a novelty and more an integral part of her personality and she has had to face major personal and financial difficulties, she has returned to the less in control, less assured Terry. Unfortunately, her fame and money have brought with them enormous problems, problems it would be difficult for anyone to handle well. Terry has been forced to wrestle with these traumas and, perhaps for the first time in her life, her miscalculations, bad decisions, and mistakes are showing, and she can't hide them. She's lost some of that iron control she once had over her life when her life was simpler, more average and normal. I think this is extremely unsettling for her, as I am sure it would be for me. (I've probably gone beyond the scope of what I was asked to write with this amateur psychoanalysis.)

I think Terry's success with The Sensuous Woman *has given her a rude awakening about human greed. I think on a subconscious level she's seen herself transformed in some people's estimation from a friend or girl friend to meal ticket. I think some of her traumatic experiences involving other people's reactions to her money have left her more cynical about people's motives in general. Terry was never a Pollyanna, but she had blind spots about what certain people were capable of in terms of lying, cheating, etc. Even today, I doubt bitterness is a feeling Terry would ascribe to herself. But I think she has plenty of cause to feel bitter; and also to examine the "blind spots" that helped her into bad situations to start with.*

Cynicism and bitterness are two emotions diametrically opposed to Terry's basic persona—which remains intact, from what I could judge on the phone this week. She is still able to laugh and discuss her despair and suicidal feelings as a thing apart, something she can subject to close scrutiny and analysis and thereby conquer.

I'll close with a string of other adjectives that apply to Terry and probably don't need further elucidation: loyal, curious, bubbly (like champagne), an up personality, friendly, poised, trustworthy, intelligent (particularly in her analytical ability), quick, and stubborn.

Maybe I should describe what I mean by stubborn. Terry is very principled and, at the same time, strong willed. The net result often makes her appear extremely stubborn, which she can be. When she becomes obstinate on an issue, there is only one way to make her change her mind—and that's through reason; and even at that, she has to want to let you change her mind. If you can give her good, solid, logical reasons why she is wrong, you can sometimes persuade her of the error of her ways. But because she is an excellent debater (another strong trait of hers), you'll never convince her unless you're a good debater yourself. One of her favorite ploys is to answer your question with a question. It's hard to put her on the spot, in other words, when she doesn't want to be put on the spot.

> Jacqueline Thompson
> New York City
> July 14, 1978

I looked up, bemused. "How strange. I barely remember the person Jacque is describing. Will I ever be this Terry again?"

"Not exactly. Endogenous depressives can regain their functioning abilities. They won't be disabled. They are 'cured' in that respect. But I think the impact of an illness of such long duration and that striking in its effect—the experiential factor—leaves a person permanently changed. As far as biochemical functioning, there are people who, once they are well, can be taken off the antidepressants. We teach them the early signs of depression so we can restart the medication immediately if the disease begins to reappear. In some people, it never does.

"In your case, Terry, the hurricane that came through your life caused a lot of destruction. You will never be the 'old Terry' again, but in many ways you can be better—more balanced, healthier, and happier. Those are our goals."

I waited . . . and waited . . . and waited for the Anafranil to take hold. Days went by, then weeks, and I lost hope again. I feared that I was tumbling into that abyss of despair and self-hatred. "There is no way out," I told Mif woodenly. "No way out."

And then gradually, very gradually, I began to notice a change.

19

*I*magine a fog so dense and so vast that you could walk for days without escaping its clammy wrap.

Imagine that you had stumbled in the darkness so long—your ears straining for clues to safety, your eyes probing the swirling mists to no avail—that you had finally succumbed to despair.

Imagine that you sat down and cradled your head in your hands and wept.

And then imagine that you finally lifted your head and, through swollen, tear-filled eyes, saw the fog somehow lifting, saw the shape of the land and the outlines of trees, and saw a large, undefined brightness filtering through the mists above you . . .

One day I noticed I wasn't perspiring steadily. I was able to stay awake longer.

And one evening, while I sat on the floor playing solitaire and half-watching *M**A*S*H on TV, I heard a strange sound and felt a peculiar sensation in my throat and chest. It was laughter. I had laughed—spontaneously, fully, out loud.

Was I getting well?

Moke wasn't sure. "Your illness is marked most characteristically by its depressive aspect," he told me, "but there is still that noticeable part which is a hypomanic state."

As usual, I rejected the notion that I ever had "highs." "I've never had unbounded energy," I insisted, "where I can just go on and on without flagging. Except for limited periods, of course, or some really exciting project. And it has to be a project where the end is in sight. . . ." I noticed that Moke was smiling at me. "On the other hand," I said less certainly, "I *am* a deadline writer. I do like to finish a project all at once, make a marathon of it. Is that hypomanic, Moke?"

He nodded. "I would think so. You don't have a total loss of control and you aren't running down the street, that sort of thing, but you show signs of hyperactivity, exaggerations, compulsive behavior."

"Then—" I hesitated. "Maybe I'm not getting well? I may just be on my upswing?"

"It's possible. Anafranil is a disappointment in one way, because it isn't controlling your compulsive behavior as research seemed to indicate it would, but Anafranil is giving you sufficient relief from your depressive symptoms so that we can now attack the stresses that trigger your episodes."

I stared at him blankly, more confused than before. "But, Moke, if I have a biochemical illness . . . what does that have to do with stress? I thought we discarded stress as a cause of my depression?"

With infinite patience, Moke tried to clarify what I saw as a paradox. "We know that it's cyclical. From your history we can even chart it, after a fashion. We know your severely depressed period is February through May, give or take a few weeks. We know the episodes are going to happen every

year. But how severe they're going to be, how long they're
going to last, that's the part that stress plays. It's somewhat
like predicting the weather. We know that a storm is coming, but we don't know exactly when or where or if it will get
out of hand."

"Then, my notoriety . . . the lawsuits with Lyle . . . my
breakup with Len . . . they *did* play a part in my depression?"

"I would think so. Stress can trigger episodes. It can cause
ordinary cycles to happen earlier and it can make them last
longer. And, of course, being depressed and unable to function well becomes a stress in itself. In your case, I think all
those major stresses camouflaged or unfocused the cyclical
nature of your illness, covered it up quite a bit. That and
your habitual masking of your true feelings and the concealment of your symptoms delayed the diagnosis."

I was a little dismayed by what Moke was telling me. I had
welcomed Anafranil as a wonder drug that would "cure" me
overnight. Now he was telling me that it was merely a medication that might ease my passage through suicidal depressions; it would not make me "stress-proof" or eternally
happy. I wasn't going to get well simply by taking a pill—I
was going to have to rearrange my life.

"*Education* is the best word for it," Moke told me. "You
have to learn what types of stress are the most dangerous for
you, how much stress you can deal with, what stresses can
trigger your cycles. You have to learn better how to tune into
your own state, how to identify your cycles and plan your life
around them. For example, I have a patient who is very
much a perfectionist, an extremely active surgeon, aggressive, hypomanic. He isn't a true manic, in the sense of thinking so fast and acting so fast that he is ineffectual, but he is
much more highly energized, and therefore achieves more,
is more accomplished than the average person, because he is
pouring so much more energy into his work. But then he hits

that block at the end where his energy system can no longer sustain itself and he falls off a cliff into the valley of depression, and there he will stay for several months. Like you, lithium did not control his mood swings, so he is having to learn to moderate his activities during hypomanic stages so that he doesn't exhaust himself, push himself into a depressive cycle, and suffer it more intensely because he's trying to fulfill commitments his hypomanic self agreed to and his depressive self is too depleted to handle. Balance and moderation are possible even when hypomanic or depressive cycles are tugging away at you.

"For years now, you have seen yourself as a victim, buffeted by forces beyond your control, and to a great extent that was true. But your illness has made you childlike, an immature person again. When a person becomes sick, he or she necessarily becomes dependent upon others—medicines, doctors, nurses, others. Your world shrinks. *You* are the world. And nothing else really matters. Typically, the sick person becomes narcissistic, self-indulgent, helpless, demanding. Just because you're walking around and people don't see the gaping wounds or scars doesn't make mental illness any different from other illnesses. Severely sick people almost invariably become childish and dependent. You will move out of your dependencies and be assertive again as your mood continues to lighten. You're ready now to begin psychotherapy to help you put your shattered life back together again. The disease was so all encompassing, so catastrophic for so long, that there is very little of your old world left. Your life-style, your habits, your social and emotional structures must all be rebuilt. And Terry and 'J' must be blended into one person."

And so, with Moke as my guide, I began, haltingly, to explore my feelings and reorder my life. I learned to recognize the danger signals—the lethargy, the passiveness, the sense of being overwhelmed by outside demands. I became more aware of my hypomanic states, too. Now, when the intense craving to shop swept over me, I went to a bookstore and spent the afternoon thumbing through books, allowing myself only paperback purchases. I fought off the temptation to buy multiple Christmas presents for all my friends and relatives. I began balancing my own checkbook again, rather than sending the bills to Arthur in New York. Knowing exactly where I stood financially made me feel more in control; bad news was easier to handle if I could see its boundaries.

"The food binges are harder to handle," I reported to Moke. "Food has always been a source of pleasure for me. It always will be. When I feel low, I can't help giving in to the desire for something absolutely delicious and bad for me."

He tap, tap, tapped his pen on the desk.

"Food is *pleasurable*," I said in a pleading voice.

"Part of the treatment," Moke reminded me, "is to identify the stresses that are most dangerous to you. We've learned that you get particularly upset if you don't feel in command of your life. Losing that sense of control creates an enormous stress for you, and if you can't control your eating . . . or your shopping . . ." He looked at me as if he expected me to finish his sentence.

"Are you saying that even pleasurable activities can be stressful? That the things I enjoy most can trigger my depressions?"

He nodded.

My compulsive attachment to possessions was not unlike my compulsive shopping. Johnny had cleared the jungle in my guest room of its heaviest growth, but there were things I had not let him dispose of—the shopping bags, for instance— and things of genuine value I had no place for. My closets bulged with size-eight and -ten designer clothes hanging on their original hangers, price tags still dangling from buttons and sleeves. The madness of paying a hundred dollars a month to store clothes and magazines in a room upstairs was finally brought home to me.

I donated a few items to charity thrift shops, but it disturbed me to see brand-new, beautifully made clothes sold so cheaply. I would visit the thrift stores and wince when I saw my expensive Bergdorf Goodman dress crushed between a faded blouse and a mildewed coat. "They don't know what it's worth," I told my Palm Beach friends. "It's crazy to give them beautiful things if they're going to sell them for five dollars!"

There was more to it than that, of course. Seeing those lovely clothes hung up with worn and grubby things was a brutal reminder that I had thrown so much money away.

One night, I was at a dinner party at my friend Ev Parker's, and Ann Carmichael, who is an island realtor, listened to my complaints and then said, "We ought to have a garage sale!"

"Fine, but I don't have a garage." I laughed.

"But I do," Ev said with enthusiasm.

Actually, the Parkers had a double garage and a long, semicircular driveway. They also had a swimming pool, a lakefront view, and a rather exclusive address—Ibis Island—that you reach by crossing a short bridge from the highway near the Palm Beach Golf Course. I was surprised that she would consider opening her garage and yard to the trample of eager garage sale mavens. "No," Ev said, "it would be great fun." She and her husband, Howard, a retired vice-president of United States Steel, still retained their Midwest practicality and lack of pretense.

"I've got scads of things I could sell," said Ann. She lived on the grounds of The Breakers in one of the rental houses that the hotel called "cottages," grand and sprawling oceanfront houses covered with shingles and decorated with turrets, gabled windows, and big porches. "They're going to tear my house down soon and build apartments. I'll have to get rid of everything."

I was still uncertain. "Isn't there a law against garage sales in Palm Beach?"

They both laughed. "What's the matter," Ann asked, "don't you like garage sales?"

"I love garage sales," I said. "I *love* garage sales."

So we had a Palm Beach garage sale.

Randy Brock, Dr. Williams's assistant and now my good friend, helped me go through all of my stuff, and he was amused that I remembered so little of my buying, that I continually discovered valuable things in boxes and exclaimed, "How beautiful! I wonder where I got it." Halfway through, I suddenly said, in horror, "Randy, some of these things may be gifts!" He thought I meant items from my inventory of gifts for Christmas, birthdays, weddings, and showers. "No, gifts to me," I fretted. "What if I'm selling something that friends have given me?" I was on the verge of dragging everything back into the guest room, but Randy pointed out that most of the items still had the original sales slips in their boxes, which proved that I had bought them. "Thank goodness," I said. I could feel my heart still racing. "This is a harrowing business."

As I began to break the bonds of my compulsive attachments, I put tags on things of real value. Vuitton pieces. Gucci. Cartier. I turned up piles of needlepoint kits that I would never get to. Carlin linens. Missoni-designed sheets. Costume jewelry. Towels. Glasses. Paperweights (although I would not touch my Baccarat collection). Handbags. Shoes. Unused cosmetics.

It was a wonderful sale. People couldn't get over how lovely everything was. Ev and I used pretty sheets as tablecloths, and I color-coded all the tickets. I bought a cashbox and brought along my adding machine so everybody got an itemized tape when they bought things. "Does one of you have a shop?" one of our startled customers asked.

"No," I said proudly, "we just like to do things right."

Randy was amazed that I told so many people that I was glad my things were "going to good homes." "You part with things as if you're placing a puppy," he joked.

"I'm fastidious," I explained patiently. "I inherited that from Mother. You don't want a precious object to go to someone who will allow it to get cracked and chipped and beat up." It gave me pleasure to see things going to people who would treasure them. I felt like a matchmaker.

A year later, we repeated the garage sale on an even grander scale—so grand, in fact, that newspapers from as far away as Miami sent reporters. The Second Annual Garage Sale was a three-day event featuring refreshments in Waterford glasses, flowers on the tables, nuns baking cookies, handpainted signs, and an incredible array of luxurious, fun, and used items for sale. We had stuffed shrimp and wine for lunch. We had fashions by Dior, Halston, Lily Pulitzer, and Diane von Furstenberg. We had a $1,500 antique gold watch, a solid gold rose pendant, an antique French telephone, a pumpkin with a happy face painted on it that Ev had just brought back from New York, and my favorite, a metallic-silver Mercedes-Benz replica housing a cut crystal decanter (when the hood was lifted to get at the shot glasses, a music box played, "If I Were a Rich Man").

Ann Carmichael best captured the spirit of the sale, I thought, when she held up a silver-and-gold incense burner. "This," she said, "was a present from the Arabs."

"This was one sale that was not boring," Linda Duffy wrote in the West Palm Beach *Post-Times*. Borrowing from Pirandello, she added, "Terry was a character in search of a garage."

Actually, I was a character in search of her sanity. The garage sales seemed to restore some of the old Terry—the

Terry of whacky publicity stunts, the Terry who painted daisies on bathroom walls, the Terry who laughed and did unpredictable things.

Not all of my old self came rushing back. The Anafranil helped—there was no question that it kept me from descending into suicidal despair—but it also kept me in a low-grade depression during my down cycles. I felt groggy, medicated. When I was "down," I couldn't handle complex mental tasks—certainly not writing—and I still felt guilty about sleepwalking my way through life. I was so concerned about the persistence of my writer's block that I asked Moke if I were permanently "disabled."

"Not exactly," Moke said. "You seem to be exhibiting a phobic reaction with regard to your writing."

In other words, he suspected I *could* write—if I weren't afraid to.

It took me a long time to accept that I *was* afraid, that I might *never* write again. I told everybody that I was working on a new book or that I was charting out a series of romance novels that I would dash off "as a lark." The truth is, I amassed mounds of notes and research materials, but no manuscript pages. When I tried to write, I felt dead inside. Writing had brought me mostly pain. It didn't stimulate me or excite me anymore.

Curiously, I had not lost the desire to communicate. "You don't *have* to write, you know," Johnny told me. "Why don't you get back into book publicity or public relations? Something where you can use your verbal skills and your persuasive powers." He pointed out, jokingly, that every industry and cause seemed to have a traveling advocate who did radio shows and newspaper interviews. "You'd be great at that," he said. "You could speak on behalf of soybeans or mobile homes or the textile industry."

I gave him a dozen reasons why I couldn't. I couldn't leave

Palm Beach. I was reluctant to travel. Short-term money problems. I was afraid I might break down in public. But he had planted the seeds of an idea.

That idea began to grow in the spring of 1981, when my friends Everett and Valerie Aspinwall invited me to host a once-a-week call-in show on their radio station, WPBR, in Palm Beach. "I think I could handle it," I confided to Johnny. "I feel well enough. And I won't have to write anything."

"Do it," he said.

"Let's Talk About Sex" went on the air on a Saturday afternoon in September 1981. It was a strange feeling, parking at the WPBR studios, which were on the beach near the old Lake Worth Casino. My first-ever radio appearance had been on WPBR, many years before, when I had participated in a reading with my Palm Beach Junior College speech class. Now the ocean and the surfers and the pier all looked pretty much the same, and *I* even felt pretty much the same: nervous.

What a debut! The first "Let's Talk About Sex" was a disaster. I said, "Uhhh," so many times that I sounded like a car trying to start. I giggled. My phrasing was strange. I spoke in patterns similar to those of my illness. I ran out of things to say a half hour into the show.

I was never in control. I mixed up the phone call-in buttons. I babbled endlessly, waiting for the phones to light up. They wouldn't. Then they would, and I would just be reaching for the buttons as they all went dark again! Why? I didn't know why!

The engineer's signals were incomprehensible to me. During a commercial, Everett Aspinwall tried to coach me. "What if I try to cut away to the network news and nothing happens?" I cried.

"Just watch the clock," Everett said soothingly.

"The clock is eight seconds off," I said. "They told me that on Wednesday."

"Then add eight seconds."

"No, subtract eight seconds," someone else ordered.

"They fixed the clock . . ."

I was wide-eyed. "They *fixed* the clock?"

"Get ready!"

"Wait!" I yelped. "Why do all the lights on the phone go out?" Everybody raced out of the studio. Ray Tronzo, my doctor guest, smiled nervously. I was more confused than before.

Tronzo, an orthopedic surgeon, was on the show to discuss the sex problems of the ill and handicapped, but somebody must have been jamming our signal when I announced that. The phone lines were clogged with quavery old ladies who had lost most of their hearing and wanted to talk about possible hip replacements. They'd pipe up, in squeaky voices, "How do you spell the doctor's name?"

When the elderly ladies' fingers flagged on the phone dials, the Moral Majority people lambasted me and the program, calling us both "disgusting," "vile," and "disgraceful."

At one point, my engineer, Rosemary, started signaling me from the control room. I looked at the clock, made some hasty calculations while saying, "Uhhhhh—" (should I add eight seconds or assume the clock was right?), and finally said, "Yes, well, we'll be back for more, but first we have to break for Mutual News. Don't go away!"

I leaned back in my chair and took a deep sigh. I was just about to say something to Ray when I looked over my shoulder at the control room. There was Rosemary making frantic hand signs for me to keep talking. There was no Mutual News!

"It was like standing on the bridge of the *Titanic* as it went down," I told everyone afterward.

Everett was very kind. He said it was a very good first program and that they were very happy. He didn't fool me.

I went straight home and cried. Then I scrubbed my face, gathered my courage, and drove over to Ruth and Rolf Kaltenborn's for a drink and commiseration. I downed a very dry martini and then asked for another drink, which surprised them. Ruth and Rolf were comforting, and I needed comforting. "It wasn't that bad," Rolf said. "The things you're worrying about, most listeners would not be aware of. The pros know, but not the average listener." Ruth said I had warmth and had shown great care with a sensitive subject. "The calls will start to come in when people get used to the program."

"How could *anybody* get used to that program?" I asked gloomily.

I was expected at a party at the Parkers', so I went there next. I asked for a drink there, too. They were all properly stunned. They stared at me with saucer eyes.

Later, I went with everybody for a nightcap at Ta-boo on Worth Avenue, and I had *another* drink. And I still wanted one after that!

When I got home, at about one in the morning, I called Johnny in Kansas City. I told him the story, not skipping a single disaster, and we laughed and groaned together. "When do I get to go to the booby hatch?" I said woefully. "I want out of this world!"

"Yeah, but Terry," he said, "listen to yourself. You're embarrassed and you feel foolish, but I can hear something in your voice. You aren't shattered by this. You know that it's just a temporary setback. You know you'll get better."

"Of course I will," I said. "I'm not giving up."

"And you spent the evening with people. You didn't go away and hide."

"Yes?" I wasn't sure what he was getting at. "Does that mean something?"

"I think it means," Johnny said, "that you're getting well."

It took a few months, but I became (I hope) a proficient

radio host. "Let's Talk About Sex" settled into a comfortable niche between "Real Estate Realities" and "Barter Board."

I didn't panic anymore. I prepared so well for my shows that I could carry the two hours even if my guest didn't show up. I still said, "Uhhh," when I was thinking, but I was generally clearheaded and in control. It bothered me that I couldn't be more lighthearted on the air—my "expert 'J'" voice was always in command—but I resigned myself to the fact that you can't reveal all your facets in a two-hour radio program. The important thing was that I was using elements of both Terry and "J" again. We had finally blended into one person.

I enjoyed doing radio. I learned something new every week, and I think I helped people become more comfortable with and knowledgeable about sex.

One afternoon, I got a call, on the air, from a very distraught woman. I took her to be middle-aged; she had a distinctive, cultivated European accent.

"I don't know why I'm calling you," she said. "A friend told me you were on . . . I've already called 'Crisis Line.' I'm thinking of taking my life." She rattled on, veering away from her emotional crisis, but she came back to the mystery of her phone call. "I don't know why I called you," she repeated. "There was something in your voice that propelled me to the telephone."

She was not "on the ledge"—she wasn't threatening to kill herself at that instant—but I couldn't let her fade back into the ether without getting help for her. I also knew that I wasn't equipped to handle her problems over the air. "You don't have to live with those feelings," I told her. "Any recurrent thoughts of suicide should be taken seriously. They're warning signs, like the red warning lights on your car dashboard. Don't let them frighten you, but don't ignore them, either." I signaled to the control room. "I want you to give your telephone number to my producer, Grey Asbury.

You don't have to give your name if you don't want to. I promise I'll call you immediately after this program."

"Thank you," she said. "I think I need to talk to someone."

People who heard the show told me later that I was very compassionate, that I had maneuvered her off the air without sounding slick or uncaring. "We knew that that lady would get help," they said.

"She did get help," I assured them.

From time to time I have reflected on the woman's call. I still wonder what it was, what the "something" was in my voice, that had made her call me, and not a doctor or a minister. Was it blind chance? Was it an exhibitionistic compulsion?

Or had she sensed somehow that Terry Garrity knew what it was like to be on the other end of that telephone line, despairing and alone?

Driving home from the studio that night, I thought, *I wish I could tell Mif about that woman's call.* And for the first time, I was aware that Mif was gone . . . *had* been gone for some time. My imaginary friend had slipped off without a word, taking his books, pipes, and tweeds with him.

I didn't need him anymore.

20

I have a particular need to change the world, a puritanical need to do right. Sometimes it drives me, sometimes it leaves me feeling overwhelmed. In *The Sensuous Woman*, I was driven to reveal the how-tos of female orgasm. At that, I was a success, no matter how badly my private life suffered in the wake of best-sellerdom. Now, I am driven to educate people about mental illness—biochemical illness in general and cyclical depression in particular. I feel that I must fight for others like myself who have been through the pain and bewilderment and who languish still, undiagnosed, suffering needlessly. It is a very personal crusade. As I told Johnny on the phone one day, "I still have anger about the way people treated me, their stubbornness, their refusal to understand."

"But, Terry," he countered, "is it reasonable to expect people to understand an illness like this? I was with you through much of your agony, and *I* certainly didn't know what was going on."

I carried Johnny's question back to Moke. *"Is* it reasonable to expect outsiders to understand?"

"Not when it's not being seen," Moke said. *Touché*. He never failed to remind me that my compulsive masking had concealed my anguish from those closest to me. "You expected people to help you, but you were not thinking all that clearly at the time. As you recover sufficiently, I think you'll recognize that you were sabotaging any help that you expected. It will become more clear why you didn't get it."

I took that as a challenge. As the months passed, my relationship with Moke changed from that of straight doctor-patient to teacher-student. I wanted to learn what I could about my disease so that I could educate others about it. I even accepted a voluntary position as regional president of the Huxley Institute, booking speakers and scheduling programs for people interested in biochemical approaches to mental illness. I gave talks on sexuality to disturbed teen-agers in mental health facilities. I tried to keep abreast of the nontechnical literature on psychotrophic drugs and innovative treatments.

Wherever I went, I encountered controversy and doubt about the "new" psychiatry. The "old" psychiatry, I learned, was grounded in something called dynamics, the theory that emotional disorders are mostly the product of psychic forces and interpersonal relationships. The old psychiatry was the world of Sigmund Freud and Carl Jung, the world of dream interpretation and repression, ids and egos, Oedipus complexes and primal fathers, neuroses and hysteria.

"Most psychiatric training, including mine," Moke told me, "stressed the dynamic theory, and once you're trained in that, it's awfully hard not to use it. Even if you become convinced of the organic or biological aspect of mental illness, you still tend to go into dynamics. And certainly the dynamic theory is perpetuated by the psychologists of the nonmedical group."

Of course, not all emotional disturbances are biochemical in nature. "And often both elements are present," Moke said, "the dynamic and the organic. As you have learned, the dynamic can trigger the organic."

I relate more to personal experience than to abstract theories, so I often quizzed Moke about my own behavior and about people I knew. At one session, I told him about the suicidal woman and the phone call to the radio station. "Do you think she sensed, from my voice, perhaps, that I knew what she was going through?"

He smiled. "You *do* belong to a select group of people."

"That's an interesting way of putting it," I said wryly. "I'd rather not have joined the world of the mentally ill, thank you."

"Understandably." He sat behind his desk, frowning myopically at the painting on the wall behind me.

"Moke, there's something I never told you." I fidgeted.

"Oh?" He didn't look surprised.

"During most of the time I was sick, I had an imaginary friend."

He blinked. Twice. Then he straightened in his chair. It was the biggest reaction I'd ever gotten from him. "Tell me about this imaginary friend," he said, trying to look disinterested. He wanted to know everything about my phantom: his name, his age, his looks, when and how often he appeared, everything. He wrote busily in my file folder with his black-and-gold pen.

"Did you have imaginary friends when you were a child?"

I shook my head. "Never. My friends had them, but not I."

He looked straight at me. "Why didn't you ever tell me about him?"

"Why didn't you ask?" I countered.

Moke didn't want to spar with me. "It's most unusual for a patient who isn't schizophrenic to have an imaginary friend. It's a delusional kind of idea. You're the first cyclical-depressive I've treated that had one."

I felt a touch of pride. I was a unique crazy person!

"Why did I create Mif, Moke?"

"You were lonely. As I've reminded you before, when you are sick, you look for help. You could not *ask* for help because that was directly opposed to what you had been taught. Maybe you were wishing for a mother—Mif did many motherlike things, like washing your tears away, rocking you—perhaps a substitute husband—these are all nurturing or protective devices which you unconsciously created to defend yourself. You needed something and you weren't asking for it from me."

"Why did I have those strange mental blanks with Burt Reynolds and on *The David Susskind* and *Mike Douglas* shows?"

"When your anxiety level is high, your ability to focus—imprint—is lowered. You hear but you don't hear. That happens to people frequently. You were aware that you weren't feeling very well and you were apprehensive about how you were going to come off. So you were concerned about your own suffering—it's like a thought boomeranging on you. Instead of your being able to hear the questions, you were taking inventories of your feeling state at the moment, which meant that you couldn't hear what they were saying because your mind was focused on how well you were doing."

"But I've had periods when I've concentrated so hard I'm in pain, and this still has happened. Is that the same thing?"

"I think so. You're trying very hard to focus, but still you're not controlling your concentration enough to keep it from wandering off beam. For example, it's similar to a radio that you've tuned so that it's barely on the band—and it will drift on and off, fade in and out."

"The mental blanks was one of my most frightening symptoms, but the loss of sexual desire was particularly hard for me to understand and accept. Is it common in endogenous depression? And why did I become so inarticulate about talking to you about my sexual problem?"

"Do you think that a man who has had his testicles cut off would be comfortable talking about sex?"

"No." I saw his point.

"You were unable to continue doing the thing that you were recognized for, so it was a painful reminder to you of the fact. Also, remember, you were in the denial stage. If you admitted to me that you had lost your ability to function sexually, that was admitting an illness.

"There are two problems that most people who have endogenous depression must deal with. One is that the disease itself can diminish sexual desire. *Everything* is depressed, including sexual function. Patients are very reluctant to admit this because they see it as a loss of manhood or womanhood. They will deny it practically down to a last-ditch stand. Two, the medicines we use to treat this illness also take away sex drive. So you have a double whammy going against you: the illness itself, and then you are treating the illness with something that is going to lower the sex drive as well. That has to be worked through with the patient when you put him or her on the medication so that you don't make the illness worse psychologically by an unexplained side effect. Also, it is very important to let patients know that when they come out of their depressed cycles, full sexual response will be possible again, as it is for you most of the time now."

"Moke, do most doctors accept the biochemical theory of mental illness now?"

"Of the schizophrenias and major affective disorders— manic depression, cyclical depression, and their variations— yes. There has been a major turnaround in psychiatry in the last five years, thanks to the leaps forward that have been made in brain chemistry research; but a small percentage of psychiatrists, perhaps ten or twelve percent, still hold with the old psychoanalytic views of these diseases, such as that schizophrenia is caused by poor mothering.

"Most of the medications we have at our disposal now to

reverse faulty brain chemistry are very primitive compared to what we will have available to us in the not too distant future. What is happening, and I find this very exciting, is that psychiatrists are beginning to use their medical training again, in conjunction with psychotherapy. The combination, when practiced well, can only benefit patients such as yourself. Talk therapy alone would have been useless with you, Terry; it couldn't fix your defective brain chemistry. But you needed more than pharmacological support to put your life in order, and that's where psychotherapy serves its purpose."

I was learning to lead a much more quiet life than before. I carefully scheduled big projects for certain months of the year when I anticipated that my energy levels would be high. When I felt down, I learned to say no to even the most appealing social events. I had to get a certain amount of sleep every day; I couldn't push myself; I couldn't afford guilt over limitations beyond my control.

"How are you doing on your diet?" Moke asked one morning, settling back in his chair.

"We-lllll . . ." I laughed. "I'm still slipping, but I'm doing better."

"And what have you bought in the last month?" The black-and-gold pen was poised, ready to make entries.

"Nothing," I said proudly.

Moke looked pleased.

"I still go through occasional periods of mental confusion when I'll pay one bill twice and another bill not at all, but it's not the way it used to be when I would worry, 'I have to do this, I have to do this,' and then think I *had* done it, when all I'd actually done was think it."

"And your perfectionist tendencies?" he asked.

"They're a luxury I can no longer afford." I laughed.

"Good." The questioning continued. My sense of time, was

it still occasionally distorted? No. Self-image? Improved. Coping? Much, much better. Libido? Returning. Nightmares and sleeping too much? Still around, and probably related to the Anafranil. ("Those might not abate until a better anti-depressant comes along," he said.) Depression? None.

Moke was pleased with my progress. I was dealing fairly well with a still-stressful life; I no longer separated Terry from "J"; my principal delusion (Mif) had vanished, and my compulsions were becoming manageable. "You will continue to need monitoring," he said, "but you seem to be responding well to both the medication and the psychotherapy."

"Then it's true? I'm getting well?"

Moke nodded. "So it appears."

I gave the goppy gold filigree tissue box a fond pat and sailed out of the office. For a certified mental patient, I felt pretty good about myself.

Until a new antidepressant comes along . . .

Those were Moke's words, and in the summer of 1982 he handed me a prescription for a new medication called Desyrel. "You'll be my first patient on it," he said.

"You mean, I'm a human guinea pig?"

He smiled. "Desyrel is a whole new compound, a different one than those that have been on the market before—the MAO inhibitors and tricyclics. Desyrel has a more direct effect on the level of serotonin* in the brain and it is faster acting.

I had read enough to know that the level of serotonin in the brain was linked to feelings of elation or depression. "But what about side effects?" I asked.

---

*Serotonin is a biochemical amine that acts as a neurotransmitter of electrical impulses from one brain cell to another.

"That's why I want you to try it. The restrictions placed upon the patient are said to be much less with Desyrel, the feeling of over-medication, the feeling of not being in command."

I no longer expected miracles. "I'll try it," I laughed, "but I bet it puts me to sleep. *Everything* puts me to sleep."

Instead, on the sixth day, I woke up . . . looked around my bedroom . . . and saw sunlight beaming through the sheer curtains and warming my white carpeted walls. I felt as if a great heaviness had been lifted from me. I felt light, but not light-headed. My mind was sharp.

I went through most of the day feeling so good—so *normal,* actually—that I was unnerved. "Don't get your hopes up," I warned myself, but it was hard not to. That night, out of habit, I gathered some of my research materials around my yellow chair, took up the yellow legal pad and the felt pens, and started to go through the motions of writing—I had never stopped pretending that I would write again—and, miraculously, I *wrote.*

I was stunned. As if by magic, the writing function was restored. I could translate thoughts into words on paper. "I don't believe it," I murmured. "I don't *believe* it!" I had given up the idea of ever writing on command again, and suddenly it was restored.

I wrote long into the night. The next morning, rising again with the same sense of lightness and normalcy, I grabbed the telephone and called Moke. "I can write again," I exulted. "The sixth day. I woke up and I could write!"

"Good," he said.

"You bet it is! But *why* is this happening?"

"Most of the other medications affect more than one chemical tract in the brain. Desyrel seems to target in more directly and leaves the other parts of the brain alone; therefore you aren't subduing such parts of brain function as those that control the ability to write. This will, indeed, make a positive difference in your life."

* * *

There's never a hundred percent happy ending. I feel bitterness still. "I lost ten years," I tell myself. "I lost the last of my youth." I'll never get those years back. Sometimes I fall into the "Why me?" syndrome and lament that so many years slipped away from me before my illness was diagnosed. It wouldn't have been that way, I think, if I had only been born later. Since 1982, doctors have had a blood test, the Dexamethasone Suppression Test (DST), that can identify organic depression with great reliability by measuring cortisol (a hormone of the adrenal cortex) levels before and after the patient has swallowed a tablet called Decadron, an adrenocortical steroid. Those people who don't have a biochemical depression stop producing cortisol for twenty-four hours. But depressed people don't shut off cortisol production, so it shows up positive in blood samples. Moke now uses it to screen all his new patients.

"No test is one hundred percent correct, but the DST has revealed many people to be depressed who we were not clinically able to identify before," he tells me. "If we had had this test available when you first came to me, we would not have wasted almost a year working around your problems." Even better tests are on the horizon.

"Within ten years," Moke predicts, "we should be able to identify organic depression at birth."

I still slip into depression—a half hour here, a half hour there. The difference is, now I can go get my medication and adjust the dosage for immediate relief. During my normal cycles I take a little Desyrel, just enough to keep it in my bloodstream so there isn't a five- to six-day lag if I should hit a stress that unexpectedly throws me back into a depression. So the seemingly inevitable side effects of antidepressants are almost nonexistent now for most of the year. This is a true blessing when I remember how miserable I was on Anafranil and other medications.

But Desyrel is no "happy drug"; I am as vulnerable to disappointment and grief and frustration as anyone else. As Moke warned me, "All of your plans to chart and rearrange your life will still be susceptible to unpredictable stresses."

He was right.

I suppose one gets over the bitterness, but I see myself in the mirror sometimes—rounder, older, less resilient, still being robbed of time in small increments—and I think, *I'm still paying for the bad years.*

But, of course, the down sides are like that. When I'm feeling good, I don't see it that way at all. And more and more, these days, I'm feeling good.

21

One morning recently, I was sorting out the contents of a large carton of odds and ends that neither Johnny nor I had gotten around to dealing with during my illness. Most of it was junk: offers to enter the Publishers Clearing House sweepstakes. Old mail-order catalogs. Paid-up department store bills. Clippings from newspapers that had no meaning for me. Unread magazines from the mid-seventies. Travel folders. Used airline tickets. Invitations to art gallery openings and charity balls long past. Letters from strangers asking for money. Letters from investment counselors soliciting my account. Recipes. A rusty safety pin. Old scorecards from rounds I had played at the Palm Beach Par-Three Golf Course. Telephone messages from people whose names I didn't recognize. Pictures of me at social events, looking fat and dazed.

But mixed in with the junk were letters from friends I never remembered receiving or reading. . . . I felt momentarily sad. All these nice people (and how many more?) had

had their feelings hurt or been insulted because I had not responded to their letters. They had no way of knowing I was unable to do so. Would I ever be able to completely tidy up my past?

I picked up a note from Jim Moran, the famous publicist and another friend with whom I had lost contact. It was a letter of sympathy written after my mother's death. Jim was suggesting that I reread William Cullen Bryant's "Thanatopsis."

> *. . . sustained and soothed*
> *By an unfaltering trust, approach thy grave,*
> *Like one who wraps the drapery of his couch*
> *About him, and lies down to pleasant dreams.*

That was what I had been seeking when I had planned my death walk into the ocean—to lie "down to pleasant dreams."

On an impulse, I dug a pair of sneakers and some socks out of the closet, put them on, and walked outside to look at the ocean. I had missed the sunrise, but the day still looked and felt new. There it was, the surf breaking and foaming close to the seawall—the instrument of release from my crazy success. I walked down to the beach and braced myself against the stiff wind, letting the sweet Florida air sweep over every pore of my body.

I stood there, shoulders back, head up, feet spread wide and dug solidly into the sand, and imagined that the pure velvet air whipping through me was purifying me, washing out all the ugliness, all the residual toxins of despair. Suddenly, I was flooded with overwhelming feelings of joy at being fully alive again. I felt like shouting, "Hey there, world! I'm back!"

Did I? An elderly woman walking her equally elderly spaniel along the sand was looking at me curiously. Did she think I was insane? How could she know I was very, wonderfully, newly sane?

"Isn't this a beautiful day?" I called out through tears and laughter.

"Why, yes, it is," she said uncertainly, looking around her. She and the spaniel padded on down the beach together, leaving a trail of footprints in the wet sand.

I walked down into the surf, letting the foam splash over my sneakers, and then edged in until the warm water was up to my waist. Then, mindlessly, I dashed myself against a big wave and let it toss me as it pleased. The same ocean that I had prayed would suck me down into a pain-free oblivion now tossed me effortlessly up into its crests and swells and then dumped me back on the shore.

I sat up and looked around me. "I get your message!" I shouted at the empty horizon.

I had a whole life yet to live.

And I am living it, with a respect and appreciation for life I never had before my crazy success.

Afterword

Our society tends to think that mood disorders, such as the one that Terry Garrity has, are rare. This is incorrect. It has been estimated that one out of every five persons over eighteen years of age suffers from a recognizable form of bipolar (manic-depressive) or unipolar (manic *or* depressive) illness.

As you can see from these statistics, biochemical mood swing is a much more significant disease than is generally known. It exists in our society in almost every home; everyplace we go there are people suffering from this illness. I don't doubt that on any given day we do business and socialize with one or more manic-depressives or unipolar depressives, many of whom don't know that they are ill, and so they don't seek professional help. The quality of life for these people could be greatly improved if they and their loved ones knew more about physiological mood disorders, so that they could learn to recognize the signs of the disease and get the person appropriate medical attention.

In the past few years, medical science has vastly improved its ability to correctly diagnose and treat biological mood disturbances. Early signs of bipolar or unipolar illness are—as in any mental disorder—a change from the norm to inappropriate behavior. In the depressed person there is withdrawal inward, not keeping up with and taking pleasure in family and personal interests, and a focus on physical ills as the reason for exhaustion and not coping. Self-recriminations often lead to the belief that "the family would be much better off without me," and recurrent thoughts of suicide can overwhelm the individual. The manic group becomes overactive physically, overly talkative, highly elated and, in the more gross stages, they may race wildly through the streets in their automobiles, engage in grandiose thinking and schemes, and go on spending sprees. These behaviors are so characteristic of the illness that almost any case history you read will describe them.

We have known for many years that bipolar and unipolar disorders have a genetic link. In the early 1900's, Emil Kraepelin found historical evidence within familial characteristics that the diseases are organic (physical). More recent studies have substantiated Kraepelin's work. The data from seven major studies of twins show that if one identical twin exhibits bipolar disease, there is a 76 percent probability that the other twin will also have the illness at some point in life. With fraternal twins, the probability is 19 percent—lower, but still quite significant.

I feel the illness is most likely to occur when a person is going through major biochemical changes, such as puberty, pregnancy or menopause, although psychological stresses and physical illness can also bring on the disease (as it did in the case of Terry Garrity). The warning signs of biochemical fragility were there, but unseen. When you look back through a person's history, you will see that there were things which were noticeable as being different but not *too* different, that, when later compared with the illness, had given clues you then recognized as being symptoms of disease. The hyperactive child often becomes the bipolar adult; the melancholy or withdrawn child, the depressed man or woman.

In the manic, symptoms may smolder for a while unnoted, but the full disease can be seen in recognizable relief within two to three weeks once the illness is florid. Manics can bankrupt themselves in that time by writing checks and signing away property while under the delusion that they have vast funds at their disposal. It is very difficult to retrieve these "gifts" under our present laws, so there can be some marked dangers involved in manic illness.

The depressives are less dangerous as far as that kind of behavior is concerned. Their danger lies in the fact that they don't share their thoughts, which may be strongly suicidal. The first clue you may have of these thoughts is a suicide attempt. That is what is so frightening about depressives—they can secrete their symptoms. This is why the usual rule of thumb is that if a person is depressed for more than a week, and there are no obvious reasons for depression, such as a death in the family or a loss of a job, that he or she should be seen by a professional for evaluation.

How can you tell if you or someone you love has a mood disorder? Three or more symptoms in the following list—occurring concurrently and lasting two to three weeks—would be indicative of a manic episode:

1. Marked increase in energy and sudden involvement in multiple activities.
2. Decreased need for sleep.
3. Overly talkative, abnormally gregarious.
4. Physically restless.
5. Unable to concentrate; easily distractible.
6. Racing thoughts; flights of ideas.

7. Inflated sense of power, knowledge, self-importance.
8. Inappropriate laughing, joking; punning and other plays on words.
9. Unwarranted optimism.
10. Reckless driving.
11. Increased sexual activity, perhaps including sexual infidelities.
12. Wild spending sprees.
13. Hyperirritability and/or bursts of anger.
14. Giving money and possessions away indiscriminately.
15. Delusions or hallucinations.
16. Lack of concern for negative consequences of acts.

Four or more of the following symptoms lasting one week or more would be indicative of a depressive episode:

1. Sleep problems: either sleeping too much or having trouble falling asleep; awakening earlier than usual.
2. Striking changes in eating habits: increased appetite and weight gain; loss of appetite and weight loss.
3. Constant feelings of exhaustion. Usual energy levels are way down.
4. Loss of pleasure in activities usually enjoyed.
5. Withdrawal from social activities because of lack of interest or feeling that they "take too much effort."
6. Decreased sexual desire. (Teenagers may show marked increase in sexual activity.)
7. Inability to concentrate.
8. Indecisiveness.
9. Feelings of helplessness.
10. Feelings of worthlessness.
11. Feelings of guilt.
12. Fearfulness; suspiciousness.
13. Restlessness; agitation.
14. Tearfulness.

15. Irritability.
16. Anxiety.
17. Persistent feelings of sadness for no apparent reason.
18. Sad, droopy, or expressionless face.
19. Absorption in physical complaints.
20. Delusions of poverty.
21. Recurrent thoughts of death from cancer or other disease.
22. Recurrent thoughts of suicide.

The most logical person to seek help from initially, if you suspect that you or a loved one is manic or depressed, is the family physician who, since he has known the patient, is able to ascertain that the person has, indeed, changed. The family physician will also be able to rule out the possibility of drugs or a physical illness as the cause of the mental and emotional disturbances.

I would like to think that in cases of this magnitude that once the patient is screened by his or her doctor, a psychiatrist would be consulted who is qualified to recognize both physical and emotional factors. Since this is a physical disease, it should be attended to by a person trained to distinguish it and treat it adequately with medications and whatever else might be indicated. Some psychiatrists treat both the medical and psychological, but many psychiatrists will treat only the medical part of the disease and call in a psychologist or counselor to handle the behavioral aspects—the adjustments in life-style.

Other sources of medical help are your community mental health clinic or, if there is a major university or medical center nearby, its psychiatric department or affective (mood) disorders clinic.

Even with good medical supervision and the newer, more efficient medications now available to the victims of a bipolar or unipolar illness, there will still be unpleasant adjustments to be made and some trying times for many patients. Some people constantly live with a cloud of imminent danger hanging over them because of the disease. They can't plan a completely normal life. They *can* learn to cope fairly well by recognizing approximations of times when they are likely to be well or sick and thus rearrange their life-styles to fit these cycles. But the victims of a mood disorder never feel completely safe; they are always walking as if the platform were going to collapse. Therefore, they live with a high level of anxiety, and that is not a very comfortable way to live. Fortunately, the patient and his or her loved ones can be educated to watch for that individual's particular set of subtle symptoms which signal a major mood shift, and the patient can then work with the doctor to get through the disruptive cycle. Terry Garrity, whose story you have just read in this book, is an excellent example of someone who has trained herself to be alert for the early warning signs that she is undergoing a biochemical alteration in mood. She has also worked successfully with her therapist to create ways of coping with the down times so that they no longer cripple her emotionally and physically.

In the future we will be able to identify the chemical pathways in the intracellular structure that are vulnerable to biochemical mood disorders and rearrange them so that the illness doesn't appear. For now, we are still faced with dealing with these diseases after the fact. Today we practice symptom control, not cure. But not too many years from now we will be able to correct faulty structures before they malfunction. Some of the more optimistic researchers predict that this will happen within the next ten years. For those of us who treat major mood disorders, and for those who suffer from them, scientific breakthroughs cannot come too quickly.

—MOKE WAYNE WILLIAMS, M.D.

Fort Lauderdale, Florida
October 1, 1983

Index

Index